Advance Praise for *Landing Page Optimization: The Definitive Guide to Testing and Tuning for Conversions*

Tim has figured out what so many people don't understand: your website can (and should) get better. Every single day.
— SETH GODIN, Author of *Meatball Sundae*

Today's diverse and ever-changing Internet marketing community can require daily, hourly and even minute-by-minute fine tuning. Tim does an excellent job at explaining common pitfalls, how to avoid them, and how to execute advanced tactics. This book is a must-read for the modern Internet marketer.
— KEVIN M. RYAN, Vice President, Global Content Director, *Search Engine Strategies* and *Search Engine Watch*

A solid, business-focused approach to turning viewers of a website into customers. This is a book written by and for business. It's not about design: it is about increasing sales, gaining customers, and retaining them. Learn how to do the measurements, learn how to conduct experiments. Revise your website by analyzing what visitors actually do. It is always good to see a former student succeed: Tim Ash provides a wonderful example. This is the best business-focused, measurement based guide to website design I have seen.
— DON NORMAN, Codirector of Northwestern's MBA + MEM program in Design and Operations and cofounder of the Nielsen Cofounder of Nielsen Norman group. Author of *Emotional Design* and *The Design of Future Things*

The days of HiPPO (Highest Paid Person's Opinion) driven website experiences are well behind us. Landing page testing finally enables experimentation so customers can help shape their own website content. The beauty is that this is a true win-win— customers get the experience they want and companies get improved conversion rates. Landing Page Optimization *will help accelerate your very own win-win journey.*
— AVINASH KAUSHIK, Analytics Evangelist and author of *Web Analytics: An Hour A Day*

Do you hear that sound? That is the sound of visitors bouncing away from your site without doing what you wanted them to do. Want a better melody? Tune your site to the sound of visitors giving you their money. Tim's Landing Page Optimization *is a must have for your bookshelf.*
— BRYAN EISENBERG, Author of *New York Times* and *Wall Street Journal* bestseller *Waiting for Your Cat to Bark?*

Landing Page Optimization

Landing Page Optimization

The Definitive Guide to Testing and Tuning for Conversions

Tim Ash

Wiley Publishing, Inc.

Acquisitions Editor: WILLEM KNIBBE
Developmental Editor: HEATHER O'CONNOR
Technical Editor: TED DUNNING
Production Editor: DASSI ZEIDEL
Copy Editor: LIZ WELCH
Production Manager: TIM TATE
Vice President & Executive Group Publisher: RICHARD SWADLEY
Vice President and Executive Publisher: JOSEPH B. WIKERT
Vice President and Publisher: NEIL EDDE
Book Designer: FRANZ BAUMHACKL
Illustrator: OSO REY, HAPPENSTANCE TYPE-O-RAMA
Compositor: MAUREEN FORYS, HAPPENSTANCE TYPE-O-RAMA
Proofreader: IAN GOLDER, WORD ONE
Indexer: TED LAUX
Cover Designer: MICHAEL TRENT
Front Cover Image: © COLIN ANDERSON/BRAND X PICTURES/JUPITER IMAGES

Library of Congress Cataloging-in-Publication Data

Ash, Tim, 1965-
  Landing page optimization / Tim Ash.
    p. cm.
  ISBN 978-0-470-17462-3 (pbk.)
  1. Web sites—Evaluation. 2. Web sites—Testing. 3. Web sites—Design. 4. Internet marketing. I. Title.
  TK5105.888.A7836 2008
  006.7—dc22
                                    2007045592

To my parents Tanya and Alexander for your love and sacrifices to get me here.

To my brother Artyom for your open heart and unfolding wisdom.

To my wife Britt for being my love and perfect partner on this wondrous journey.

To my children Sasha and Anya for showing me that joy is endless.

Acknowledgments

I want to thank Brett Crosby and Avinash Kaushik from Google for getting me into this fine mess. Without their chance intercession, this book would have never come to pass.

My appreciation to the professional team at Wiley/Sybex including Heather O'Connor, Dassi Zeidel, Liz Welch, and Pete Gaughan, who broke in a newbie book author very gently. Special thanks to acquisitions editor Willem Knibbe for having the vision and courage to let me write the book that needed to be written instead of the one that you were originally planning.

I am grateful to the Google Website Optimizer team including Peter Harbison, Ariel Bardin, and Jon Stona for giving the whole landing page optimization field a giant push forward. A special thanks to Tom Leung for your consummate professionalism, ongoing support, and review of the appendix material.

Kudos to Guy Davis, Nancy Lents, Brad Feuer, and the rest of the SiteTuners.com crew for your help and dedication over the years. This book is the distillation of all of your experience and hard work. Additional thanks to Ted Dunning for doubling as our chief scientist and the book's technical editor. I know that it was not easy making sure that I did not put my foot too far into my mouth. To my business partner and friend Robyn Benensohn, what can I say... through three start-up companies and a dozen years I have enjoyed your love and support. What a long strange trip it's been—I would not be here without you. Thank you for everything.

I would like to thank my amazing wife Britt for her patience and support through the writing of this book. I had expected no less from my spirit warrior woman, but I know that it was not easy. You will always be my true north. My dear sweet children Sasha and Anya, thank you for putting up with my extended absences. Now it is all finished. No more writing "night shifts" at the office—Daddy is coming home to tuck you in starting tonight.

Dear Reader

Thank you for choosing *Landing Page Optimization*. This book is part of a family of premium quality Sybex books, all written by outstanding authors who combine practical experience with a gift for teaching.

Sybex was founded in 1976. More than thirty years later, we're still committed to producing consistently exceptional books. With each of our titles we're working hard to set a new standard for the industry. From the authors we work with to the paper we print on, our goal is to bring you the best books available.

I hope you see all that reflected in these pages. I'd be very interested to hear your comments and get your feedback on how we're doing. Feel free to let me know what you think about this or any other Sybex book by sending me an e-mail at nedde@wiley.com, or if you think you've found a technical error in this book, please visit http://sybex.custhelp.com. Customer feedback is critical to our efforts at Sybex.

Best regards,

NEIL EDDE
Vice President and Publisher
Sybex, an Imprint of Wiley

About the Author

Tim Ash is an experienced Internet marketing thought-leader, entrepreneur, and co-founder of several Internet related start-up companies. He is the President of SiteTuners.com and its parent company, Epic Sky. During his long involvement with the Internet, Tim has worked with American Express, Sony Music, American Honda, Coach, COMP USA, Harcourt Brace & Co., Universal Studios, Homegain.com, Eaton, Guidant, ProFlowers.com, SAIC, Pyxis, Veoh Networks, and B.F. Goodrich Aerospace to develop successful Internet initiatives. Before starting Epic Sky he co-founded Future Focus, an Internet business accelerator. Prior to that, he worked in a variety of management and technical roles at SAIC, HNC Software (now a division of Fair Isaac), NCR, and the U.S. Navy.

He has chaired Internet conferences and spoken internationally at numerous industry events including Search Engine Strategies, Affiliate Summit, eComXpo, PC Expo, and Internet World. Tim has written several articles on harnessing the power of the Internet for business and is a contributing columnist for several industry publications including *Search Engine Watch*.

After attending the University of California, San Diego on a U.C. Regents full academic scholarship, he received his B.S. in Computer Engineering and Cognitive Science "with highest distinction." Tim also completed his M.S. and C.Phil. degrees during his PhD. studies in Computer Science (specializing in neural networks and artificial intelligence) at U.C. San Diego.

He lives and works in San Diego, California, with his wife and two small children. In his nonexistent spare time, Tim is an avid photographer, artist, and a certified Tai Chi Chuan instructor. He can be reached by e-mail at tim@sitetuners.com.

Contents

Introduction

The train is pulling out of the station—will you be on it?

Landing page optimization is no longer a secret. It has rapidly become the most powerful method that smart Internet marketers use to build a lasting competitive advantage.

Well-optimized landing pages can change the economics of your business overnight and turbocharge your online marketing programs.

Don't *guess* at what your visitors want. Turn your landing page into a dynamic laboratory to find out what they *actually respond to*.

But you must orient yourself quickly to learn a number of new skills:

- What is the real value of my landing page?
- Can I see the world from my visitor's perspective?
- How do I uncover problems with my website?
- What page elements should I test to get the best results?
- Which tuning method is appropriate for me?
- Can I build the necessary team and action plan for my project?
- How do I avoid the biggest pitfalls when running my test?

If any of these questions ring true, then you have found the right book.

Who Can Benefit from This Book

If you are looking for an instant fix for your landing page, then put down this book and look around for a "Top 10 ways to increase conversions" entry on someone's blog. You will not find any quick or easy prescriptions here. To truly benefit from this book you will need to commit to understanding all of the important fundamentals of this challenging and rewarding field.

If you are involved in any way with making your company's Internet marketing programs more effective, this book is for you. If you have already gotten your feet wet in landing page optimization, this book will take you to the next level and provide you with a solid framework for repeatable future success.

This book will benefit people in the following roles:

- Web Designer
- Media Buyer
- Copywriter

- Webmaster
- User Experience Engineer
- Affiliate Manager
- Web Analytics Manager
- Product Manager
- Advertising Manager
- Marketing Manager
- Director of Online Marketing
- Media Director
- V.P. of Online Marketing
- CMO

What's Inside

Landing page optimization does not fit neatly into any box on an organizational chart. It requires a truly diverse set of knowledge and perspectives in order to be effective. Among other topics, you need to be familiar with Web design, human psychology, copywriting, statistics, usability, team building, and the scientific method.

This book is a guide to this strange and wondrous land. My colleagues at Site-Tuners.com and I have spent a lot of time exploring up ahead and we've come back with a comprehensive map. Like many pioneers, we have suffered setbacks and endured many painful lessons along the way. My sincere hope is that this book can shorten your own learning curve and help you become a more effective landing page tuner.

Here's what you will find inside.

Part I: Background

- **Chapter 1: "Setting the Stage"**

  Helps you understand how landing page optimization fits into the larger picture of online marketing.

- **Chapter 2: "Understanding Your Landing Pages"**

  Helps you understand the different types of landing pages, key target audience segments, conversion actions, and how to calculate their economic value.

- **Chapter 3: "Understanding Your Audience"**

  Helps you understand your Internet visitors more fully through both objective measures and psychological styles. Introduces a comprehensive framework for meeting the needs of your visitors.

- **Chapter 4: "Understanding the Decision Process"**

  Takes you through the four steps of the online decision-making process with extensive examples drawn from a variety of websites.

Part II: What and How to Tune

- **Chapter 5: "Why Your Site Is Not Perfect"**

  Presents methods for uncovering landing page issues. Introduces the fundamentals of Web usability.

- **Chapter 6: "Selecting Elements to Tune"**

  Presents a comprehensive framework for evaluating and selecting the best page elements to tune.

- **Chapter 7: "The Math of Tuning"**

  Introduces the math behind landing page testing, and addresses important questions related to proper test design.

- **Chapter 8: "Tuning Methods"**

  Provides a framework for describing tests and their setup. Surveys all important tuning methods along with their strengths and weaknesses.

Part III: Getting It Done

- **Chapter 9: "Assembling the Team and Getting Buy-in"**

  Reviews all important stakeholder roles and company politics common to landing page testing. Suggests several strategies for getting started and discusses the decision to use in-house staff or outsource.

- **Chapter 10: "Developing Your Action Plan"**

  Lays out a detailed framework for putting your plan into action.

- **Chapter 11: "Avoiding the Pitfalls"**

  Describes several common pitfalls that can derail your testing program.

- **Appendix A: "A Closer Look at the Google Website Optimizer"**

  Provides background, a hands-on walkthrough, and an analysis of this important landing page testing platform.

- **Glossary**

  A comprehensive glossary covering all important landing page optimization terms.

This Book's Companion Website

This book covers a lot of material, but it cannot be the last word on landing page optimization. The Internet is always changing and evolving. The companion site for this book can be found at http://LandingPageOptimizationBook.com.

On it you will find additional resources, guides, and links to help you get the most out of your landing page testing and tuning.

Landing Page Optimization

Background

I

All of us have our own unique perspectives and biases when dealing with landing page testing. The knowledge and belief systems that you bring to it will largely determine your success. As you study the topic of landing page optimization, you first have to get the right perspective. The first part of this book lays this groundwork. Leave all of your assumptions at the door, and let's get started. Part I consists of the following chapters:

Setting the Stage

*Life is like a sewer...what you get out
of it depends on what you put into it.*
—Tom Lehrer, American humorist, singer, and
songwriter

*What does a landing page look like from your
perspective? How does it fit into the overall
marketing picture? Can you really convert every
single visitor? Are you devoting enough attention
to your landing page?*

*This chapter will examine these questions and
set the stage for understanding landing page
optimization.*

1

Chapter Contents
A Few Precious Moments...
The Three Keys to Online Marketing
The Myth of Perfect Conversion
What's Wrong with This Picture?

A Few Precious Moments...

The following is a true story.

My Online Shopping Adventure

I was looking to buy a new camcorder online. First I used the Web to gather information about desirable features. Then I researched appropriate models. I invested hours of my time making sure that I bought the best possible one. After deciding on the one for me, I started looking for a place to buy it by typing the specific camcorder model name into a search engine. I got back a page of search results and started investigating the promising ones.

As I clicked on each link in my mission-oriented hunter mode, I looked for intangibles that would cause me to stick around. One site was too cluttered with confusing links and options; another featured obnoxious colors and was plastered with banner ads; the next looked too cheesy and unprofessional. Other websites' failings were subtler. I gave them a little more of my time and attention, but ultimately abandoned them as well. Click, backtrack, click, backtrack, click, backtrack—and so it went...until I found a company that was just right, and I bought my camcorder from them.

Sound familiar? The fact is that most of the companies that I had briefly visited sold the model that I wanted, had it in stock for quick shipping, and were in a similar price range. So why did one particular company get my money while most of the others got just a second of my attention?

Imagine that you are in charge of online marketing for your organization.

You have slaved for months to tune and optimize your campaigns. Countless hours and days have passed in a blur. You have constructed keyword lists, written pay-per-click ad copy, properly set your bid amounts, bought additional banners and exposure on related websites, optimized your site for organic search engines, created a powerful affiliate program with effective incentives, and set up the website analytics needed to track the return on your investment in real time.

You are standing by with a powerful series of e-mails that will be sent to prospects or customers who respond to your initial offer or leave their contact information on your site. This should significantly increase the lifetime value of the relationship with your website visitor.

The first visitor arrives—and leaves in half a second. The next one lands on your site, clicks another link, and is gone as well. More and more visitors flash by—a virtual flood. Yet only a tiny percentage will take the action that you would like them to take. What's wrong?

It's hard to figure it out:

- You have their fleeting attention for a split second.
- You don't know who they are.

- You don't know what they are thinking or feeling.
- You don't know why the vast majority of them leave so soon, empty-handed.

It seems like a hopeless situation. You are forever doomed to suffer from the poor marketing program economics that result from a low website conversion rate.

All of your hard work comes down to the few precious moments that the Internet visitors spend on your website...

But all is not lost. This book is about those few precious moments, and what you can do to make them count.

"On the Internet, nobody knows you're a dog."

You can (within the limits of ethics and accuracy) represent yourself in any way that you want on the Internet. Your landing page is not written on stone tablets. In fact, it is the most ethereal of objects—a set of bits that resides on a computer hard disk that is accessible to the whole world. No one is forcing you to use the particular colors, page layout, pictures, sales copy, call-to-action, or headlines that comprise your landing page now.

The only things stopping you from creating more compelling landing pages may be a lack of attention and imagination.

You are as free as an artist in front of a blank canvas. Maybe you will create a masterpiece that will move most people who see it. Maybe you will create bland and uninspired mush that will bore and turn away everyone. This freedom can be both energizing and scary at the same time.

The promise of better performing landing pages is often tempered by a fear of making things worse than they already are. How are you to know in advance what will or won't work better? Yet you are supposed to be the "expert." Shouldn't your landing page already be perfect based on your extensive online marketing experience? What if your landing page design knowledge was exposed as nothing more than pompous subjective posturing and guesswork?

Don't be afraid. You actually have access to a real expert—in fact, thousands of them. You are interacting with them daily already, but you have mostly ignored their advice to date.

The real experts on the design of your landing pages are your website visitors.

You may never be able to answer why a *specific* person did or did not respond to your landing page. But there are ways to determine what your website visitors respond to. In fact, landing page optimization can be viewed as a giant online marketing laboratory where your experimental subjects voluntarily participate in your tests without being asked. Their very actions (or inactions) expose them, and allow you to improve your appeal to a similar population of people.

Websites have three desirable properties as a testing laboratory. Let's look at these in turn:

High data rates Many websites have significant traffic rates. The supply of test subjects is ample. Some of the traffic is free, while other sources are paid. In aggregate, all of your traffic sources result in a particular traffic mix that is unique for your website.

A relatively steady and large stream of visitors allows you to use statistics to find and verify the validity of the best landing page designs. The best versions are proven winners. Unlike previous designs, they are no longer based solely on subjective opinions. Nor are they the results of popularity contests within your company.

> With high website traffic volumes, statistical analysis allows you to find verifiably better landing pages and to be confident in our answer.

Accurate tracking Web analytics software supports the accurate tracking and recording of every interaction with your website. Each visit is recorded along with a mind-numbing amount of detailed information. Reports can tell you the source of the visitors, their path through your site, the time that they spent lingering over certain content, and whether they were persuaded to act. Although Web analytics software is not perfect, it provides a standard of data collection accuracy that is almost unheard of in any other marketing medium.

Easy content changes Internet technology offers the ability to easily swap or modify the content that a particular website visitor sees. The content can be customized based on the source of the traffic, the specific capabilities of the visitor's computer or Web browser software, their behavior during the particular visit, or their past history of interactions with your site. In other experimental environments it is very expensive or time-consuming to come up with an alternative version or prototype. On the Internet, countless website content variations can be created and managed at minimal cost for a landing page optimization test.

The Three Keys to Online Marketing

Before we focus on the specifics of landing page optimization, let's get oriented. Online marketing can be divided into three key activities:

- **Acquisition** Getting people to your website or landing page
- **Conversion** Persuading them to take the desired action(s)
- **Retention** Deepening the relationship and increasing its lifetime value

Each step feeds into the next. The efficiency of each online marketing activity can be viewed as a funnel like the one in Figure 1.1.

Inefficient acquisition activities will limit the traffic to your site. An inefficient website with low conversion rates will restrict the number of leads or customers. Inefficient retention follow-up activities will fail to extract additional value from your current prospects or clients. Ideally you would like each step to have the highest possible yield. Let's discuss them each in more detail here.

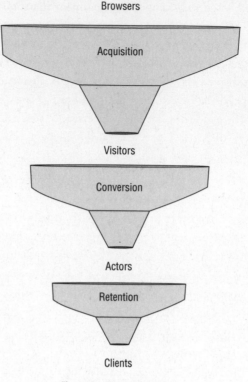

Figure 1.1 The activity funnel

Acquisition

Acquisition activities focus on generating traffic to your website or landing pages. The goal is to create an awareness of your company or products and enough interest for your target Internet audience to actually visit your site.

Web marketing experts use a variety of methods to generate traffic. I've listed the traffic sources in this section, to convey the range of possible acquisition activities. They can be broadly grouped into online and offline methods, although there is often some overlap and mutual reinforcement between the two.

Online Acquisition Methods

Web marketers typically use the following *online* methods for driving traffic:

Search engine optimization (SEO) Search engines like Google, Yahoo!, and MSN provide an excellent source of traffic for many companies. Contrasted with most *interruption marketing*, people using search engines show focus and a specific intention to act. They may be actively gathering information about a topic, selecting the right product or service, or looking for a place to make an immediate purchase.

The process of making your website pages appear near the top in search engine search results for words and phrases (also known as *keywords*) that are relevant to your business is known as *search engine optimization (SEO)*. This process is also referred to as getting organic listings in search engine results. SEO involves initial activities to enhance your website content and get other highly ranked sites to link back to yours. Once your SEO campaign has achieved your initial visibility goals, ongoing maintenance is required to keep you near the top of the search results.

One of the key ways to increase your SEO website traffic is to have important and credible sites in your industry link back to you. Links are usually requested from the webmasters of other sites. You contact them and ask them to add a relevant link back to your site from the appropriate spot on theirs.

Getting such *back links* from other popular websites in your industry has many benefits. As part of your SEO link-back activities it can result in higher placement in the search results and more visibility. Outside links can also enhance your credibility to people browsing the Web and drive motivated visitors to your site. Links can appear in industry directories, on the websites of your business partners, and in news-related blogs (which I will discuss in a moment).

Banner and text ads Many popular or special-purpose websites reserve space on their pages for advertisers. This is usually in the form of short text advertisements, or rectangles of various sizes containing images designed by the advertiser (*banner ads*). Advertisements on multiple websites (*run of network* campaigns) are possible through a number of online distribution companies. Such distributors can also target your ads to websites that have a specific theme. In some cases, advertisements can be further tailored to appear on only certain sections or even individual pages of a desired website. Typically banner ads are sold on a *cost per thousand impressions (CPM)* basis. This means that you are charged a set fee based on a preset *rate card* for every time a visitor to the site sees your ad on a page. You pay even if *nobody* ever clicks on your ad and visits your website. This has begun to change as leading companies in the industry are moving toward an auction model (where the ad real estate is sold to the highest bidder). Some experimental programs have even sold ads on a pure performance basis. Under this business model the advertiser only pays if a specific action such as a sale or completion of a lead inquiry actually happens downstream.

Pay-per-click (PPC) Pay-per-click (PPC) is a very popular online advertising model. PPC ads are typically short text advertisements along the top, sides, or bottom of a Web page. PPC text ads appear in two major contexts. When featured on *search engine results pages (SERPs)*, the PPC ads are targeted to the particular keyword that the searcher typed in. Other text PPC ads occur by insertion into targeted Web pages whose themes are associated with the keyword in question. In contrast to the way that search results are normally presented, the advertiser controls the exact title and text of their ad within the editorial guidelines and policies of the PPC program.

Most PPC search engines charge advertisers using some variation of a live auction model. In other words, your position in the paid search results depends on how much you and other advertisers are willing to pay per click. The more you pay, the more prominently your ad will appear.

Many PPC campaigns involve a large number of keywords (ranging from dozens to tens of thousands). Each keyword has a different value based on its focus and relevance to the advertiser's business. Because of the live auction environment, the position of each ad in the paid search results can change based on the actions of other advertisers. If the position gets too low, the amount of traffic from that keyword can drop very quickly. Typically, many advertisers will compete for the top few positions and bid the prices up over time. Specific software tools have been created to maintain the proper pricing and position for each keyword in the face of changing circumstances. Even with these automated tools, maintaining PPC campaigns can be extremely time-consuming. Because of this, some companies hire dedicated staff to run the campaign or outsource to a search engine marketing (SEM) agency.

Banner ads may also be bought on a PPC basis. Regardless of the format of the ad (text or banner ad), the advertiser is only charged when a Web surfer clicks on the ad and follows the link to their website or landing page. With pay-per-click ads, the advertiser controls how much they are willing to pay for a click on their ad.

Affiliates Many midsize and larger companies have well-established affiliate programs. An *affiliate program* is essentially a form of pure-commission selling. The affiliate directs a visitor to a website or landing page. The affiliate that the visitor originated from is recorded. If that visitor converts by taking the desired action (e.g., purchases, fills out a form, downloads something, or clicks through to another Web page), the affiliate gets credit and payment for the action. For sales, the payment is typically a fixed amount or percentage of the sale. For other actions such as sales leads or special offers, the payment is typically a fixed amount. There are often volume tiers, with higher payouts for top-performing affiliates. Affiliates vary widely in their sophistication and traffic-driving tactics. The bottom line is that they send traffic to your landing page and get paid only if that traffic subsequently converts.

Third-party e-mail lists Many companies purchase third-party e-mail lists from a number of sources and send a single e-mail or multiple e-mails to the list. The quality and targeting of the lists varies widely. Some are clearly low quality and will be perceived as spam by the recipients. Others can be well targeted and provide a good overlap with your intended audience. Very targeted e-mails can be sent (e.g., to the readership of a particular focused blog). Since repeated mailing to the same list can lead to *list fatigue* and lower response rates over time, responders to e-mail are not typically used as traffic sources during conversion tuning tests (which require a steady flow of new and unbiased visitors).

Blogs Blogs are public online diaries. The number of blogs is continuing to explode. They exist on an incredibly wide range of topics, and are often focused on deep coverage of their subject matter. Some blogs are informal and conversational in tone. Others are more akin to a regular magazine or newspaper column, with in-depth coverage of a specific event or topic. Once a blog author has a reputation as a "thought leader" and an expert in a certain field, their readership can grow quickly. They may mention, or "cover," your company in one of their online entries, or "posts." The resulting exposure may mean high-quality ongoing traffic from their reader base as people read and reread the post over time.

Social networking Social networking sites such as MySpace and Facebook allow people to connect in communities of shared interest. If members of the community recommend your products or services or describe them in a positive light, they can influence other people with similar tastes and interests to visit your website. Key members of these online communities can have significant audiences and followings similar to popular bloggers.

Collaborative authoring Collaborative authoring sites include news and discussion forums, client-authored product reviews on e-commerce sites, user reviews on various city-guide websites, and extensive encyclopedias such as Wikipedia.org. Anyone can add content to such websites (and in the case of Wikipedia even remove the content of others). Links embedded in informational posts on such sites can direct visitors to your website or landing page.

In-house e-mail lists You can construct in-house mailing lists by asking people for information while they are visiting your site. If used properly, in-house lists can become an asset that grows in value over time. In-house mailing lists are rarely used to create traffic for conversion tuning tests because each person on the list has already interacted with your company and may be biased in some way. They have been exposed to your marketing, messaging, and current website or landing pages, as well as previous e-mails that you have sent them. In-house mailing lists are at the core of retention activities and will be discussed in more detail later in this chapter.

Online video ads Online video content is growing quickly with the increased penetration of high-speed Internet connections in many businesses and homes. Many video clips and programs now include short promotional messages or commercials.

Offline Acquisitions Methods

The offline methods that you use to drive traffic will lead to a Web visitor directly typing in your *universal resource locator (URL)* (or Web address) into a Web browser. It is difficult to accurately attribute traffic coming from offline sources to their original source (with the exceptions noted below). A single visitor may be driven to your site from multiple sources at different times.

Common offline tactics include:

Brand awareness Brand awareness is demonstrated by someone typing in your company's Web address directly into their Web browser or when somebody uses your brand names as a Web search. This means that the person is specifically looking for your company. Although not strictly an offline traffic-driving method, brand awareness traffic is usually achieved as a result of multiple exposures to your company in diverse settings. A high proportion of brand awareness traffic is an indication that your brand is strong in your industry sector and that you are "top of mind" for prospective customers. It usually results from a combination of all of the other online and offline activities.

TV and radio advertising Many TV and radio commercials specify a URL as one of the possible response mechanisms (along with a telephone number and mailing address). Some Web addresses add a specific trackable landing page (e.g., http://YourCompany.com/tv) to attribute the traffic correctly to its source. This is not a foolproof method since many people may drop the last part of the URL and just type in the company name.

Print ad magazine advertising Almost all print advertising includes a URL. It is standard practice to direct the traffic to a specific landing page. Since the print medium offers more permanence (unlike a fleeting TV or radio ad), people may be more willing to type in a longer landing page URL.

Public relations and media coverage Various public relations activities can result in mentions of your company in print and broadcast media. Typically your site will experience a spike of coverage-related traffic after such events. Afterward you may also get additional traffic from people who later come across the information.

Industry analyst coverage Many complex industries (especially in high technology) have key industry analysts and market research firms that routinely put out reports and analyses of emerging trends, products, and services. If your company is included in these publications, you will be considered by a very interested group of prospects as they research their buying decision. If you are not part of the industry analyst reports, your company will be invisible to these prospects.

Industry tradeshows Industry tradeshows can provide the opportunity to speak and exhibit in front of a targeted audience. Many key influencers and decision makers also attend networking and social events held in conjunction with such shows.

Event participation Event participation and sponsorship may raise awareness of your company with a particular audience or group. You can choose the demographics and psychographics of the events that you promote.

Point-of-sale (POS) promotions Many companies conduct promotion and advertising at the point of sale or the point at which the service is delivered. Common forms include sweepstakes, contests, and games of various types. The Web is used as the mechanism to complete the promotional transaction, allowing you to accurately gauge its impact.

Client referrals Current and past clients can be an excellent source of additional traffic. If a company has a specific incentive program to reward them for referrals, the mechanism for completing the referral transaction is done via the Web.

Outdoor advertising Billboard advertising is typically used to promote the company or overall brand. Its limited ability to convey deep information means that it is usually limited to building awareness.

Promotional items Company promotional items can feature a Web URL. Typically such items enhance your type-in traffic but cannot be tracked directly. However, you can have a dedicated domain name on the promotional item for certain events (e.g., for a new product launch).

Direct marketing and catalogs Sending out specialized flyers or catalogs by mail is a proven way to market to prospective and existing customers. Activities can be tracked through to the Web by specifying unique landing pages in the printed materials. A *promo code* that is entered by the recipient on the landing page can serve to identify them. Most people will type in this additional information in exchange for receiving the benefit of the promotional offer.

The resulting mix of traffic hits your website or landing pages in a number of places. Some visitors will arrive on your home page, while others may land deep within your site, or even on specially designed single-purpose landing pages that are not connected to your main website at all. The particular composition of traffic, and where it lands, depends on your current acquisition marketing activities. Each site's traffic mix and landing pattern is unique.

Conversion

Since conversion is the main topic of this book, I'll briefly define and summarize it here.

Let's start with the basics. A *landing page* is the point at which an Internet visitor lands on your website. Landing pages can be stand-alone with no connection to your main website. They can also be specialized micro-sites that are focused on a particular audience and desired outcome. The landing page can also be a specific page deep in your main website. For purposes of this book, the term *landing page* will be used for all of these cases unless noted otherwise.

A *conversion* happens when a visitor to your landing page takes a desired *conversion action* that has a measurable value to your business.

The desired action can be a purchase, download, form-fill, or even a simple click-through to another page on your website. Conversions can also be measured by having someone interact with a particular feature of your site (such as a product demo tour). A conversion can also be measured in more subtle brand interaction terms by looking at the number of page views, repeat visits, and the time spent on your site, or by interactions with content that includes product placements from your company. The main point is that the conversion action must be trackable and its value can be calculated or estimated.

A *conversion rate* is the percentage of visitors to your website or landing page who take a desired action that has a measurable value to your business.

Conversion rates vary widely across different industries and even between competitors in the same industry. There are many reasons why they may vary, and many of them are not related to the visitor's direct experience with your website.

External Conversion Factors

Conversions do not happen in a vacuum. Before people even get to your site, they will be inclined or disinclined to act by factors that have nothing to do with your site directly. Several external factors affect conversion rates:

Brand strength Visitors to your website are more likely to act if they are familiar with your company or products and trust your brand promise. Many companies spend enormous sums of money to have their brand penetrate the visitor's awareness. If they are successful, the brand serves as a permanent shortcut and aids in decision making. Other companies without this status are simply not in the game, and will not be considered by many people despite their objective parity or even advantages over established rivals.

Degree of commoditization If your industry sells nearly identical generic products as your competitor does, then the main factor in visitors' minds will be price. There may be many competitors who offer identical products, and it pays for the visitor to shop around. So the likelihood of a particular visitor converting is lower. If you offer a very specialized or unique product or service, your website visitors will be much more likely to act simply because there may not be many choices, or because the effort required to find viable alternatives may be too high.

Seasonality Some products or services are in constant demand because they are either consumable (you will use them up) or perishable (they have a limited effective shelf life or a specific expiration date). So people will reliably replenish their supply or renew the appropriate subscription. Other products are highly seasonal or are only needed for a single event or purpose. For example, the cut flower business has a steady flow of year-round occasions (dates and anniversaries), but is largely driven by the ordering frenzy that precedes Valentine's Day and Mother's Day. During such peak demand times, conversion rates will be higher because the product or service becomes a "must have." For many seasonal businesses, the limited supply of available product can also drive up its value and desirability (e.g., scarce hotel rooms in high-demand locations, or airline seats on popular routes).

Physicality and uniformity The lament is often heard among e-tailers: "Why are we only converting 2% of our site visitors to buyers? We get much higher conversion rates in our retail locations. We must be doing a lousy job to lose 98% of potential customers."

Of course this is an apples-to-oranges comparison. The visitor to a physical store typically has already decided to invest more time and energy to the visit than a Web visitor. Many of the visitors to a website who don't purchase anything would never visit a physical store at all since they just don't care enough to make the effort. The physical experience in a real store can never be duplicated online and involves many experiential and sensory details. Before we even decide to buy something in a physical store, we must carry out a number of tasks—drive to the store, park, walk inside, take in the décor, experience the lighting level and temperature, compare our appearance to other customers, react to whether we are greeted or ignored by store employees, physically interact with potential products that we are considering, and so forth.

This is a completely different experience than sitting in front of a computer and surfing the Internet. We stare at a tiny screen (compared to our normal field of vision), and decipher information that is organized typically not around our needs, but along the organizational and usability concepts of others. We rarely get to interact with the products beyond clicking on their small *thumbnail image* to get a larger zoomed view.

Some products and services must be experienced before they are bought. Imagine buying an expensive suit without feeling the texture and thickness of the fabric, and feeling the construction and drape of the materials over your particular body. You will probably need to have the suit customized and tailored to your build, and would not wear the pants unhemmed out of the store.

Other products (like books or bottles of wine) cannot be sampled without consuming them and are more easily sold online. You are buying their contents based on the packaging and reputation. They depend on their cover (or label), and the recommendations and reviews of trusted friends or expert authorities. Because they can be reduced to images and written text, such products translate well to a Web buying experience and are much more likely to have higher conversion rates. You do not typically worry about their contents since they should be uniform.

Intention and commitment Not everyone who visits your site has the same intention and commitment to act. As you will see in the following chapters, visitors' frame of mind depends on their demographics, psychographics, personality type, role, time of day, day of week, physical environment and the presence of distractions, and their position in the buying/decision cycle. Someone who is surrounded by coworkers and researching a gift idea on their lunch break at work will behave very differently than someone who is alone at night in their home and is looking for the lowest price vendor for a specific product. People are often looking for an intangible package that represents the best value proposition. Of course, price is often an important consideration, but other factors such as the warranty, in-stock availability, shipping speed and methods, positive reviews, available financing and payment terms, and accepted payment methods all enter into this equation.

People arrive at your website with all of these factors already influencing them to various degrees. And all of this happens before they even see your landing page. So don't forget that your website does not exist in a vacuum. Your online visitors, like any other traveler, are already bringing a lot of baggage with them.

Onsite Conversion Factors

As we just discussed, visitors will arrive at your website with their own needs, perspectives, and emotions. Since you don't know very much about them individually, how can you influence them with the design of your site?

This is not exactly new ground. The field of direct marketing (DM) is all about getting people to act and respond to offers. Since basic human nature has not changed, we can apply the well-tested lessons of DM to the online sphere.

People do not often make rational decisions. In fact, the capacity for abstract rational thought is only a recent evolutionary addition to our brains. We have mainly gotten by on our emotions and gut feelings. We may think that we are approaching something rationally, but most of the time we use after-the-fact rationalization to justify our intuitive and emotional decision making.

It is a well-known maxim in marketing that people who are comfortable enough with their current situation (like the hound dog in the story) are not good prospects for buying goods, services, or ideas—they simply don't care enough to make a change.

All of the specific strategies and tactics that you will learn later in the book are aimed at influencing basic human emotions and moving your visitors off their comfortable spot. Direct marketers Bob Hacker and Axel Andersson have defined several key copywriting concepts that motivate people to act: fear, greed, guilt, exclusivity, anger, salvation, or flattery. Not one of these motivations is rational—all of them are rooted in our fundamental and unchanging emotional nature.

> The best way to get visitors to act is to appeal to their fundamental *emotional* motivations.

At SiteTuners.com we have developed a set of hierarchical scales to help us rate websites. They are not precise instruments, but rather tools that help us to focus outward (on our website visitors) and then inward (on their emotional state). Each scale is a continuum of feelings and internal states.

A specific design change proposal must be explainable within these scales, and should attempt to "move the needle to the right." Although the scales are distinct, changes that affect one scale will often have an impact on the others as well.

Anxiety vs. Trust This is the most basic scale and addresses our feelings of safety and security. You would not think that sitting in front of a Web browser would produce much anxiety, but you would be wrong. Giving up personal information, allowing people to contact us, and paying by credit card all have significant fears associated with them.

How will my information be used? Will I get on a spam list? Will I be the victim of identity theft? Will the purchase arrive undamaged and on time? Will I actually get what I ordered? Will unexpected fine print charges be added to my order without my knowledge? Will anyone respond if I have a problem after buying? Will it be easy to dispute or cancel my transaction?

Anything that you can do to minimize anxiety will help conversion. This includes clear privacy policies, detailed shipping directions, unconditional return policies, client testimonials, certifications, and trust symbols that show that you conduct business with integrity.

Confusion vs. Clarity Some sites are simple and intuitive. Most are akin to a busy marketplace with loud hawkers vying for your attention. You are assaulted with bright colors, boxes, flashing advertisements. You are overloaded with too many choices and links. You are drowned in too much text displayed in tiny fonts. You are not sure how to navigate the site and find the information that you need.

Is this a button that I can click or just a graphic? Does "Buy it now" just put something in my shopping cart or does it actually charge me and place my order? Where am I in the site? How do I get back to the page that I read earlier? Which of these 20 links should I click? Why does this page text not address my particular needs?

Often too many internal company interests compete for real estate and prominence on important pages. Over time nothing ever gets taken away—new items are simply added to the Web page. Unfortunately, this often leads to a phenomenon know as "The Tragedy of the Commons." If too many shepherds have unrestricted access to the unregulated common grazing lands, the sheep will overwhelm the grass's ability to regenerate itself—destroying it for everyone. The individual self-interests of shepherds undercuts the common good.

By emphasizing too many items on a Web page, we destroy visitors' ability to find key information and paralyze them from making a decision.

Most sites and landing pages have very poor information architecture and interaction design. Fixing major usability, coherence, and cognitive problems can have a major conversion rate impact.

Alienation vs. Affinity   Even if we get over our anxiety and confusion to find the information that we need, we still have to deal with affinity and alienation. We want to be
recognized for who we are, understood, and valued. These are subtle issues of identity,
tribalism, self-esteem, and belonging. We are members of many formal and informal
tribes in our lives: fans of a specific sports team, employees of a certain company, drivers of a particular make of car, occupants of a specific zip code, and graduates of a certain school… the list is endless. Some of these tribes we chose consciously, others
unconsciously. Still others chose us (e.g., the "tribe" of orphaned children, or being a
member of a specific racial/ethnic group).

> A sense of belonging and being understood is a powerful motivator for people.

The editorial tone of the landing page needs to conform to the visitor's values and
beliefs. Any images of people should also help them to self-identify. Graphics color
schemes should match the appropriate palette for their sensibilities. Button text and
calls-to-action should also use the language of the target community. By segmenting
your visitors and personalizing information for them, you are much more likely to
appeal to their sensibilities and move them to action.

Online and Offline Combined

Although I have tried to separate conversion-related factors into offline and online, the
world is not really that neatly organized. There are very important interactions among
the two, and they often play complementary roles. Many people will conduct extensive
research online and then convert offline. So the online channel serves as a key influencer, but not as the point of conversion. If an online marketing program has no way
to track these subsequent conversions, the apparent economics seem much less favorable. One way to close the loop is to create specific incentives (such as printable
coupons), which can be redeemed at the point of purchase and can be used to encode
the exact online origin of the transaction.

   The influence can extend the other way as well. Many people will see a product
in the physical world and then track it down and purchase it online.

   Every contact with a potential customer can impact their eventual behavior. This
often involves a complicated and tangled thread with multiple exposures to your brand
and products across several online and offline channels. Accurate tracking and measurement in this kind of environment can become nearly impossible. Even if you could
track everything properly, it often comes down to interpretation about how to assign
the proper marketing credit. For example, should you always count the initial source of

the visitor, or assign credit to their last point of interaction before the conversion action happens? There are no clear answers or rules about such chains of contact over extended periods of time. The point is that you should be aware of the multiple influences on each Web visitor, and understand the real value of each customer conversion regardless of where it happens.

Retention

Retention is the third key online marketing activity. Once someone has become aware of your company and made initial contact, you must deepen your relationship with them in order to extract value in the future. In his excellent book *Permission Marketing: Turning Strangers into Friends and Friends into Customers* (Simon & Schuster, 1999), author Seth Godin accurately lays out the changing balance of power between consumers and companies. Consumers are in almost total control and are increasingly impervious to traditional advertising assaults. They tune out most interruptions and focus only on what is important to them. If they notice you at all, they will give you very limited "permission" to interact with them.

Retention programs should seek to build on the initial permission with anticipated, personal, and relevant ongoing communications. Over time, as you earn the consumer's trust and continue to provide value, you are granted higher levels of intimacy and permission in return.

Retention programs start immediately after the initial conversion action on your site has been taken. This initial action may have been an e-mail sign-up for your newsletter, or a whitepaper download. It will often not be the actual initial purchase of your products or services. But you can leverage the right to contact the person by educating them and leading them closer to the ultimate desired action (an initial sale or a repeat sale).

The basis for all retention programs is the ability for the user to receive information from your company on an ongoing basis. So the minimum requirement is that they have given you their e-mail address or added your blog or news source to their data feed.

E-mail has three disadvantages from the user's perspective. You typically do not restrict the list of people or entities that you are willing to accept e-mails from, you are not anonymous, and you cannot control the contents of the messages that are sent to you. Of course, there are ways to *blacklist* certain senders, or receive e-mails only from a *whitelist* of approved addresses. There are also ways to create anonymous or even disposable e-mail addresses. Unwanted content can also be fought by spam-filtering software. But none of these solutions are perfect, and it is difficult to strike the right balance among intrusiveness, extra effort and work, and access to the right information.

News feeds and blog readers address some of the problems with e-mail and are increasingly the preferred choice for getting information from companies. Feeds allow you to specify your news sources and modify them at will so you can control the mix of information that you receive. You can also filter the results and flag only those news entries that mention specific keywords that interest you. You can also remain anonymous and read about events without the originating company knowing your identity. There are a growing number of readers available. Most new blogging software allows you to subscribe to feeds and blogs in a number of the most popular formats.

Retention marketing takes on several forms online:

E-mail E-mail is probably the most widely used of all retention media. A clear distinction must be made between unsolicited spam versus true opt-in lists that are carefully collected and built by companies over time. Spam has no place in this discussion (or ethical online business) and is actually a form of acquisition marketing because you have no prior relationship with the e-mail recipient. In-house mailing lists, on the other hand, are a powerful resource that grows in value over time. Sophisticated e-mail campaigns can be set up to touch specific recipients with a preprogrammed sequence of messages. The presentation of information can even be modified based on reactions to previous contacts (such as opening an e-mail, clicking a link, or actually responding to a particular offer).

Newsletters Newsletters are a close cousin and a specific use of e-mail retention marketing. They tend to be sent on a regular schedule, and their main purpose is to educate a prospect about the details of more complex products or services, and enable the reader to make an informed buying decision at some point. Their editorial tone is generally informational, and calls to action subtly nudge the reader to take the next step in the buying process.

Blog feeds Online diaries or blogs exist on a very wide range of topics. Some of the authors of blogs have large followings and are considered authorities in their respective domains of knowledge. Blogs can be very timely and are often updated several times per day. Getting someone to subscribe to a blog is the desired goal for a retention marketer. After that, all new posts to your blog will automatically become available in the recipient's blog feed.

News feeds News feeds are similar in concept to blogs, but the source of content is different. The information often comes from accredited news sources and major publications, and is typically less varied in quality, length, and editorial tone than blogs.

Rewards and loyalty Various "points" programs are used to incentivize people to act. These include frequent-flyer miles or simple promotions like "every fifth car wash is free." Online tracking allows retention marketers to reward very granular events such as responding to e-mail promotions, clicking on certain pages, participating in surveys, or referring others.

Retention marketing is critical to an online company's profitability. Effective programs can have a multiplier effect on revenues by increasing lifetime value of the client relationship. You will also typically have much higher profit margins with repeat customers because the incremental cost of marketing to them is minimal.

But it is important to realize that every experience with your company contributes to your success. Well-designed e-mail campaigns may fail because of a user's poor experience with your product or service, or negative interactions with your customer support or billing staff. So it is critical to keep your nose clean and sweat the details of every customer or prospect "touch point." Otherwise, you can undermine the success of your retention programs.

The Myth of Perfect Conversion

Don't make the mistake of assuming that every visitor is a potential prospect or buyer for your goods or services. That would be a delusion. The mythical 100% conversion rate simply does not exist.

There are three types of visitors to your website:

1. Noes—Those that *won't ever* take the desired action
2. Yesses—Those that *will always* take the desired action
3. Maybes—Those that *may* take the desired action

You should completely ignore the first two and concentrate on the last group. Let's examine this more closely.

Some visitors to your website are not prepared to take action. They may be unable to afford what you sell. They may work for your rival and are merely conducting competitive research. Or they may have been simply surfing the Web and thought that it was worth a second of their time to look at your landing page. There are countless reasons why someone will not take the desired action. The important realization is that there is *nothing that you can do to influence them to act*. For most landing pages, this group is by far the largest of the three.

There is also a group of visitors who will always take the desired action. There is ample evidence for this. People will put up with maddeningly difficult registration or checkout processes. They will seek out links and information that are buried deep within websites. In general, they will display a degree of tenacity and will that is staggering. Why do they do this? There are a variety of reasons. Some of them have willful personalities. Others are already sold on what you are offering due to outside influences. Still others have searched far and wide and have been able to find only your company as a viable answer to their immediate and burning needs. Others are just tired of looking further and have settled on your company as the best alternative that they have seen. Regardless, short of a broken website nothing will deter these people from taking the desired action on your landing page. The main point is that *these people do not need any convincing by you.*

The final group of undecideds contains a wide variety of people. Some of them are almost there—a small improvement in your landing page or website might get them over the hump and result in the desired action. Others may need significant additional persuasion and hand-holding in order to come around. Figure 1.2 shows the range of possible visitor dispositions towards the desired conversion actions

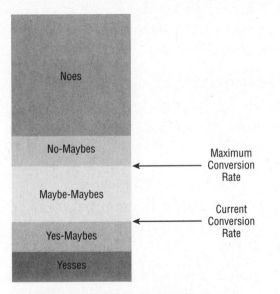

Figure 1.2 Visitor conversion action dispositions

Unless your website is truly ineffectual, you are already converting some of the maybes. This segment of "yes-maybes," along with your yesses, makes up your current conversion rate. However, even with the best landing page you will not be able to convert all of the people in this group at once—they have contradictory needs. Landing page changes that sway a particular person might repel another. So at best you can hope to convert only a portion of the undecideds. The remainder (the "no-maybes") will forever be out of your reach. So the maximum conversion rate improvement that is possible for your business is limited to capturing the rest of the "maybe-maybes" that are still up for grabs.

Of course, it is impossible to precisely measure or even estimate the sizes of these segments for a particular landing page or website. But you should understand that your actual conversion rate "ceiling" is well below 100%.

What's Wrong with This Picture?

What's wrong with this picture?

Acquisition   Conversion   Retention

In the marketing world, a lot of time and resources are spent buying media, tracking pay-per-click (PPC) campaigns, driving organic traffic via SEO to landing pages, and installing and customizing Web analytics software to properly track all online marketing activities. Dedicated in-house or agency staff craft keyword lists, write ad copy, and manage keyword bidding to achieve the proper profitability, cost per action (CPA), and return on investment (ROI). Copywriters adjust our sales copy to improve click-through rates (CTRs). Every aspect of performance is scrutinized under a microscope as we drill down on mind-numbingly detailed reports.

Once someone converts, extensive retention e-mail campaigns are set in motion to persuade visitors to deepen their level of engagement. We worry about every single word in our e-mails as we test headlines and offers. We analyze "bounce rates," "open rates," and "unsubscribe rates" with almost religious fervor in order to extract the last penny of revenue and profit possible over the lifetime of our interaction with someone.

But we have almost completely ignored our website and landing page. Sure, we occasionally do facelifts or even wholesale redesigns of our sites. But these changes are rarely tested, and are simply assumed to improve the situation. They are just a cost of "doing business." And even though we spend obscene amounts of money to buy traffic, the effort that we devote to the landing pages to which it is sent is negligible. A couple of hours of graphic designer and copywriter time are often all that the landing page merits. With a cursory review by the higher-ups, the landing page goes live.

Worse yet, we assume that the quality of the landing page cannot be changed. So we do not even look to it for improvements. We turn all of the other knobs and dials at our disposal and continue to neglect the biggest profit driver under our control—the conversion efficiency of the landing page. And this is costing a lot of money in the form of missed opportunity. Double- or triple-digit conversion rate gains are routinely realized through engagements at my company, SiteTuners.com. Yet there is still a widespread perception among online marketers that their landing pages are already solid and can't be improved through testing.

> Your website and landing page conversion rates have been neglected for much too long—costing you a lot of money.

Because of the large amounts of money spent on acquisition and retention, sophisticated systems have been created to maximize the ROI of these activities. But the efficiency of the website or landing page has been largely neglected. Many companies are now beginning to understand that website and landing page conversion can have a dramatic impact on online marketing program profits. That's where the new battleground is in the coming years.

In the next chapter we will examine the important aspects of your landing pages.

Understanding Your Landing Pages

Begin with the end in mind.
—Stephen R. Covey, author of The *Seven Habits of Highly Effective People*

What is the purpose of your landing page?

This seems like a simple question. But the vast majority of us cannot answer it in a simple and cogent sentence.

Most of your websites and landing pages have become overgrown like a dense jungle. They have no clear purpose, and are instead a grab bag of unrelated tidbits—each one hoping to compete for visitors' attention.

Let's take a close look at what your landing pages are, and ask a series of questions about what they ought to be.

2

Chapter Contents

Landing Page Types

The landing page is the first page that a visitor lands on as a result of your traffic acquisition efforts.

Landing pages come in three main flavors:

Main site The landing page might be part of your main corporate website. Such pages have the same navigation and page layout as all of the other pages on your site. The specific landing page might be buried several layers deep within your site organization, or it might be your home page.

Microsite The landing page is part of a *microsite* specifically designed for a single audience or purpose. A microsite usually has one main call-to-action (such as a purchase or information request), and all of the information on the site funnels the visitor back to this desired conversion action. A microsite usually contains a few pages of supporting information that allow a visitor to make an educated decision about the topic in question, and request further information or buy something. Such information includes a detailed description of your product or service, buying guides or wizards, downloadable whitepapers, comparisons to similar products or services, case studies, testimonials, and other validation. Microsites can be branded as part of your main company or can have their own stand-alone brand.

Stand-alone Some Web pages are specifically designed for a particular marketing campaign. Such pages usually have specific information related only to the offer or action that you would like your visitors to take. Usually there is a clear, single call-to-action. If the desired action is not taken, stand-alone landing pages may employ an exit pop-up window with a secondary desired action, or a repeat of the original call-to-action.

The type of landing page that you deploy is largely dictated by your traffic source, as well as the type of product or service that you offer.

Ideally your traffic can be specifically directed to a particular page and tracked in significant detail. For example, a PPC campaign allows you to specify the exact landing page for each keyword. This information can be tracked through the conversion process, and allows you to calculate the ROI at the keyword level. Such traffic should generally be directed at goal-oriented, stand-alone landing pages. The advantage of stand-alone landing pages is that they are targeted. They do not overwhelm your visitor or distract them with irrelevant information. This usually results in the best bang for the buck and highest conversion rates.

In the case of an online catalog, this may be harder to do. When you prepare large PPC campaigns, you create a mapping indicating exactly where each keyword should land. A good rule of thumb is to always *deep-link* the PPC traffic within your main site (place the visitors as close as you can to the information that they requested). Even though the traffic will land in different places on your site, at least you can control the exact landing page for each keyword. For example, if you were operating an online shoe catalog, you might use the following landing pages:

- "shoes"—Website home page
- "women's shoes"—Women's shoes home page
- "hiking boots"—Hiking boots category home page
- "reebok sneakers"—Reebok brand home page
- "bruno magli ranuncolo"—Product detail page for this particular shoe model

Some main-site traffic cannot be easily controlled. If you achieve a high ranking for a particular keyword as a result of good search engine optimization (SEO), visitors will land on the most relevant page on your site (as determined by the search engine). This may mean that the traffic enters through what you might consider a side door and not the main page on your site. Many websites make sure that such popular SEO landing pages offer supplemental navigation to quickly link to important parts of your site. This in effect converts the landing page side door into another front door.

Other traffic is more generic and anonymous. For example, most traffic from offline sources is likely to end up on your home page for the simple reason that visitors will not bother to type in a long and convoluted URL. Even if you give them a specific landing page, many visitors will shorten it and drop everything except your top-level domain name.

In general (unless you operate an online catalog), landing controllable traffic sources on your main website should be a last resort. By definition your main site must serve many audiences, so it is likely to be somewhat generic and cluttered. Each page must also include all of your cumbersome navigation and page layout conventions in order to have a consistent look and feel throughout the site.

Single products or services are ideal for stand-alone landing pages. Many products have been successfully sold via the online equivalent of a long direct-mail sales letter. Much of online lead capture likewise depends on a single page to start (and ideally to complete) the information-collection process.

Microsite landing pages fall somewhere in between. They are typically used when the product or service in question requires a lot of supporting information. Microsites work well because they are separate from the main corporate site and focus exclusively on the needs of the visitors, who care only about their immediate goal. They create more intimacy and a feeling of belonging, while still providing important supporting information.

What Parts of Your Site Are Mission Critical?

Mission critical activities on your sites can easily be identified. All you have to do is ask yourself the following question:

You must be very sober and ruthless in answering. Very little of the content on your site meets this definition. For the most part, only activities that drive business revenues and sales fall into this category.

Here are some examples of typical site content that is *not* usually mission critical:

- Investor relations
- Company mission statement
- Open job listings
- Management bios

I am sure that counter-examples can be brought up to each of these (e.g., job listings for a recruiting company, or management bios for a professional services firm). But as a rule of thumb, supporting company information is not mission critical.

Still not sure whether something is mission critical? Use this test:

Does the content create a *meaningful transaction* or *deepen your relationship* with the visitor?

A meaningful transaction does not have to be your ultimate conversion goal. It can be a small incremental step that creates psychological momentum toward that goal. Deepening your relationship means that you have been given a higher level of trust by the visitor. Tangible evidence of this includes spending more time on important parts of your site. So does increased page views of key content. Of course, the most important indicators are the sharing of information by filling out forms, calling, or chatting; downloading written materials or computer programs; signing up for free trials and promotions; or actually buying something.

All other content on the site is at best irrelevant, or at worst a distraction from the mission critical parts. As you will see later in the book, this deadwood content should be eliminated, or at least reduced in scope and emphasis as much as possible in order to streamline the important parts of your landing pages.

What you should be left with are the mission critical parts that you will test and tune to improve conversion rates.

Who Is Your Landing Page Designed For?

Your business attracts a number of possible visitor classes to your site. These may include the following:

- Prospects
- Clients
- Current business partners
- Potential future business partners
- Competitors
- Members of the press
- Job seekers
- Current employees
- Past employees
- Investors

The usual practice (especially if your landing page is your main site home page) is to provide a comprehensive view of your company and to give each of these visitor classes equal billing. The company is often portrayed along product lines or as client-facing functional departments.

This tendency to be even-handed is actually counterproductive. Your landing page should be modified to best serve the mission critical visitor classes. Everyone may want real estate on the home page, but they do not necessarily deserve it in equal measure.

Moreover, some visitors are more motivated to find the relevant information on your site. Job seekers will discover the page with available open positions no matter how deeply it is buried in your site. Likewise, potential affiliates will join your program regardless of whether you label the link "affiliates," "webmasters," "partners," or "referral program."

> Important classes of visitors are the ones who interact with the mission critical parts of your website.

What Is the Desired Conversion Action?

Conversion actions are measurable events that move a visitor toward the mission critical activities that you have identified. Many people view conversions as large-scale or "macro" events, such as product sales or sign-ups for a service. In fact, most conversion actions are incremental micro-events that reduce friction and allow a visitor to continue moving toward your ultimate desired outcome. That outcome may not occur during their current visit and may be delayed for many months or even years.

The key criterion for defining conversion actions is that they must be measurable and have a clear value (see the next section for details on how to calculate and estimate this value).

Examples of conversion actions along with their measurement and efficiency metrics follow:

Advertising This includes advertising online, such as banners, text ads, and sponsor links. Measuring advertising effectiveness usually involves tracking the number of times that an ad was seen or clicked on. Another measure is the average advertising revenue per page view for alternative ad page layouts.

Click-through As discussed earlier, only a few parts of your website are mission critical. A click-through can measure the effectiveness with which you funnel visitors to the desired actionable pages, and through the conversion process. Click-throughs can serve as intermediate gauges of progress. The *click-through rate* (CTR) is the percentage of visitors who click through to a desired page.

Education Some websites have ultimate conversion steps that require a lot of up-front education. They provide resources and online guides to fully explain their products and services. If education of visitors is your primary goal, the key metrics are the time spent on your educational pages and the number of page views.

Downloads and printouts Many websites want visitors to take away free content without having to leave behind any personal information. Visitors may be able to download and print (where applicable) any number of items from your site: whitepapers, coupons for offline redemption, samples, or computer software. The download or printout rate of the desired content is the best measure of efficiency.

Form-fill rate Often the conversion goal involves gathering data about the visitor. This can range from a minimum of data (e.g., asking for an e-mail address to which to send future e-newsletters), to full disclosure involving a lot of personal information (e.g., a lengthy online application for a mortgage loan). Regardless of the length or complexity of the form, the form-fill rate is used to measure the efficiency of this process.

Purchase Many companies measure sales efficiency by looking at their sales conversion rate (the percentage of unique visitors who complete a purchase), or their shopping cart abandonment rate (the percentage of people who start the checkout process but never finish it). In many circumstances, the revenue per visitor and profit per visitor are more useful metrics.

For example, if you sell multiple products at widely varying prices, you can bias the mix of products that you sell intentionally. This may mean that you choose to lower your sale conversion rate to focus on higher-ticket items. Conversely, you may seemingly raise your sales conversion rate by emphasizing smaller-ticket items. The merit of the trade-offs involved in such situations can be evaluated by focusing on the revenue per visitor metric. Measuring revenue instead of conversion rate can help make these trade-offs properly.

If the products that you sell have different profit margins, the revenue per visitor metric can be deceiving. This can happen when you boost your revenues by selling very low-margin or even unprofitable loss-leader items. It is possible to boost your revenues while at the same time actually lowering your overall profits. A more sophisticated metric for such situations is the profit per visitor. Instead of assigning the full revenue value to the sale conversion action, you use only the profit margin on the sale.

Multiple Actions The situation is more complicated when multiple conversion actions are involved. For example, your site may sell a service, offer a free trial, and have a sign-up form for a free newsletter (which may eventually lead to future sales). These three conversion actions are all appropriate and roughly correspond to a visitor's position in the buying cycle. It is important to track and measure each of them. By assigning a dollar value to each action, you can see if your overall profit per visitor increases (see the previous list item "Purchase").

Sometimes visitors must make a mutually exclusive choice. For example, they may choose to fill out your information request form, start an online chat session with a customer support representative, or pick up the telephone and call your toll-free number. All three advance your agenda, and allow visitors to select the most appropriate response medium for them.

What Is the Lifetime Value of the Conversion Action?

The *lifetime value* (*LTV*) of a conversion action is the total financial benefit that your company will receive from your relationship with the visitor over the course of the current interaction and all future interactions. In some cases, this is easy to calculate; in other cases it is very difficult.

The easiest cases are when the conversion action is your ultimate goal and its value does not change after the action occurs. For example, if you sell a onetime-use or durable product and the client is unlikely to buy another one from you (e.g., aluminum siding with a lifetime warranty), then the LTV of the conversion action is your profit margin on that sale.

For most businesses, there are many factors that need to be taken into account to properly understand the LTV of your relationship:

Length of relationship How long will your relationship last on average? How many future transactions does this represent?

Repeat buyer rate Are you more focused on hunting for new prospects or tending to existing clients? What is your ratio of repeat to new buyers? What percentage of new clients will become repeat buyers?

Value of repeat sales What is the average value of a repeat customer? What additional products do you use to cross-sell or up-sell to existing clients?

Economies of scale Are there significant economies of scale that you can achieve by raising your sales to a certain level? Can you negotiate better terms with suppliers once you hit certain volume breakpoints?

Changing product/service mix Do follow-on services involve more profitable reduced service levels? Are potential product up-sells at a higher margin than the original purchases?

Referral business How likely are the clients to refer additional business? What is the value of a referral?

The Financial Impact of Conversion Rate Improvement

The total financial benefit of an improved conversion rate depends greatly on your business model and margins. The increases in sales revenue or the increased conversion rate are only an indirect measurement of it.

At SiteTuners.com we have developed a simple model for determining the potential financial impact of a landing page optimization test. The profit impact is based on three quantities. Although the definitions that follow may not strictly match traditional accounting practices, they allow you to quickly establish the potential profit impact of your conversion test and focus your energies on the correct landing pages:

Revenue (R) is the annualized run rate of the full LTV of the conversion actions on the landing page in question, and come from the traffic sources being considered for the test.

The annualized run rate is used to remove the strong seasonal effects of many industries. LTV allows you to see the true future revenue stream as opposed to focusing only on the initial conversion transaction. It is important to take into account only the revenue that is generated through the landing pages and traffic sources that you are considering for the test. Do not include revenues that pass through other pages or that result from other traffic sources.

For example, let's assume that the immediate conversion action is a $20 sale, that an average initial sale leads to additional revenue of $30 over the course of your three-year ongoing relationship with the typical client, that 10,000 clients per year convert through your pay-per-click campaign, and that all of the traffic is directed to the landing page in question. The revenue in this case would be ($20 + $30) × 10,000, or $500,000.

Variable Cost Percentage (VCP) Variable Cost Percentage (VCP) is the total of variable costs on an incremental sale as a percentage of revenue (as defined previously).

Include your cost of goods sold (COGS), affiliate commissions, customer service, shipping, credit card charges, return and allowances, front-line staff salaries (sales, product production, service delivery, and customer service), and other variable costs as a percentage of the total revenue.

Do not include your fixed costs such as rent, utilities, administrative expenses, and non-front-line salaries.

Do not include current online media spending because this will remain unchanged even if your conversion rate improves. Normally this would be considered a variable expense. But your online marketing media buys are in effect part of fixed costs because they are not required to produce an incremental conversion action. The action is happening because of the improved efficiency of your landing page—not because of additional media spending required to produce it.

Also note that VCP is not directly related to your current profit margins (for example, if your profit margins are 10% this does not mean that your VCP is 90%). This is because your current fixed costs are also being included in calculating your overall profit margin. Since these costs will not change as you add incremental sales or conversion actions, they are not included. Only costs directly associated with the incremental conversion action should be included.

If we continue our earlier example, let's assume that the cost of the product and upsells over three years is $15, and the credit card fees and customer service cost another $5. The VCP would be [($15 + $5) × 10,000] ÷ $500,000, or 40%.

Conversion Improvement Percentage (CIP) is the percentage improvement of the measurement criteria of the new (challenger) landing page versus the original (baseline) landing page.

The measurement criterion is the appropriate one for your test and depends on your conversion action. It can include average time spent on site (for educational goals), number of page views (for advertising supported websites), or revenue per visitor (for e-commerce).

Of course, it is impossible to precisely calculate the impact of your landing page optimization ahead of time. But if you use a wide range of possible improvement percentages, you can get a sense of the possible financial impact and the appropriate resources to apply to the effort.

Let's assume that in our example we expect at least a 20% potential improvement in revenue per visitor over our original landing page. Our CIP would then be 0.2.

To conclude our earlier example, the estimated minimum profit increase would be $500,000 \times 0.2 \times (1 - 0.4)$, or $60,000.

I am often asked why fixed costs are not included in the SiteTuners.com financial model. The simple answer is that the fixed costs get canceled out when you subtract the profitability of your improved landing page from the profitability of your original. Since you only care about the *net* impact of the conversion test, it is not important to accurately calculate (or even include) the fixed costs in the financial model.

Resource: Conversion Improvement Profit Calculator

Once you have calculated the revenue and variable cost percentage values, you can use this free calculator to produce a table of profit increases across a range of possible conversion rate improvement percentages: http://sitetuners.com/conversion-rate-improvement-profit-calculator.html

conversion profit improvement report

XYZ Company
(6/29/07)

Conversion Rate Improvement	Baseline	5%	10%	20%	30%	40%	50%	75%	100%	200%
Revenue	20,000,000	21,000,000	22,000,000	24,000,000	26,000,000	28,000,000	30,000,000	35,000,000	40,000,000	60,000,000
Variable Costs	13,000,000	13,650,000	14,300,000	15,600,000	16,900,000	18,200,000	19,500,000	22,750,000	26,000,000	39,000,000
Fixed Costs	4,000,000	4,000,000	4,000,000	4,000,000	4,000,000	4,000,000	4,000,000	4,000,000	4,000,000	4,000,000
Gross Profit	3,000,000	3,350,000	3,700,000	4,400,000	5,100,000	5,800,000	6,500,000	8,250,000	10,000,000	17,000,000
Profit Improvement		350,000	700,000	1,400,000	2,100,000	2,800,000	3,500,000	5,250,000	7,000,000	14,000,000
Profit Improvement Percentage		11.67%	23.33%	46.67%	70.00%	93.33%	116.67%	175.00%	233.33%	466.67%

Report Assumptions:

Revenue — 20,000,000 — Total annual sales revenue or the value of all conversion actions that are affected by the proposed conversion test.

Fixed Costs — 4,000,000 — Include all of your fixed costs such as rent, utilities, administrative expenses, non-customer-service-related salaries, and your online marketing media buys (these costs are considered "fixed" because they will remain unchanged even if your conversion rate improves).

Variable Cost % — 65 — Variable Cost Percentage (VCP) - Include your cost of goods sold, affiliate commisions, customer service, shipping, credit card charges, and other variable costs as a percentage of the revenue. Do NOT include current online media spending or PPC costs because these will remain unchanged if your conversion rate improves. Note: Your VCP is NOT directly related to your current profit margins (for example if your profit margins are 10% this does not mean that your VCP is 90%). This is because your current "fixed" costs (such as overhead and marketing) are also being included. Since these costs will not change as you add INCREMENTAL sales or conversion actions, they are not included. Only costs directly associated with the incremental conversion action should be included.

CHAPTER 2: UNDERSTANDING YOUR LANDING PAGES ■

Each business has its own unique particularities, which may make constructing the financial model more difficult. Don't be paralyzed by your inability to create a perfect model. Some of the data that you need may not be tracked or easily reportable within your organization. Or you may simply not have access to it, or have the clout or resources to have it properly compiled.

Nevertheless, online marketing is a numbers game, so the closer you get to a correct model, the more strongly you will be able to make the financial case for conversion testing and tuning. Just remember that your goal is not to create a super-detailed and accurate model that would pass an accounting audit. You only need to understand the high-level economics of your business well enough to determine the value and impact of conversion testing. So get the best numbers that you can, and make conservative assumptions about the missing information—but definitely build a financial model.

To help you find a way to come up with some numbers, I'm providing the following examples for common types of businesses.

The numeric example scenarios are for illustrative purposes only. Although they may not exactly match your specific situation, they should provide enough guidance for you to develop your own model. The parenthetical abbreviations are not commonly used in accounting. They are simply shorthand used in the illustrative calculations and formulas. The computations are calculated and derived in different ways to fit the available information for each example business.

Purchase of Consumer Product

There are two main types of *business-to-consumer (B2C)* e-commerce websites: direct-to-consumer or retailer catalog. Some companies use the Internet to bypass the normal distribution channels and sell their specific narrow product line directly to consumers. Other companies try to compete with traditional retailers by carrying a wide inventory of available products from all leading manufacturers in their online catalog. In many cases, such aggregators never even take physical possession of inventory and rely on the manufacturer or distributor to drop-ship directly to the consumer.

Possible issues for e-commerce sites include:

In-store sales Many online retailers are not Internet "pure plays." They started as a physical store and decided to add a website. Because of the extensive information available on websites, many people will research the product on the Internet and then buy it at the retail store location. In some consumer product categories, such crossover sales dwarf the online component and are inaccurately attributed simply to in-store sales. Market research is available for a number of industries documenting the amount of crossover. In the absence of specific numbers for your business, you can use such industry research as your starting point.

Another tactic for accurately tracking in-store sales is to provide an incentive on your website (such as a special promotion or coupon code) that can be entered at the physical store point of sale. However, you will probably be underestimating the crossover since many people will not bother with your special offer. This is similar to coupon clipping in the newspaper—even though the coupon is available to everyone, only a fraction of households receiving the paper will take advantage of it. Of course, the value of the incentive will affect its participation rate, but most businesses cannot afford to offer huge discounts just to be able to track offline sales that originated online.

Print catalog sales Many businesses will mail catalogs to lists of prospects. This can create the reverse of the problem we just discussed—catalog sales may be falsely attributed to direct online sales and inflate the effectiveness of the website. This is especially true when catalogs are regularly mailed to a large base of existing clients who are frequent repeat customers. Even though most catalogs include special incentives for ordering online, the revenue of the catalog sales will probably still be understated. One way to estimate this effect is to document the size of any online sales spikes following each catalog mail drop. If you can estimate the increased Web sales compared to a similar period without a catalog drop, you can use this factor to lower your online sales estimates accordingly.

Phone sales If a significant portion of your sales come over the phone, it is very important to track this accurately. By assigning a separate toll-free number to each inbound traffic acquisition campaign, you can ensure that this happens. Do not use a single number for all channels and campaigns because you will improperly attribute sales to direct call-ins. There are limitations to this approach if you want to maintain a high degree of granularity in your tracking. For example, it would be difficult to track every keyword in your PPC campaign since you might potentially have to assign a unique number to each one.

Example Scenario: Purchase of Consumer Product

You run an online catalog selling consumer electronics. You do not have a physical store location or print catalog. Your sales revenues are on an annualized run-rate of $5 million. Your wholesale costs average 65% of retail price, and the customer pays for the shipping (which is not included in the revenue number). Credit card fees and refunds average 4% of your sales. Your average initial online sale is $85. Some 40% of your business comes from repeat purchases, which average $120 per sale.

Example Scenario: Purchase of Consumer Product *(Continued)*

You run an SEO campaign for your website in-house, and outsource your PPC management to an agency with a budget of $500,000 per year including media costs and agency fees. Some 20% of your sales are closed over the phone by your staff. The salaries of your phone sales and support people are $120,000 per year. Affiliates represent 35% of your sales and you pay 10% of the initial sale amount as the commission. You are interested in tuning the checkout process of your website to reduce your shopping cart abandonment rate.

Revenue (R)

$5,000,000 (annual revenue)

× 80% (since 20% are phone sales)

= $4,000,000

Since only the checkout process is being tuned, phone sales do not count. They must be considered as a parallel sales channel that is not affected by changes to your online checkout process (most people will not even see the checkout process if they call you to complete the sale). If pages further upstream of the checkout (such as your website home page) were to be conversion tuned, then the impact on phone sales should be tracked, and the phone sales revenues and associated costs included in the model.

Average revenue per initial sale (ARIS)

$85 (average initial sale amount)

× 60% (percentage of initial sales)

= $51

Average revenue per repeat sale (ARRS)

$120 (average repeat sale amount)

× 40% (percentage of repeat sales)

= $48

Average revenue per sale (ARPS)

= ARIS + ARRS

= $51 + $48

= $99

Continues

Example Scenario: Purchase of Consumer Product (*Continued*)

Cost of goods sold (COGS)

$99 (average revenue per sale)

× 65% (average wholesale cost percentage)

= $64.35

Credit card charges (CC)

$99 (average revenue per sale)

× 4% (average credit card fees)

= $3.96

Variable cost of affiliate sales (VCAS)

$51 (commissionable revenue − initial sale only)

× 10% (avg. affiliate commission rate)

× 35% (percentage of sales due to affiliates)

= $1.79

Variable Cost Percentage (VCP)

= (COGS + CC + VCAS) ÷ ARPS

= ($64.35 + $3.96 + $1.79) ÷ $99

= 70.80%

Third-Party Lead Generation

If you run a lead-generation website, it is typical that you would be paid a fixed dollar amount for each lead. If the leads are exclusive (i.e., they are not resold to multiple buyers), the LTV is the dollar amount of the lead. If the leads are nonexclusive, the LTV depends on the number of times that an average lead is resold.

Possible issues include:

Different values for specific regions Some leads (e.g., from specific states) are more valuable than others. Use a blended average based on the mix of leads that you are currently selling. Some locations do not allow or support the use of leads at all. You can determine a percentage of leads that go to waste in this manner, and use it in your calculation of lead value.

Capped number of leads Some buyers may not be able to handle additional leads past a certain number. Incremental leads past such a cutoff point may have a reduced value (if other buyers still exist for them) or none at all. You can build the cap into your economic formula.

Returned leads Many lead buyers reserve the option of determining whether a lead is valid (after attempting to contact the person and qualifying them). Buyers typically get credit in full for such bad leads.

Example Scenario: Third-Party Lead Generation

You run a nonexclusive lead site for life insurance. You spend $240,000 per year to run your own PPC campaign, which generates 40% of your form-fills. The other 60% come from your affiliate program. You pay a flat $15 per lead for valid affiliate leads that are sold at least once. Your site averages 140 form-fills per day. Some 20% of your leads are from states where you are not allowed to sell them, or have no buyers. The average lead is worth $25 and is resold once an additional 30% of the time. Some 10% of leads are returned as unusable or bogus by buyers.

Revenue (R)

140 form-fills per day $\times$ 365 days (annual form-fills)

$\times$ 80% (since 20% are unsellable)

$\times$ 90% (since 10% are returned)

$\times$ $25 (average lead value)

$\times$ 130% (since a lead is resold 30% of the time)

= $1,195,740

Average revenue per sale (ARPS)

$25 (average lead value)

$\times$ 130% (resold an additional 30% of the time)

= $32.50

Variable cost of affiliate leads (VCAL)

$15 (avg. affiliate commission)

$\times$ 60% (affilate leads as a percentage of the total)

= $9

Variable cost of nonaffiliate leads (VCNL)

= $0 (your PPC costs are considered fixed)

Variable Cost Percentage (VCP)

= (VCAL + VCNL) $\div$ ARPS

= ($9 + $0) $\div$ $32.50

= 27.69%

Subscriptions

Subscriptions can apply to both services and products. Consumers agree to be billed on a regular basis during the term of the subscription agreement. Often the term only includes the initial sale and can be "canceled at any time" in the future. The value of a subscription lies in extending the term of it. Typically there is a drop-off in customers each time a billing event occurs as more and more customers cancel their subscriptions. Subscription businesses that do not add a lot of real value are in a constant race to replenish the ranks of their customers before existing ones cancel.

Example Scenario: Subscriptions

You sell a unique "natural" weight loss pill (manufactured under contract) through a dedicated website. You offer a free 30-day trial of the product (for a $7 shipping and handling fee billed to the client's credit card). Some 40% of trials become paid customers who will purchase an additional three months' worth of product after the initial trial. Each monthly supply sells for $30, including shipping and handling. The cost of the pills is $4 for a month, and the shipping and handling adds another $4. One hundred new clients per day sign up for the trial. Half of your sales come from affiliates to whom you pay $20 for each new customer. An additional 25% of sales come from your PPC campaign, on which you spend $120,000 per year. The remaining 25% come through direct type-in of your URL by people who have heard of your product name.

Revenue from trials (RFT)

100 free trials per day $\times$ 365 days (annual trials)

$\times$ $7 (revenue from a trial)

= $255,500

Revenue from sales (RFS)

100 free trials per day $\times$ 365 days (annual trials)

$\times$ 40% (trial-to-sale "closing" percentage)

$\times$ $90 (revenue from average 3-month sale)

= $1,314,000

Revenue (R) = RFT + RFS

= $255,500 + $1,314,000

= $1,569,500

Example Scenario: Subscriptions *(Continued)*

Unit Cost (UC)

$4 (cost of pills)

+ $4 (cost of shipping and handling)

= $8

Trials Units (TU)

100 free trials per day $\times$ 365 days (annual trials)

=36,500

Paid Units (PU)

100 free trials per day $\times$ 365 days (annual trials)

$\times$ 40% (trial-to-sale "closing" percentage)

$\times$ 3 (average number of paid refills)

= 43,800

Cost of Product (CP)

$= UC \times (TU + PU)$

$= \$8 \times (36,500 + 43,800)$

$= \$642,400$

Affiliate Cost (AC)

36,500 (trials units shipped)

$\times$ $20 (affiliate payout per trial)

$\times$ 50% (percentage of affiliate sales)

= $365,000

Variable Cost Percentage (VCP)

$= (CP + AC) \div R$

$= (\$642,400 + \$365,000) \div \$1,569,500$

$= 64.18\%$

In this example, there is an actual financial loss on the free trial (when considering the product, shipping, and affiliate costs). This results in negative short-term cash flow for the business until the money is recouped in subsequent months from refill clients.

Intermediate Conversion Actions

In many cases, the ultimate desired conversion action may occur months or even years after the initial visitor contact with your website. To complicate matters further, there may be several intermediate actions following the initial contact. This is typical of many high-ticket business-to-business sales. In such cases, the website serves as a tool for educating the prospect early in the sales cycle and identifying who they are.

To properly track such activities, you will probably need some way to note the whole history of an interaction with your company by an outside visitor. This may require having some sort of *sales force automation* (*SFA*) or customer relationship management (CRM) software.

Most of the time, as an online marketer you will not have all of the information required to make decisions. Perhaps the data may need to be periodically compiled for you by other people at the company. This is the riskiest type of conversion action to value. You must make a series of assumptions to arrive at the value of the most upstream conversion action available. This is also your most frequent and least-delayed conversion action. Of course, these assumptions should be conservative. In addition, they must be verified once real data starts flowing in.

But this is confounded by three additional issues. First, the time lag between initial contact and downstream intermediate conversions can be significant, and you must wait until properly "aged" data is available. For example, if someone downloads a whitepaper, they may read it immediately, but may not sign up for a pilot study of your product until the next fiscal year's budget has been approved and funded. Second, the number of ultimate conversion actions may be very small, making it hard to determine an accurate conversion rate. Third, the value of each sale can also vary dramatically, making it difficult to estimate the revenue per sale accurately.

Example Scenario: Intermediate Conversion Actions

Your company sells a complicated suite of special-purpose computers and custom software applications aimed specifically at managing human resources for large state and federal government departments. The sales amount depends on the size of the installation and the specific modules that the customer orders. It can range from $100,000 to $10,000,000. The product is sophisticated and requires a lot of education before a prospect understands the full benefits of your solution and how it differs from those of your competitors.

Ten thousand visitors per year to your website will give you their contact information to get an informational whitepaper about human resource management systems like the one you sell. All of the website traffic originates from a PPC campaign costing $20,000 per month.

Example Scenario: Intermediate Conversion Actions *(Continued)*

After downloading the whitepaper, visitors start receiving ongoing informational e-mails that cover developments in your industry and encourage them to contact a sales representative. Some 8 to 10% of people on your e-mail list will eventually contact a sales person. Some 20 to 25% of sales contacts will lead to free trials. About 15 to 20% of free trials will continue on to become paid sales.

Your CFO cannot give you accurate variable cost percentages, but instead provides you with the following information based on last year's annual report. Your sales salaries and bonuses equal 10% of your revenue. Customer service is approximately 25% of revenues. Hardware and the cost of configuring your systems is 20% of revenues.

Value per download (VPD)

$250,000 (your estimate of average sale amount)

× 15% (low end of trial-to-sale conversions)

× 20% (low end of contact-to-trial conversions)

× 8% (low end of whitepaper-to-contact conversions)

= $600

Revenue (R)

10,000 (number of whitepapers per year)

× $600 (value per download)

= $6,000,000

Variable Cost Percentage (VCP)

10% (sales salaries and commissions)

+ 25% (customer service)

+ 20% (hardware and system cost)

= 55%

Now that you understand your landing page, let's take a closer look at the people who visit it. In the next chapter, you will get a much better perspective on your online audience.

Understanding Your Audience

I could be you, you could be me
I could walk a mile in your shoes...
And you could walk a mile in my
bare feet
—Michael Franti and Spearhead, "What I Be"
song lyric

Who are you trying to influence?

What are they like?

Can you see the world from their perspective?

*   Before you can even look at the specific issues*
and problems with your landing page, you must
try to see it through the eyes of your audience.
This chapter will give you that foundation.

Chapter Contents
Empathy: The Key Ingredient
Covering the Complete Story
Demographics and Segmentation
Behavioral Styles
User-Centered Design
The Matrix

Empathy: The Key Ingredient

We are all familiar with the Golden Rule: "Do onto others as you would have them do onto you." This ethical guidepost exists in many variants among the world's major philosophies and religions. But it is missing an essential component by presupposing that everyone is the same. Moreover, it makes *your* behavior and beliefs the standard by which all conduct should be judged and measured.

> *Do onto others as they would have you do onto them.*
> —*The Platinum Rule™*, by Dr. Tony Alessandra

I ran across this more powerful formulation at a sales training workshop many years ago and it resonated deeply for me. Here was the missing component: empathy. People are not all the same. If we want to understand them, we should try to step outside of our own needs and experience the world from their perspective.

The rest of this chapter should help you get into the minds and hearts of your website visitors. All of the following frameworks require an openness and flexibility on your part. The more flexible and imaginative you are, the more powerfully you can wield these tools.

But let me inject a note of warning: no matter how you might try to put ourselves in others' shoes, you are bound to be wrong. You can never replicate their bodies, brains, or formative experiences. This realization requires a certain humility, wide-eyed wonder, and willingness to be constantly surprised.

"You're Wrong"

After conducting hundreds of usability tests for a wide range of clients, Larry Marine, usability expert and founder of Intuitive Design & Research, delights in being constantly surprised by his audience. The viewpoint of a single person can never fully capture the perspective of others. During a talk in San Diego, Larry used the following presentation points to remind us about the difficulty of our task as online marketers:

- Everything you think you know about the user is probably wrong.
- The users aren't who you think they are.
- They do things differently than you think.
- They have different reasons for needing your product than you think.

Nevertheless, let's continue.

Covering the Complete Story

Like a solid news report, you must understand the basics of the story and be able to articulate the following particulars about your audience:

- Who
- Where
- When
- Why
- What
- How

    Let me explain:

Who is your audience? Where do they come from? The *who* of your audience is defined by their demographics and segmentation. Because you can't meet every visitor to your site in person, you are limited to using aggregated information. You understand the traffic sources hitting your website and the specific landing pages. Extensive information is also available about these visitors and their behavior. From a landing page optimization perspective, it is important to exactly determine what subset of your traffic will be used for the test. You should pay particular attention to its stability and consistency over time. The following section, "Demographics and Segmentation," will cover this in more detail.

Where on your website does the interaction occur? As you learned in the previous chapter, the *where* of your landing page optimization test should occur on your previously identified mission-critical landing pages. Sometimes the where may be an offline call-to-action such as a phone call or an in-store sale, but the mechanism for it (e.g., displaying a special dedicated toll-free number, or creating a printable coupon for redemption in a store) is still part of the website.

When do your visitors make their decision? The *when* should be seen not as a specific time event, but more generally as a position in a decision process. Some visitors feel a vague unease about a concern that they may have, but have just begun to look around and try to formulate a response to their problem. Others know exactly what they want, and may only be concerned with completing whatever transaction is required to obtain their specific product. There needs to be appropriate information for a visitor regardless of their place in this process. The decision process (consisting of awareness, interest, desire, and action) is discussed in detail in the next chapter.

Why do visitors behave the way they do? You do not have intimate and accurate information about your individual visitors. The *why* can be understood by imagining the categories of behavioral styles. Many psychologists and philosophers have proposed fundamental archetypes or frameworks for describing the basic human temperaments, and our consequently different ways of relating to the world. I'll examine behavioral styles, "personas," and their limitations in the "Behavioral Styles" section later in this chapter. The notion of *roles* is more pertinent to Web design and conversion, which I'll discuss further in the "User-Centered Design" section.

What is the task that you are asking them to complete? The *what* is the specific task that your visitor is trying to complete on your website. Tasks and how to properly define them are described in the "User-Centered Design" section that follows. Chapter 4, "Understanding the Decision Process," will also review the micro-steps necessary to move your visitors through each task.

How does your site operate in order for visitors to complete their tasks? The *how* is the actual design of your website or landing pages. It is the medium through which each task must be accomplished. Specific page elements include layout, organization, and emphasis of key information, text copy, the call-to-action, and hundreds of other factors. All of them combine to influence the effectiveness of your landing page. In Chapter 5, "Why Your Site Is Not Perfect," I will cover ways to identify specific problems and issues with your website. Chapter 6, "Selecting Elements to Tune," will help you figure out exactly what to include in your conversion tuning tests.

Demographics and Segmentation

Information about your site visitors comes in two main flavors: objective and subjective. Because almost everything on the Internet can be logged or recorded, it provides a wealth of objective information. The goal of the effective online marketer is to determine which specific metrics are good predictors of success, and to monitor them properly to focus your programs in the right direction. As with all numeric information, you should treat demographics with proper respect and be aware of the following issues:

Data-gathering methods and limitations Depending on the exact technology used, software packages will track the activities of your visitors differently and come up with different numbers for the same metrics. Be aware of the limitations of the software that you choose.

Gathering enough data Many online marketers do not wait to gather enough data before making decisions. Just because one out of the first four visitors to your website bought from you, it does not mean that you have a 25% conversion rate to sale. Wait to gather enough data to get statistically valid answers.

Web Analytics

You already know a lot about your audience. Your website logs record information in mind-numbing detail about every request for information from your Web servers:

- The Internet Protocol (IP) address of your visitors
- Which pages they viewed
- How long they spent looking at your site
- Which browser software they are using
- Whether they have been to your site before

All of this information is analyzed by *Web analytics* software. Web analytics packages have a wide range of capabilities and power. The simplest ones are glorified counters. High-end packages are very powerful but often require months of laborious and expensive customization to create the right set of live online reports for key people on your staff. Such packages can tie into other systems within your company to give you a more complete picture of the ongoing interactions with your audience. For example, many analytics systems connect directly to a company's *customer relationship management* (*CRM*) systems.

In general, there are three main uses of Web analytics software: canned reports, data mining, and dynamic content presentation. Let's discuss these further:

Canned reports Specific reports can be generated (typically on the fly or at specified intervals) to report on a number of activities. The set of reports does not typically change. They normally report simple statistics about the number of visitors, popular entry pages, and distributions of traffic by time of day. Some offer *clickstream analysis*—showing the popular sequences of clicks and pages that users take to navigate your site. The efficiency of your sales funnel can also be measured by examining the conversion rate of every step in your sales or checkout funnel.

Data mining Some systems have flexible reporting and scripting languages that allow you to construct your own specialized reports based on historical data. This supports open-ended discovery and ongoing questioning. Do our search engine visitors buy more often than our banner ad visitors? What is our repeat order rate within a six-month window of an initial purchase?

Dynamic content presentation Many Web analytics systems have begun to overlap with Web content management systems and support the ability to change content on the fly. They encode business rules within your Web pages that can change specific portions of your content based on the actions of a particular user. In addition to testing landing pages, you can also introduce up-sells or cross-sells to your buyers, or display special offers to repeat visitors. The possibilities for personalizing your content are almost endless.

Web analytics packages can be used for almost any purpose. In recent years many of them have increased their focus on tracking the effectiveness of online marketing programs. They offer built-in reports for tracking separate marketing channels. Pay-per-click spending and return on investment (ROI) can be measured down to the keyword level. Support is typically included for simple landing page testing.

Traffic Sources and Their Variability

Your audience is not homogenous or uniform. Streams of diverse people visit your site as a result of your current and past marketing activities. None of these streams fit together very well, so it is dangerous and misleading to stitch them together into a unified picture. If your audience consisted of a six-year-old in San Diego and a seventy-four-year-old in New York City, it would be silly to describe your "average" visitor as a forty-year-old from Kansas. Yet similar conclusions are often drawn from Web analytics data. Try to keep your traffic sources separated and analyze them only within their peer group. The most appropriate segmentation may be to focus on specific roles and the tasks that you want your visitors to complete on the website. In other words, do not look at your overall site traffic, but focus instead on the demographics of the people who are actually interacting with the mission-critical parts of your site.

However, if you segment too finely, you may have problems as well. When you analyze within a particular traffic source or marketing segment, be sure that there is enough data to draw valid statistical conclusions.

Not only is your audience composition diverse, but these people act differently under different circumstances and conditions. Time of day can have very strong behavioral effects. Someone browsing surreptitiously at work will spend less time on your site than the same person on the computer in her home during the evening. Time zones can cause a shift in your audience at different hours of the day, as more international visitors have *their* daytime.

Likewise, weekend behavior is different than that of the workweek. There are well-known differences in direct response e-mail marketing conversion rates based on the specific day of the week that a mail drop is done. However, the best days are completely different depending on the audience and the offer in question. So day of week turns out to be another unknown factor that must be considered in your testing.

Such effects can be mitigated by running conversion tests in whole-week units. But longer-term time variations such as external event-driven behavior or seasonality can also play a strong role and are much harder to deal with.

For example, a flower website will do a hugely disproportionate business in the two to three weeks leading up to Mother's Day every year. As the actual event date approaches, the audience becomes segmented and changes—all of the planners in the group will have completed their transactions and secured the best prices and appropriate delivery dates. At the last minute, the less price-sensitive procrastinators will descend on the website and spend more money than they probably should in order to get express delivery.

Seasonal trends are also seen in many discretionary spending consumer categories, with the fourth quarter accounting for a majority of the year's sales. But even companies whose products have no natural seasonality to speak of may see slowdowns in the summer (when many people are away on vacation and do not have the same access to the Internet) or at other times.

Sometimes, your seemingly homogeneous audience is really not the same at all. For example, in the winter people from colder climates will tend to vacation in warmer places. In the summer this pattern reverses and Southerners head north to escape the heat. As a result, many travel-related sites have strong seasonality, coupled with a changing audience mix. In such circumstances it is difficult to conduct certain types of conversion testing (primarily having to do with your content or offers).

> Some websites have such extreme audience changes and vicious seasonality factors that content conversion tuning is simply not possible. The predicted best answer will simply not hold up over time.

However, even such difficult vertical industry sites can often derive some benefit from conversion testing. Instead of focusing on the specifics of their business, the variations tested can focus on the basic usability of their websites and effective and frictionless flow through the important tasks (such as booking a reservation or purchasing).

The TicketsNow.com website (www.ticketsnow.com) shown in Figure 3.1 will have the strongest conversion effects based on the contents of the highlighted featured offers. Since there is a limited supply of tickets for certain events, the featured promotions change frequently and would make it difficult to even test the offer. However, the underlying page layout and site usability could be tuned independently of the featured offers.

When you look at the suitability of the traffic mix for conversion testing, you should watch for three important characteristics: recurring, controllable, and stable.

Figure 3.1 The TicketsNow.com home page

Recurring The traffic must come from a replenishable resource. For example, PPC or banner ad traffic is essentially endless—you can get more of it as long as you are willing to pay. This supply of "fresh meat" is important because you typically want to run conversion tests on new people who have not been exposed to your company or website before. It is okay to have a high percentage of repeat visitors in your test, as long as the mix of visitors does not change and represents a roughly constant percentage of your traffic. However, this is different from the traffic coming from a single e-mail drop to a finite in-house list. E-mail campaigns come under the category of direct marketing and have their own methods for testing and improving effectiveness. However, nonrecurring traffic sources like e-mail have many drawbacks for traditional landing page optimization and must be used cautiously (if at all).

Controllable It is easy to control paid search and other online media buys. Unfortunately, other traffic sources are not under your command. For example, organic SEO depends on changes in the ranking algorithms of the search engines, and you cannot predict what mix of currently high-ranking keywords your traffic will arrive from. You also cannot control the context in which your site was seen (i.e., the text of the search result that was shown alongside your link). Nor can you directly specify the pages on which the traffic will land. However, SEO traffic can still be used for tests if it has a record of being historically stable in terms of the volume and mix of landing pages.

Stable Even if your traffic is recurring and controllable, it may not be stable. For example, you may see a periodic traffic spike as one of your marketing partners pushes a special recurring campaign that drives visitors to your site. Or the turnover in the composition of your affiliate program results in a rapidly changing traffic mix. SEO traffic can also disappear overnight as the ranking algorithms are adjusted.

Behavioral Styles

Your audience can be spoken of in the abstract, but in fact it is like a continual snowfall of visitors landing on your site—no two snowflake crystals are exactly alike. You do not have access to the individual thoughts, fears, or motivations of your visitors, yet you must try to understand them.

Since the individual level is not appropriate, some online marketers look for meaningful commonalities at a group level. One way to do this is by using behavioral frameworks. Behavioral frameworks sort people into exclusive categories based on observable behavioral styles or personality types.

Any attempt to characterize your visitors is bound to be incomplete, but that's okay. You are just trying to understand them well enough to come up with more effective landing pages. Within this limited scope and purpose, online marketers commonly turn to approaches that might help them to better understand their audience: Myers-Briggs, Keirsey-Bates, and the Platinum Rule. Remember, no single framework is definitive or complete. No one has a complete corner on "the Truth"—all you can hope for are better insights into your audience.

Behavioral frameworks are excellent tools in helping to understand a real-life person. Unfortunately, they have significant problems when applied to landing page testing. Their focus is on improving an individual's self knowledge and approaches for interacting with others. But landing page optimization deals with very large numbers of visitors. So each major category of visitors within a behavioral framework will be represented in your audience. This means that you cannot tune for a specific category without making inevitable compromises that affect all others. I will discuss a more appropriate framework of roles and tasks later in this chapter.

Myers-Briggs

In 1923, noted Swiss psychiatrist Carl Jung wrote *Psychological Types* and outlined his classification of different types of people ("Theory of Personality Preferences"). According to Jung, many of the differences among people did not stem from mental illness, abnormalities, or problems. Rather, he suggested that people had more or less innate ways of relating to the world. These built-in filters would color every social interaction, and dictate someone's effectiveness in a particular circumstance or environment. They also help explain to a large degree why we are attracted to or frustrated by other people. Jung's very dense writing style unfortunately made his work inaccessible to most readers, and it languished for many years.

This research was picked up and expanded in the 1930s by Katharine Cook Briggs and her daughter Isabel Briggs Myers. They worked through World War II to develop a specific testing tool that would classify people reliably according to Jung's basic theory. They culled through thousands of potential questions, and were able to tease out ones that predicted personality types reliably. The final questionnaire and rating method was named the *Myers-Briggs Type Indicator* (*MBTI*).

The MBTI examines people on four independent scales. Each scale is anchored by two opposite extremes. Where someone falls on a particular scale is not supposed to change over the course of a lifetime. In other words, your basic personality type is pretty much set in stone. This does not mean that as you learn and grow you will not express your type differently. It only means that your underlying world view shifts very slowly. Each of the scales (also called dichotomies) that follow indicates preferences and tendencies only. Very few people are the caricatures typically described by the two extremes of each scale. There are no value judgments associated with someone's innate type. Obviously, each evolved and took hold in a significant portion of the human population because it had some kind of evolutionary or survival value. None of the types are absolutely better or worse than others. The main goal of the Myers-Briggs method is to understand yourself. Through MBTI you can predict how you might perform in a specific environment or role. It also gives you the basis to find effective communications strategies with people of a different type.

It is beyond the scope of this book to go into detail about this field. The following sketches are meant simply to illustrate the basic concepts and taxonomy of the MBTI.

The source of energy: Extroverts (E) vs. Introverts (I) Extroverts draw their energy from the outside world and other people. They love social interactions, and are gregarious and communicative. They expend a lot of personal energy and tend to speak before thinking.

Introverts prefer limited social relationships. They conserve their personal energy and are more internal and focused. Introverts are more reflective and notice their own internal reactions to events. They tend to think first and then speak.

Information gathering: Sensors (S) vs. Intuitives (N) Sensors live in the present moment. They prefer orderly sequential planning, and are practical, down-to-earth people who pride themselves in being realistic. They insist on what is actual and specific.

Intuitives live in the future world of possibilities. They are conceptual, scattered, and like to see the big picture. They are comfortable with randomness and disorder, and are often viewed as impractical dreamers.

Information processing: Thinkers (T) vs. Feelers (F) Thinkers tend to be objective and just. They prefer the clarity and detachment provided by firm rules, and they are not afraid to critique others.

Feelers are subjective and social. They prefer to be involved and operate based on harmony and social values. They try to mediate based on the changing circumstances and come to conclusions that are deemed to be humane and that maintain harmony.

Lifestyle orientation: Judgers (J) vs. Perceivers (P) Judgers like control, definitiveness, closure, and structure. They plan, resolve, and decide the smallest aspects of their lives. They like to schedule their time and are comfortable meeting specific deadlines.

Perceivers prefer flexibility and a tentative, open-ended orientation to making decisions. They are adaptable and spontaneous, and do not like to be hemmed in by deadlines.

The resulting four components can be combined in 16 individual personality types or "role variants." By convention, a descriptive profession has been attached to each one along with a label describing the primary orientation:

- Teacher (ENFJ): Educating
- Counselor (INFJ): Guiding
- Champion (ENFP): Motivating
- Healer (INFP): Conciliating
- Fieldmarshal (ENTJ): Mobilizing
- Mastermind (INTJ): Entailing
- Inventor (ENTP): Devising
- Architect (INTP): Designing
- Supervisor (ESTJ): Enforcing
- Inspector (ISTJ): Certifying
- Provider (ESFJ): Supplying
- Protector (ISFJ): Securing

- Promoter (ESTP): Persuading
- Crafter (ISTP): Instrumenting
- Performer (ESFP): Demonstrating
- Composer (ISFP): Synthesizing

Keirsey-Bates

While Myers and Briggs focused on people's internal mental states, David Keirsey and Marilyn Bates focused more on easily observable behavior patterns. This led Keirsey to develop a descriptive temperament framework that he later merged with the MBTI. He focused on the primary S-N (abstract-concrete) dimension, which he mapped to the "observant" and "introspective" qualities, respectively. These were combined with another dimension (cooperative-utilitarian) to create the four primary temperaments of the Keirsey Temperament Sorter:

- Artisans (SP): Tactical—Observant and pragmatic
- Guardians (SJ): Logistical—Observant and cooperative
- Idealists (NF): Diplomatic—Introspective and cooperative
- Rationals (NT): Strategic—Introspective and pragmatic

For purposes of Web design, the four temperaments are a much more manageable set. It is difficult to try to consider 16 distinct personality types.

Platinum Rule

Dr. Tony Alessandra states his Platinum Rule as follows: "Do onto others as they would have you do onto them." Like other personality typing and behavioral frameworks, his seeks to clarify people's operating styles. Like Keirsey, Alessandra focuses on observable behaviors and provides us with two primary dimensions:

- Open versus guarded
- Direct versus indirect

The resulting quadrants form the four foundational styles. Like the MBTI there are two additional scales to further subdivide each quadrant into 16 total styles. The primary styles are:

- Relater—Indirect/open
- Thinker—Indirect/guarded
- Socializer—Direct/open
- Director—Direct/guarded

Table 3.1 provides an overview of the four basic styles.

► **Table 3.1** Four Foundational Styles of the Platinum Rule

	Director Style	Socializer Style	Relater Style	Thinker Style
Pace	Fast/decisive	Fast/spontaneous	Slower/relaxed	Slower/systematic
Priority	Goal	People	Relationship	Task
Seeks	Productivity Control	Participation Applause	Acceptance	Accuracy Precision
Strengths	Administration Leadership Pioneering	Persuading Motivating Entertaining	Listening Teamwork Follow-through	Planning Systematizing Orchestration
Growth Areas	Impatient Insensitive to others Poor listener	Inattentive to detail Short attention span Low follow-through	Oversensitive Slow to begin action Lacks global perspective	Perfectionists Critical Unresponsive
Fears	Being taken advantage of	Loss of social recognition	Sudden changes Instability	Personal criticism of their work efforts
Irritations	Inefficiency Indecision	Routines Complexity	Insensitivity Impatience	Disorganization Impropriety
Under Stress May Become	Dictatorial Critical	Sarcastic Superficial	Submissive Indecisive	Withdrawn Headstrong
Gains Security Through	Control Leadership	Playfulness Other's approval	Friendship Cooperation	Preparation Thoroughness
Measures Personal Worth By	Impact or results Track record and process	Acknowledgements Applause Compliments	Compatibility with others Depth of contribution	Precision Accuracy Quality of results
Workplace	Efficient Busy Structured	Interacting Busy Personal	Friendly Functional Personal	Formal Functional Structured

© Dr. Tony Alessandra, www.Alessandra.com, 1-760-603-8110, Reprinted with Permission

One of the key uses of this framework is for adapting a sales presentation or process to an individual's style, so among behavioral frameworks it is especially well suited for persuading or selling on the Web. For additional information, please visit the website platinumrule.com.

User-Centered Design

During my Cognitive Science undergraduate studies at U.C. San Diego in the mid-1980s I had the pleasure of taking classes from Dr. Don Norman. He is considered one of the foremost usability experts in the world and is the originator of *user-centered design (UCD)*. UCD is an approach to designing objects and interfaces that considers the needs, desires, and perspectives of the intended users as primary. Instead of enforcing the designer's view of the world on the users, this approach tries to adapt to the way that users actually want to use the product in question.

It is an iterative approach that refines the existing design through a series of progressively more effective versions. Significant research is conducted up-front to understand the needs and goals of the intended user audience. Each revision is tested on actual intended users to see if the designer's underlying assumptions hold up, and to see whether the design meets the stated measurable performance criteria. Real testing is necessary because it is often difficult or impossible for the designers to step outside of their own competencies. Because they are so familiar with the design, they cannot imagine what naïve first-time users may do or how their behavior may change once they have been repeatedly exposed to the design.

A series of specific user interactions can form a larger *user experience (UX)*. For example, an e-commerce site may require a user to add an item to the shopping cart, specify a shipping address, and correctly enter payment information. These individual interactions combine into a larger "checking out" user experience. Each of the component interactions must be usable and must also combine into an overall effective user experience.

Usability Testing

At the heart of UCD is usability testing. During this process, representative users are given a prototype or mock-up of your design and asked to complete a specific task. The number of users is typically small (three to six). A specific task (also called a "use case" or "scenario") is developed (with objective measurable goals and tied to the overall business objectives), and the user is asked to complete the task. The designers quietly observe the test (and optionally record it or take handwritten notes).

The test is often carried out on a nonfunctional prototype, a wireframe model, or even on a hand-drawn flipchart representation of the product. This allows the users to focus on the task and not worry about offending the designers who have invested a lot of time in preparing it. There is less invested in such early-stage prototypes, and they are easy to discard, refine, and modify. The real product build should not happen until the testing goals have been achieved and a workable design identified.

If the goal for the task has been met, the testing is complete and the current design is adopted. If the goal has not been met, the designers include their learnings from the current test in a revised design to be used for the next test.

Personas

One of the tools commonly used in usability testing and UCD is a persona. A *persona* is a fictional person who acts as a representative stand-in for a large class of representative visitors to your site.

Personas should be developed by observing usability tests, conducting contextual interviews (working in their actual typical environment), online surveys, focus groups, and regular interviews (where you do not observe people working).

Typical elements of a persona include:

- A name and picture
- Demographics (age, education, ethnicity, family status)
- Job title and major responsibilities
- Goals and tasks in relation to your site
- Environment (physical, social, technological)
- A quote that sums up what matters most to the persona with relevance for your site

The following persona is an example from a usability test for a consumer technology comparison website:

Ned Adams ("Ned the Nerd")

Ned Adams is a "thought leader" for people who are interested in emerging consumer technologies.

- 24-year-old college drop-out; studied computer science
- Single, not in a relationship; lives at home with his parents
- Clerk at the local computer game arcade and Internet café
- Influencer for new gadgets among his peers
- Spends a lot of time on the Internet
- Has his own consumer technology blog
- Always upgrades his high-tech gear to have the "latest and greatest"
- Quote: "If it's cool and new, I want to know about it!"

The advantages of personas in UCD are:

- They help everyone have a consistent view of major audience groups.
- They are easy to communicate.
- They increase empathy toward the audience and help focus on their needs.
- They help prioritize possible new product features (based on how well they would meet the needs of a particular persona).

However, personas are not generally not appropriate for large-scale statistical landing page optimization tests. In this setting, personas have several significant drawbacks and limitations:

Basis for construction The proper basis for constructing personas are usability tests, contextual interviews (seeing users work in their actual native environment and not a controlled usability lab setting), focus groups, and surveys (telephone, in-person, or online). Personas should always be representative of key audience classes and grounded in experiences with real people. Unfortunately, some Web conversion companies have begun fabricating personas based primarily on their personality types or behavioral styles, with no reference to actual classes of visitors to a website. Without access to real people, these personas basically become window dressing around the Keirsey temperament types that I discussed in the preceding section.

Difficult to understand other cultures Many website audiences are worldwide in scope and include a significant percentage of international visitors. It is difficult to emotionally connect with people from other cultures and backgrounds and to even begin to understand their motivations. In such settings, attempting to construct international personas would be difficult, while modeling them with standard local counterparts is bound to be inaccurate.

Diverse visitor populations Most consumer-oriented websites have a diverse audience. Large websites have visitors whose demographics and psychographics closely mirror the population mix of Internet users as a whole. Since a given temperament or behavioral type represents only a small fraction of the overall population, any attempt to span the whole audience with a small number of personas is bound to fail. Whole segments will be missed.

Of course, this is less of an issue for some niche and special-purpose sites. For example, I am pretty confident that returning visitors to a bungee jumping coupon site (I'm pretty sure that such a thing must exist somewhere on the Web...) can be effectively modeled by a young thrill-seeking male persona. But in most cases the visitors to your website are a pretty bland mix of standard people.

Competing needs You will find that each persona has differing and conflicting needs and desires. This is not so much of an issue when one persona can be used as a stand-in for a whole visitor class—then the landing page and conversion task is designed around them.

However, as discussed earlier, many websites have diverse populations, thus requiring multiple personas to effectively capture the characteristics of a single visitor class.

Unfortunately, this implies compromise and suboptimal landing page designs. Instead of a consistent user experience based on a single persona, the landing page becomes a hodge-podge of features and trade-offs designed to appeal somewhat to each relevant persona. The clarity and integrity of the design is bound to be destroyed via the resulting additional clutter. In many cases, what helps one persona will actually undermine the needs of another.

Addressing the wrong question Personas allow you to ask, "What is best for this persona?" Even if your answer to that question produced the best results possible, you would still not be addressing the needs of all visitors who do not match the persona.

Since you do not know whether a particular visitor to your site is well represented by the persona, you must deal with the audience as a whole. The appropriate question then becomes, "On average, which of the tested alternatives does this audience prefer?" This is exactly the question that large-scale statistics-based testing can answer.

At odds with the spirit of testing Personas, as often applied to landing page testing, include some hidden assumptions: that users can be divided into a small number of key classes and that if you create detailed personas you can come up with the perfect design to address their needs. The only real validation conducted is to determine if the recommended new solution is better than the original.

The persona-based design may well perform better than the original (often simply because the original was so poorly designed in the first place). But why would you restrict yourself to a single design alternative? Remember, in UCD personas are used to run a *series* of usability tests. It is rare that the first proposed solution is accepted as is.

Unfortunately, personas are commonly used on a one-shot basis in landing page optimization to create a new landing page design. There is no iterative redesign and testing process. When practiced this way, you will get one alternative design choice that is the best educated guess of an expert or outside consultant. This is radically different than the large-scale statistical testing perspective. Statistical testing looks for the needle in a haystack and can identify which of a million possible page versions is the best performer. No human expert can guess at the answer under such circumstances and hope to consistently predict the winner. In my experience, I am often wrong about which final landing page version (or even individual test variable setting within it) will end up as the winner. This sobering and humbling realization is the reason for trying many alternatives in the first place, and antithetical to the notion that any one person can come up with the right solution. Your audience must vote through their actions on the page to guide you to the solution.

Roles

Earlier in this book you identified important classes of visitors to your landing page. These can be expanded into the roles that people take on when interacting with your site. The role breakdown can be basic, or it may need to be slightly more nuanced depending on your circumstances.

Here are some representative examples of possible roles:

Plumbing-supply company Retail customers (looking to buy an individual replacement part), plumbing contractors (need an array of parts for a specific customer job), wholesale buyers and real estate developers (need large volume price breaks and extended payment terms)

Dating service Prospective member (has not signed up yet), new member (has paid but has not set up a complete personal profile), experienced member (has done multiple searches and contacted other members)

Educational-saving-plan provider Future recipients (children under age 18), parents of recipients (who typically establish the plan), relatives and friends (who may contribute money to the plan)

Consumer e-tail company New visitors (who have not been to your site before), returning visitors (who have been there but have not bought yet), first-time buyers (trying to complete their first purchase), repeat buyers (who already have their information stored in your system), e-mail list members (who have signed up to hear about future special offers)

> ### Roles vs. Personas
>
> Roles are different than personas.
>
> In one sense they are more changeable. A persona is usually treated as a monolithic person with a formed personality that does not change. In fact, most people play many different roles in their daily life. In each role, their competencies, mental frameworks, and attitudes can shift dramatically. For example, I may be confident, gregarious, and quick to make decisions during the workday. After work I may leave the office to buy a present for a friend's birthday party. In this setting, I may become unsure of myself, deliberate, tentative, and afraid to make the wrong decision. So even though I am the same person (and would presumably still be represented by the same persona), I behave completely differently in my roles as businessman and shopper-for-a-friend's-birthday-gift.
>
> In some other circumstances, roles are actually more stable than personas. This is often the case in landing page testing. For example, regardless of the personalities involved, all website visitors to an e-commerce catalog site still need to complete the same functional tasks as part of their role as shoppers (e.g., placing items in a shopping cart and checking out). So the role of shopper can subsume the specific personas who might be functioning in this capacity.

Tasks

In UCD, tasks (also known as "use cases" or "scenarios") represent a sketched-out problem statement that is used during a usability test. It is important that the tasks have measurable and quantifiable objectives, and that these objectives are based on the high-priority goals of the business. Individual features should not be tested (too narrow). Whole websites should not be tested (too broad). Tasks should represent common activities that users might want to engage in that have significant value to the business.

Example tasks include the following:

Insurance comparison site Find three, $1-million term life insurance quotes for a healthy 30-year-old single man living in California.

Network security company Download and open the whitepaper on "Remotely Diagnosing Security Threats."

E-commerce site Determine the cost of a Model-XYZ laptop computer when configured with the optional DVD drive.

Photo-sharing site Activate your free account and upload a picture from your local computer.

Notice that none of the tasks specify *how* a user is expected to accomplish them, only *what* needs to get done.

The Matrix

Yes, *The Matrix* is a science fiction movie. But this section refers to a different one. At SiteTuners.com we have developed "The Matrix" as a way to describe our approach to large-scale statistical landing page testing. Although it is loosely based on UCD, two additional elements are introduced.

The Matrix = ROLES × TASKS × AIDA

The basic steps in creating The Matrix are:

Define key user classes and roles. From your understanding of your website visitors you should have already identified the classes of users who perform the mission-critical tasks on your site.

Define critical conversion tasks for each class. You have already determined what your key conversion actions are. The tasks are simply an assignment of key activities leading to the conversion actions to the appropriate roles.

Determine required decision process support for each task. In the next chapter, you will learn about the key steps in the decision process (AIDA). During each task, you will map out what specific help, information, and resources will be needed by the visitors in the prescribed role to accomplish the required task (and complete the corresponding conversion action).

> Basically The Matrix ensures that you have thought through in detail how to guide the *right people*, through the *right activities*, in the *correct order*.

Of course, the testing methodology itself is also very different from usability testing. Instead of observing a small number of representative users and extracting qualitative information, The Matrix relies on large numbers of anonymous visitors to your website, and judges them strictly on their conversion actions (or lack thereof).

As you can see, we have already covered two critical pieces of The Matrix (roles and tasks). So let's keep moving forward and learn about the decision process.

Understanding The Decision Process

A-I-D-A. Attention, interest, decision, action.
—Blake (played by actor Alec Baldwin) in the 1992 movie *Glengarry Glen Ross*)

People naturally follow a similar mental trajectory when they make decisions. If we are trying to persuade them to take action, we must also have a firm grounding in this entire process.

Chapter Contents

Overview of the Decision Process

In 1898, Elias St. Elmo Lewis pioneered a framework for describing stages of consumer interest and behavior. In effect, he created the modern concept of the sales funnel. All people were thought to progress through four stages covered by the acronym AIDA.

Awareness (Attention)

Interested

Desire (Decision)

Action

In 1911, Frederick Sheldon added a fifth post-sale stage called "Permanent Satisfaction," and thus extended the model to AIDAS. The final *S* in AIDAS is mainly a function of your user's experience with your actual product or service, and is the key to repeat sales. However, since this is a book about landing page optimization, you should be concerned mainly with the steps leading up to the first conversion action. This is where the design of your landing page (in the absence of other experiences with your company) plays the most decisive role. Because of this, the original AIDA framework will be the primary focus.

The key to properly applying this model is to make sure that there is continuity and flow to support a visitor's progression through each of the steps. None of the steps can be skipped, and all of them must happen in sequence. That is not to say that equal emphasis should be placed on each within your landing page, nor that visitors will spend an equal amount of time in each step. But there should be a clear path, and the proper support to keep them moving forward toward your conversion goal.

In his book *Submit Now: Designing Persuasive Web Sites* (New Riders Press, 2002), Andrew Chak closely follows the AIDAS model and applies it specifically to website visitors. He correctly suggests that the website or landing page should be designed for four main user types corresponding to the mind-set of each stage:

Browsers May not know exactly what they want, but have an unmet need

Evaluators Know enough to compare the available options, and are looking for detailed supporting information

Transactors Have made buying decision, and need to quickly go through the mechanics of the actual transaction

Customers Have completed their transaction, and need to sustain their satisfaction level until they transact again in the future

It is also helpful to realize that AIDA applies to different scales of tasks and different time frames. If I am a consumer researching the next computer to buy, I may take days or weeks to make my decision. My interaction with your website may be only one of dozens. I may have long ago forgotten about your website by the time I make my ultimate decision (depending on when I visited it, the intervening research that I have conducted, and the uniqueness of your company and its selling proposition).

At the other extreme, the Web supports small-scale and short-duration micro-tasks that may happen in a fraction of a second. Sometimes the task that you want the user to perform is simply to click through to another page on your site. Yet the same four steps must still happen during the visit for the conversion action to occur.

Ultimately you must help to answer two questions for a visitor to pass through all of the AIDA stages.

- Do you have what I want?
- Why should I get it from you?

This process may not happen during a single visit or interaction. The ultimate goal may be weeks or months away. But you must provide a clear path to that goal, as well as support along every step of the way. If your conversion action typically has a long delay, then try to provide mechanisms to record your visitors' progress, and restart them in the most recent and relevant state upon their subsequent return visits to your landing page.

As you will see in the sections that follow, the typical time spent in the awareness and interest stages on the Web is very short. Most of the "Do you have what I want?" question is answered during the desire stage. However, without attention and interest, desire cannot even happen. Similarly, although the bulk of "Why should I get it from you?" is answered during the action stage, it cannot even be reached without passing through the other three stages in order.

Awareness (Attention)

Awareness and its close cousin attention are scarce commodities in our fast-paced world. We are constantly bombarded by information and strong sensory impressions. Unceasing advertisements haunt us from our first waking moments to our exhausted slumber at the end of the day. The pace of change keeps increasing and threatens to overwhelm us. The Internet has given us access to a vast wealth of information, but has not helped us to organize or make sense of it.

> *What information consumes is rather obvious: it consumes the attention of its recipients. Hence, a wealth of information creates a poverty of attention and a need to allocate that attention efficiently among the overabundance of information sources that might consume it.*

—Herbert A. Simon, noted interdisciplinary computational and social scientist

There is only one possible response: build walls. People learn to tune everything out. You can call them cynical, jaded, or media savvy. But it really boils down to the same thing—they have to get desensitized to survive. So it takes more and more effort for an advertiser to break through the clutter and the noise to reach their target audience.

You're not paying attention. Nobody is.
—Seth Godin, *Permission Marketing*

As Seth Godin points out in his excellent book *Permission Marketing*, this type of *interruption advertising* may still be necessary to make initial contact, but it should only be followed up with voluntary *permission marketing* once a visitor lands on your site. Permission marketing is a selfish and voluntary activity on the part of your Web visitor. Over time you can trade things of greater value to the visitor in exchange for more information and a deeper level of relationship with them.

Permission marketing has three key attributes:

Anticipated Your prospects actually want to hear from you.

Personal Your messages are tailored to each person.

Relevant Your messages relate directly to visitors' needs.

Let's look at the mind-set of visitors during the awareness stage. They have just arrived at your site. Their level of commitment is very low and they may click away at any moment. They are looking for reassurance, recognition of their needs, and a clear path to follow. If something catches their eye, they may stay and explore further.

The Rules of Web Awareness

- If the visitor can't find something easily, it does not exist.
- If you emphasize too many items, all of them lose importance.
- Any delay increases frustration.

Unfortunately, instead of going into a permission marketing mind-set, most companies stay in interruption marketing mode on their landing pages. The elements of the landing page continue to scream, shout, and demand the visitor's attention. This is done through the use of bold color blocks, bright images and graphics, and large font headlines—all trumpeting different items to click on.

Banner Ads

A big awareness thief is the third-party (or in-house) ad on your own landing pages. It is an invitation to throw away your visitors' attention and transport them to another website. Ads are specifically designed to grab awareness. Visual banner ads in particular are known for using bright, dramatic colors and provocative headlines. Many banner ads include animation and flashing colors to get noticed. Since most websites do not control the exact ads that will run on their pages, this is an invitation for disaster. A single banner ad can radically shift the attention away from your intended conversion action. Unless your primary business model is advertising supported, ads should be eliminated from your site, or at least radically deemphasized.

Entry Pop-ups

The absolute best way to destroy someone's attention is the use of entry pop-ups. These are floating windows that appear in front of your landing page as soon as it loads into the visitor's browser. Such pop-ups typically include a call-to-action such as filling out a form or clicking on a link leading to a special offer. Regardless of how they are technically implemented, they require an interaction by the visitor in order to deal with them. This means that the visitor must complete the intended action, or at least click on the pop-up in order to close and dismiss it from your computer screen. In effect, entry pop-ups prevent you from getting to the content of the landing page and are seen as an unwelcome surprise by most Web users.

Entry pop-ups represent the most blatant kind of in-your-face interruption advertising. They will anger, annoy, frustrate, and distract your visitors before they even see your landing page. Worst of all, using entry pop-ups shows really poor thinking on the part of the marketer responsible for their creation. If the pop-up's desired conversion action is your most important one, then it properly belongs on the landing page itself. If the conversion action on the landing page is different than the one in the pop-up, then the two can be displayed on the landing page side by side, instead of resorting to use of the pop-up. By emphasizing one or the other through the use of visual cues on the landing page, you can control their relative importance and steer people toward the more desirable one.

Entry pop-ups are an indication that your ability to prioritize is severely impaired and that you do not trust your actual landing page to get the job done on its own. It is absolutely unnecessary to compete with your own landing page, and in the process alienate the vast majority of your visitors.

Exit Pop-ups

The effect of exit pop-ups is not as clear. These are similar to entry pop-ups but appear only when someone is clicking *away* from your landing page or website. Exit pop-ups may try to entice you with a last-minute promotion, ask you to sign up for an e-mail newsletter in exchange for your contact information, or gather survey information about your reason for leaving. All of these can be seen as secondary conversion actions that have value to you. Since your primary conversion action did not happen, you can at least try to extract a little extra value from your visitor stream (especially if you are paying to get them there).

This may seem to contradict what I wrote earlier about competing for attention with your own landing pages. But in fact it does not—you are competing for attention with your Web visitors' next destination. They have already made the decision to move on, and in a sense you have nothing to lose. So a final dose of interruption marketing may salvage a tiny fraction of these people. Of course, taken to an extreme this may frustrate people and leave them with a negative impression of your company. So be judicious in your use of exit pop-ups.

Home Page Awareness

Single-purpose landing pages are relatively easy to streamline for attention. By contrast, home pages are hard. Home pages are often burdened with demands put on them by every functional department within a company. One of their many duties is to serve as a landing page (for type-in traffic, SEO traffic, some PPC traffic, and inbound links from other websites). Because of their many other legitimate functions, they are often severely compromised as landing pages. Consider Adorama's home page (www.adorama.com), shown in Figure 4.1. It illustrates many of the common home page issues.

Adorama sells a broad array of photography-related gear, and the visitor is presented with a bewildering array of choices. There are 146 clickable items on this page! Product shots feature a dozen disparate items that range in price from $24.95 to $799.95. Bright graphical banner ads across the top and right side of the page clamor for attention, leading to specific items on the site. A scrollable news ticker and rotating banner ads draw the eye through motion.

Which of the following actions are visitors expected to take?

Read the scrolling news bar? They probably did not come there for photo industry news.

Buy a replacement lithium-ion battery compatible only with certain Nikon cameras? This is limited to a very small segment of the visitors to the home page (who already own the compatible models of cameras).

Click on the cryptic "Photo Essentials" category? Even if they read down to the 13th position on the left navigation bar to reach this item, they would be hard-pressed to figure out what it means.

Figure 4.1 Adorama.com home page

Click on "Copiers/Printers/Fax Machines"? Most people would not have a compelling reason to buy these kinds of items from a company whose tagline is "The Photography People."

Read the "How to master dog photography" article by "Bowser"? This is probably not a pressing concern for most visitors.

I can imagine that while sitting in a company staff meeting somebody approved the addition of all of these items to the home page. Each item may be useful to a subset of your audience and may be logical in its own right. But the cumulative effect of all of this clutter is that you are squandering precious milliseconds of *every* visitor's attention. They are forced to wade through a lot of muck to even understand if there is any relevant information for them on your page. Will they do this? No. Many will simply throw up their hands in frustration and try another website.

The main goal of a broad-selection online catalog should be to efficiently direct all visitors to a relevant set of product choices, and to help them decide among them. The Adorama page does not do this effectively. A better alternative would be to focus on a smaller number of choices that apply to everyone and to funnel visitors deeper into the site.

Figure 4.2 shows the top of the home page for B&H (www.bhphotovideo.com), a company similar to Adorama in its breadth and scope of product offerings.

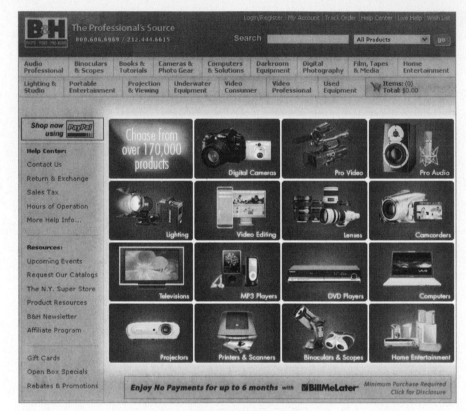

Figure 4.2 B&H Photo and Video home page

This home page has many of the same fundamental problems as Adorama's, and I am not holding it up as some paragon of effective landing page design. However, it handles one critical task significantly better: the attention of the user is directed to the block of high-level category images near the center of the page (see the highlighted area). Each main category is given equal weight, and the representative photos and descriptive text make it easy to see at a glance the breadth of the product line available on the site. The rest of the page is visually relatively mild and does not compete as much for the visitor's attention. Even though visual clutter also appears on this page, most of it is not visible without scrolling (and is not shown in Figure 4.2).

Keys to Creating Awareness

We'll revisit some of the suggestions in this section later in the book as we discuss timeless testing themes.

Stop screaming at your visitors.   Get out of the interruption marketing mind-set. Imagine your Web visitors as guests who have just arrived at your home. Would you scream at them? Turn down the volume by eliminating gaudy and flashy visual elements on your landing pages. Everything on your landing page does not deserve special emphasis.

This does not mean that you should not have a larger headline or clear call-to-action. Your desired conversion action should be prominent and clear. But in the absence of competing elements for the visitor's attention, this will happen naturally.

Eliminate unnecessary choices. Now that you have clearly defined your conversion action(s), you must take a hard look at your landing pages. Anything that does not directly support the conversion goal must be eliminated. If you have more than one conversion goal, you must emphasize the ones that have the highest value per visitor. These should receive a disproportionately large amount of screen real estate and prominence. Minor or supporting conversion goals should be minimized.

"Unclutter" what remains. Now it is time to become a word miser. Ruthlessly edit your remaining text copy. Simplify concepts. Shorten prose paragraphs to easy-to-scan bullet lists. Organize information with short headlines so visitors do not have to read unwanted topics. Create room to breathe with lots of whitespace on the page.

Interest

On the Web, interest is very fleeting. A world of other websites is just a mouse click away. People at this stage are in an "If it's interesting I'll check it out" mind-set. The level of commitment is very low. Interest is often tied very closely to awareness. The attention of the person flits like a butterfly across all of the available points of interest on your landing page. So awareness can also be described as an ongoing scanning process.

Interest is akin to the butterfly alighting for a moment on a particular flower. Interest can be viewed as a transient pull and concentration of the attention on a particular object. Often, interest on the Web is expressed in a split-second decision to click on something. If the attention surge is strong enough, you will take the action of clicking. If not, your attention will subside back into a more diffuse scanning mode. If your needs are not being met and you grow frustrated enough, interest can peak instead as a desire to leave the current Web page.

The key to creating the interest is to focus on the visitor. Elements of your landing page must be relevant to them, and they must self-select because they recognize this relevance.

The Rules of Web Interest

- Understand who the visitor is.

- Understand what the visitor is trying to accomplish.

Web interest comes in two main flavors: self-selection and need identification.

Self-Selection

In order to self-select, I must be given a discrete choice of specific classes of visitors to your site, and the appropriate path to follow. In effect, I have to raise my hand and say, "Yes, I identify with this label." Figure 4.3 shows the home page for the University of California, San Diego (ucsd.edu), my alma mater for undergraduate and graduate studies. Several navigation methods are available. One of the most prominent ones is the list of typical visitor classes near the upper-left portion of the page. It allows a visitor to self-select and proceed down the correct track.

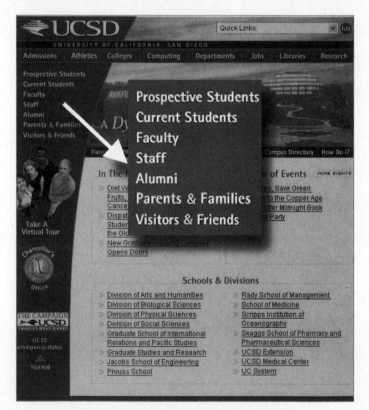

Figure 4.3 University of California, San Diego home page

Self-selection is another way of describing the appropriate role that someone takes on in relation to your landing page. Roles are described in more detail in the "User-Centered Design" section in Chapter 3.

Need Recognition

Another way to increase interest is to have people identify with a specific need that they currently have. Needs can change more quickly than roles. The highlighted portion of the Southwest Airline home page in Figure 4.4 (www.southwest.com) prominently features a needs-based navigation section.

To the right of the large photo, visitors are invited to select among the following choices:

- Book a Flight
- Check In Online
- Check Your Flight Status
- View or Change Your Flight

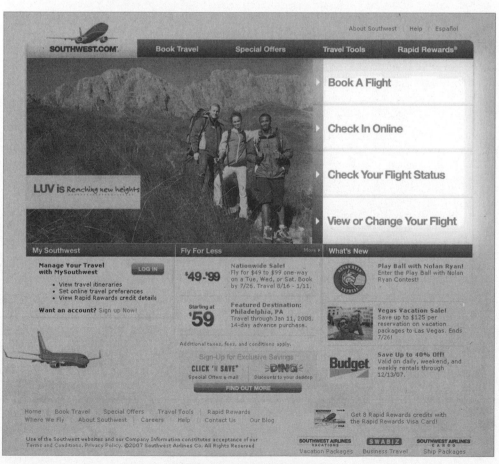

Figure 4.4 Southwest Airlines home page

Note that these choices are aimed at two classes of users: prospective travelers and booked travelers. The last three choices apply only to booked travelers. So the visitor's role alone is not enough to distinguish among them. However, on any particular visit, a booked traveler will likely to need to complete one of the three tasks.

Need recognition is another way of describing the specific task that someone is trying to complete on your landing page. I explored tasks in the "User-Centered Design" section in Chapter 3.

Desire

The mind-set and attention span of the visitor in the desire stage is different from those in the preceding stages. Whereas the attention and interest stages may have lasted only a few seconds, visitors in the desire stage may give you their full attention for minutes or even hours. They are in research mode and are willing to take more time.

With visitors in the desire stage, you get the precious gift of having them spend time on your landing page or website. You have piqued their interest and they are now going to check you out. You are engaged in a subtle seduction to continue to increase your visitor's desire.

Just as in an interpersonal setting, seduction is a tricky and tenuous activity. You can't move too fast without seeming off-putting. Yet we see this all the time on the Web. Have you ever visited an e-tailer website, and after being shown some random featured product on the home page, been instructed to "Buy It Now"? This can be seen as premature and inappropriate. So what should you do instead? Follow these basic rules for building desire:

The Rules of Web Desire

- Make the visitor feel appreciated.
- Make the visitor feel safe.
- Understand that the visitor is in control.

Make the visitor feel appreciated. The Web allows you to provide your visitors with all kinds of useful information at minimal cost to you. This information, if properly used, can make them feel knowledgeable, powerful, and understood.

Make the visitor feel safe. The Web is a scary place, and your landing page or website is often a total stranger to your visitors. You must do everything you can to let them get to know you better. It is important to be completely open, honest, and transparent.

You must also do everything you can to alleviate their fears by transferring credibility from others in the form of testimonials, awards, and trust symbols.

Understand that the visitor is in control. Visitors should be able to dictate the terms of the relationship with you. This includes the timescale of the interaction, the order in which things get done, the option to stay anonymous for as long as possible, and the ability to look for information in whatever format is easiest and most appropriate for them.

Do You Have What the Visitor Wants?

To determine whether you have what they want, a typical visitor will pass formally or informally through several steps:

- Research
- Compare
- Get details
- Customize

Although the following examples are drawn mostly from e-tailing, the principles and steps are the same for all landing pages and websites.

Research

Understand what features of the product or service are important to visitors. Rank their importance as must-have, nice-to-have, and nonessential. During the research step, people may have only vague notions of what they want. They are looking for a guide or a knowledgeable expert to help them get oriented. Once they understand the lay of the land better, they can compare the available options against their perceived needs. These needs themselves may undergo change during the research process. As new information becomes available, additional needs may arise. Alternatively, former needs may become irrelevant in light of some new discovery or understanding.

As long as your information is useful and objective, you get to define the rules of the game, and can present key features that are a source of competitive advantage and a differentiator for you.

This information can be presented in a variety of formats:

Whitepapers Informational articles (typically used in a business-to-business setting) to educate prospects about important and complex topics

Buying guides Articles written to educate consumers about important features and differences among a certain class of products or services

Wizards Automated tools that help visitors zero in on the right solution by asking them a series of questions related to their specific task

Demonstrations Videos, animations, or presentation slides that showcase a particular product or service

I recently visited Shoes.com (www.shoes.com) in search of new hiking shoes (see Figure 4.5). Their home page informed me that there were 11,478 types of shoes available in the men's department. I steeled myself for the inevitable slog through dozens of pages featuring endless arrays of tiny thumbnail images and descriptions. Instead I was guided within seconds by using the "Narrow By" navigation bar (highlighted on the left of the page) to two specific shoe models that met my needs.

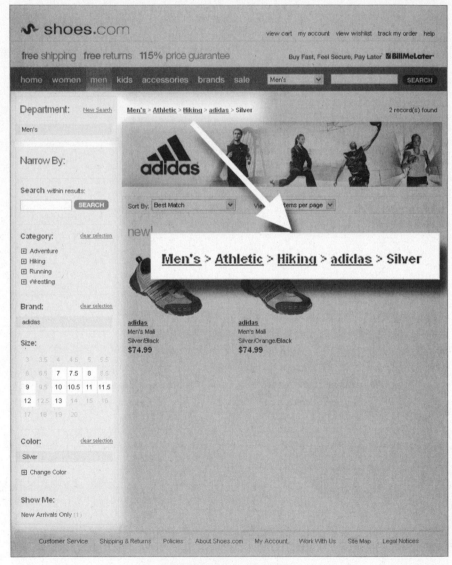

Figure 4.5 Shoes.com home page

The "Narrow By" features included:

- Text search
- Category
- Brand
- Size
- Color
- Filters for "new arrivals only" and "on sale only"

Breadcrumbs are normally a navigation aid to show you exactly how you got to the current page within the site, and allow you to backtrack and retrace your steps. They are usually displayed based on the static navigation scheme of the website as documented in its sitemap (a special page with an indented outline view of every other page on the site). As I continued through my narrowing-down process, the breadcrumbs at the top of the page changed to match my preferences (see the callout in Figure 4.5). In other words, they adjusted dynamically and did not force me to fit into a single fixed notion of how the site should be navigated.

Although the site's functionality is simply an advanced form of search, it is so useful that it qualifies as a wizard for the product-selection task. Several features combine to make it more powerful than the sum of its parts:

Flexible search options As I mentioned earlier, six ways of searching were provided. The only obvious missing search method is price range.

Context sensitivity All of the search options were "aware" of each other. For example, if I made a choice of brand, and certain sizes were not available, this would be reflected in the shoe size chart. If the search had narrowed to include no on-sale items, the "on sale only" option would no longer be shown. This allows for iterative (i.e., incremental) drilldown and refinement.

Order independence I could choose to use any of the remaining search methods in whatever order I wanted. There was no rigid search methodology forced on me.

Reversible I could always easily undo any of my prior choices, and re-widen the scope of my search. As I mentioned earlier, the other remaining search options would also reconfigure to show me their available settings in the revised search context.

The end result is radically different than simply offering multiple advanced search options on a website.

Zappos.com (www.zappos.com) is another online shoe retailer that features a wide selection. On the surface, they also offer an advanced search with seemingly similar options to Shoes.com. Within the Men's Athletic category I was able to specify shoe size, width, color, and price range.

Men's:	Athletic ▾	- All Men's Athletic -	▾		Save This Search

Men's Athletic - no items found

| | 10 ▾ | E (W or Wide) ▾ | Silver ▾ | 70.00 to 99.99 ▾ | GO |

However, when I selected my options, I got the result shown here:

Sort by Popularity | New | Name | Low Price | High Price **Show** 12 per page | All one page

Sorry, no results found.
Please try a different combination of searches.

Notify Me of New Sizes!

Sign up to be notified when new shoes in your size and/or width become available! Just enter your email address, pick whether you are looking for mens or womens shoes and pick your size and width.

Email Address: [ ]

Gender: ○ Men's   **Send Updates:** ○ Weekly
        ○ Women's   ○ Daily

Size: Pick Size ▾   **Width:** Pick Width ▾

[Notify Me!]

Imagine my frustration. I had wasted my time, and gotten nothing for my efforts. I also began to question the breadth of inventory available on Zappos.com. The no-results message is cryptic and made me feel stupid, as if I had done something wrong. There was no attempt to salvage the situation and provide me with additional assistance at this critical juncture—I felt like I was on my own. To add insult to injury, I was asked to volunteer for daily e-mail spam every time men's shoes in my size and width became available. My options at this point were to try to figure out how to change my search to produce some results (akin to shooting in the dark), or to do a very general search with lots of results and laboriously scan them all until I found something useful. There was a third option, and it is always available to even mildly frustrated Internet users: punch out and visit a competitor's site instead.

It all adds up to an unpleasant brand experience that could have been easily avoided. At every step of the way, Shoes.com told me how many products were left within my current search scope. I did not have to specify everything at once only to be told that I had reached a dead end. I could never be surprised by a no-results message because the forward-looking, context-sensitive search options remaining would only display choices that still led to valid results.

Some companies make searching so difficult (or do not provide any search functionality at all!) that visitors must spend a lot of time looking through seemingly endless clearly inappropriate search results. The Men's Athletic category page on Zappos.com features 12,504 items. It is a pretty safe bet that the 12 particular shoes on any given search results page are unlikely to match most people's needs. It is also safe to assume that no one will want to step manually through 1,042 matching results pages by using the "Previous Page" and "Next Page" links.

The proper solution is to detect this information overload situation and help guide the visitor to a smaller number of items before displaying any of them in more detail. You want to provide them with door-to-door service—not drop them off within a few miles of their destination and have them walk the rest of the way. In the previous example, if the number of matching shoes is still above a reasonable threshold, further search refinement should be suggested.

If this was the last website on the Internet, and their life depended on finding the correct item, then you could expect your visitors to put up with this kind of nonsense. But the reality of the Internet is usually the polar opposite: users have a world of choices, and the items they are searching for are mostly of passing casual interest.

The following mock-up screenshot offers Zappos.com an alternative way of dealing with this situation:

> **Your search for:** Men's > Athletic Shoes
> Returned **12504** matching items
>
> Would you like to...
>
> Refine your search: See all 12504 matches
>
> [Any Size ▽]
>
> [Any Width   ▽]
>
> [Any Color   ▽]
>
> [Any Price   ▽]

Visitors are presented with a clear choice and can still get to the full list of results. But they are not distracted prematurely and are given the option to narrow the scope of their search. If they choose a refinement from one of the drop-downs below and the number of matching items is still above the thresholds, they would simply be shown an updated version of this page.

The bottom line is that there is no excuse for poor search features. Giving visitors too many choices and forcing them to wade through them is the Web equivalent of being sprayed with a fire hose. Giving them no matching search results is admitting your incompetence in providing useful guidance in helping visitors to narrow their choices.

Is it slightly more difficult and time consuming to provide thoughtful support during the search step? Of course it is. But you must do it to avoid a huge drop in conversion rate.

Compare

Check out alternative solutions or products to see how they stack up against the previously determined feature set. Once visitors have been educated about the desirable features of the product or service, they usually find more than one acceptable alternative. The key must-have features have all been satisfied. So the decision to narrow their choice does not depend on these previously considered features. They need additional "tie-breakers," although these may be secondary or even tertiary in their ultimate importance. But, in the absence of the primary selection criteria, they serve as differentiators. Giving as much side-by-side detailed information during this step is critical. This is usually done in the form of a comparison matrix.

Because comparison sites are specialized and focused on this step, they obviously play an important role and have a definite advantage in influencing the ultimate decision. They fulfill one of the ultimate promises of the Internet: aggregating the full range of choices for a particular industry or product type and helping to guide consumers. Most comparison sites also cover the research and desire steps, and seamlessly hand off to the ultimate recommended e-retailer or service provider.

There are two ways that comparisons can be skewed: choice of features, and choice of competitors. We have all seen television car commercials and we know that the comparison features are hand-picked and skewed in favor of the advertiser's product (e.g., "Our car costs thousand less *and* has four more cup holders!"). Internet consumers are generally too sophisticated or cynical to fall for heavy-handed approaches like this. They are used to getting detailed objective information, and can find it in a variety of places. To compete with comparison sites, single-brand or single-product sites must duplicate this deep and detailed content on their websites. Better yet, they can get the objective information from a trusted third party and feature the source prominently to lend extra credibility to their data. Include a wide range of realistic competitors. If possible, allow the selection of more than one competitor in your matrix.

For many marketers, the comparison step represents an internal tug of war. The instinct to carve out a competitive advantage through information hoarding or biased slanting is strong. Yet this is exactly the wrong impulse for the Internet and must be consciously resisted. Internet consumers are often more knowledgeable about products and services than the so-called experts who sell them.

Some online marketers also live on a steady diet of self-inflicted in-house brain-washing and propaganda. They actually believe that their products really are the "world-class leader" in their category. The consumer does not labor under this delusion. In fact, they seek out not only objective data and reviews, but also the opinions of third-party experts and existing users of a particular product or service. Many online marketers would be shocked to find that their precious product claims are regularly savaged in online forums, discussion groups, and special interest communities.

Much of this criticism is well deserved and as you will see in the next chapter should be looked at as a source of ideas for improvement. Comparison information must be complete, objective, and easily digested by your target audience. The conclusion is unavoidable: if you don't provide support during the crucial comparison step, then your competitor or some other influencer will.

Get Details

Make sure that *you* understand everything about the total experience with the chosen product or service. Once visitors select a product or service from a list of finalists, they want to make sure that they are making the right decision. At this step, even more detailed information should be provided including:

- Detailed description
- Features
- Specifications
- Compatibilities, standards compliance, minimum requirements
- Configuration options, available service levels
- Photos, diagrams
- Accessories and suggested add-ons
- Third-party media reviews and endorsements
- User reviews and client testimonials
- Case studies or survey results
- Suggested alternative products
- Delivery and setup options (shipping, installation)
- Service plans and customer care levels
- Accurate costs and payment terms
- Availability and in-stock status

Niche product or service sites often provide extensive information on their product-detail pages. A perfect example is specialty e-tailer JoggingStroller.com (www.joggingstroller.com). The site features many of the top brands of baby strollers and simple "Help the visitor choose" guides to identify the right one. The product detail pages are chock-full of information that will help visitors make a good decision: detailed staff-written reviews, pricing, shipping costs, specs, features, pictures of all available color choices, suggested upgrades, accessories, alternative competitive models, and extensive reviews from actual customers (with ratings of how helpful other visitors found each one).

It is important to provide complete and objective information, even if this means reporting something negative. Chances are if someone is going to do their homework about your product or service on the Web, they will run across the negative information anyway. By presenting it yourself, you are seen as more trustworthy. You also have the opportunity to frame the concern on your own terms, and partially mitigate its impact.

The user reviews are especially useful because they provide insights about real-world use in situations that a first-time buyer may not have considered. The reviews are not always flattering, but unless they are clearly inappropriate or offensive they should be left on your site. Having negative reviews shows a well-rounded picture, and indicates that the information on the site is more or less unfiltered (and therefore more trustworthy). When user reviews (or other forms of user-generated content) reach critical mass on these kinds of sites, they can serve as a defensible barrier to entry against other competitors (who may only feature stock descriptions or specs from the product manufacturer).

Customize

By configuring or personalizing a product or service to your particular needs or circumstances, you are mentally envisioning yourself enjoying its benefits, and may be nearing the action stage. Once visitors have decided on a particular product or service, they should be given the opportunity to customize it. By personalizing the solution to their specific needs, they are vicariously "trying it on for size." This gets visitors involved in imagining exactly how they might use it in the future. Personalization and configuration put visitors in control and create momentum toward the action stage.

The laptop configurator on the Sony website (www.sonystyle.com) allows me to choose from a deep list of options: CPU, memory, hard drive, optical disc drive, display, TV tuner, operating system, wireless local area network, battery, preinstalled software, music software, photo software, video software, finance software, other software, and service plan. A number of available accessories can also be added (adapters, batteries, carrying cases). I even chose two lines of text that will actually be engraved above the screen. The exact price is subtotaled after every change. The monthly financing option is displayed along with the estimated shipment date. Estimated tax and shipping costs are optionally shown if I enter my zip code.

Action

Desire and action are not really distinct stages, but rather a continuing give-and-take. Increasing desire pulls us to take successively larger steps toward the ultimate conversion goal. Each of these steps is in itself an action. After each action, we build on its momentum to create enough desire to jump to the next level of action and commitment.

Even if your website can answer the "Do you have what I want?" question in the affirmative, you still have to get past the "Should I get it from you?" hurdle. Some additional desire is usually needed to propel us through the ultimate conversion transaction.

Should the Visitor Get It from You?

Before I am moved to action, I must believe that I have found the right solution for my needs, and also that I have found a reasonable and trustworthy company to deal with. Notice that I did not say "the best" company. As you will soon see, this is not a prerequisite for transacting.

Finding the best solution, and finding the best provider for that solution, are largely independent decisions. Just because you have gone to great lengths to help visitors research, compare, review, and customize a good solution does not mean that they will buy it from you. Especially if the item in question is a commodity, or widely available from a number of online and offline sources, many people will comparison-shop to find the best price and terms. There is growing evidence that online consumers are getting savvier, and that the median online purchase times for many industries are steadily increasing because of comparison shopping.

There are claims by some that the Internet will eventually subsume every offline category and transform it. This is hyperbole. However, some industries and activities are certainly more Internet-friendly. These are usually the ones where detailed and formerly-restricted information is the key to a buyer's decision. Real estate has experienced this onslaught. Two information-related tasks have gotten much easier with the wide adoption of the Internet: finding a property and arranging for the financing. Secret multiple listing service books (MLSs) containing all for-sale houses were once the exclusive purview of licensed real estate agents. Now consumers can sign up on comprehensive national websites and be instantly notified when a new property matching their needs hits the market. The time-consuming, paperwork-intensive process required to arrange for a mortgage loan has also been streamlined by online applications. Formerly standard 6% commission rates have fallen as discount brokers and agents have proliferated. These discount brokers are simply offering more abbreviated and streamlined services to sophisticated consumers who have already done the hard work of finding potential properties and who arrive with their pre-approved financing already in hand.

Similarly, consumers in other industries often use the Internet for a portion of their decision process, but then prefer to conclude the transaction offline. In many instances, offline is in fact your biggest threat. When my family was looking for a stroller we researched it online and found the JoggingStroller.com website extremely helpful. We settled on a hard-to-find model made exclusively by a manufacturer in New Zealand. We then called a local retailer and, after determining that they had the right model and color in stock, decided to visit their store and examine it in person. We came well prepared and very much liked our physical test drive of the stroller. Even though it was slightly more expensive than online, we ended up purchasing it on the spot.

Were we disloyal to JoggingStroller.com? In a way we were. They did provide us with a free education, and yet we still did not buy from them. However, this is the harsh reality of Internet sales, and a significant reason why shopping cart abandonment rates will remain stubbornly high. But in our defense we also had a number of other considerations. We wanted to see the physical product and experience how heavy, solid, and maneuverable it was. It is very difficult to convey this ergonomic information—even with the help of detailed product images and specifications. We were also excited by the prospect of our purchase, and wanted to immediately take our baby for a walk in it. We were also consciously choosing to support a physical "brick and mortar" retailer who took the risk of carrying this manufacturer's product line in stock on the off chance that someone like us would walk into their store.

This does not mean that you should not bother to provide all of the pre-conversion supporting information on your landing page. By doing so, you narrow the range of your likely online competitors. Ones that do not have similarly deep and rich content will simply not be in the running because visitors are less likely to spend significant time on their websites. It then comes down to a decision of your company versus offline alternatives. And offline is not always an option. Unless you live in a large city, your choice of specialty products or services may be very restricted (or nonexistent). In such circumstances, the best online company actually has a huge advantage.

There is a continuum of goods and services that range from concrete to vague. Many services fall toward the latter end of the spectrum. In his excellent book *Selling the Invisible: A Field Guide to Modern Marketing* (Business Plus, 1997), Harry Beckwith describes the fundamental difference between selling services and tangible products. When people buy services, they are usually looking for specialized knowledge and expertise that they do not possess themselves. In the case of many professional occupations (such as lawyers, architects, or doctors), people only infrequently need the services and do not know how to objectively evaluate the merits of the service provider. But the consequences of making a poor decision are very high. So they are forced to rely on the personal relationship, referrals, and any other tangible clues of quality that they can find.

It is important to remember that the landing page itself is simply a visual representation of a service promise that you are making to the visitor. The promise can be very different depending on your conversion actions: that you will follow up on your contact request promptly (lead-generation forms), that you will not spam visitors but will instead send them useful information (e-mail newsletter sign-up), that the product they are seeing is accurately represented (online auction sites), and that their purchase will indeed arrive before that special occasion (e-commerce).

Often the ultimate conversion action is actually offline, and the intermediate online step is simply designed to pass the visitor on to a live person on the telephone, to schedule a callback, or to arrange for a subsequent face-to-face consultation or group event.

The factors that I discuss in the next sections weigh heavily on whether someone will transact with you.

Brand Strength

As I discussed in Chapter 1, brands are very powerful. Well-known marketers Al Ries and Jack Trout correctly point out in their classic book *The 22 Immutable Laws of Marketing: Violate Them at Your Own Risk!* (HarperBusiness, 1994) that brands serve as a shortcut to decision making in our busy lives. Each product or service category only has room for a tiny number of established leaders, and they capture disproportionate value in their respective market categories. When a brand is firmly established in the mind of a person as a market leader, it becomes almost impossible to dislodge.

The halo provided by the brand's promise means that a person can devote much less attention to evaluating items related to the brand. The same presumption is not accorded to lesser-known or unknown competitors. Although their products or services may be objectively just as good, they require additional attention to evaluate. Because of this, they may be disqualified from consideration simply because people will not choose to spend the required time investigating them.

Brands take enormous amounts of time and money to build. Take a hard look at your brand. Most likely it is not that strong. Even if your company is one of the online leaders in a category, that does not mean that your brand awareness has spread to most people in your industry (or to the public at large for consumer products and services). The relative weakness of many online brands is the primary reason that their offline competitors often win the battle for the customer's mindshare. Since there is no short-term way to impact the strength of your brand, it is essentially outside of your control.

Previous Resource Investment

I think that my approach to finding something on the Internet is representative of many people's. I poke around in my favorite search engine, briefly visit promising sites, focus on one or two key sources of information, get educated, make a decision, and live with it. Have I found the optimum answer? Clearly not. But I am tired of looking, and there are endless additional choices to explore. Usually the solutions or products that I find are acceptable—although not always the best.

Economist Herbert A. Simon coined a term for this phenomenon: *satisficing.* It is a combination of the words "satisfy" and "suffice." Most people do not want to invest additional time without a strong sense that they will find a better answer. As soon as they find a solution that is good enough, they often stop looking. The more effort they have previously invested, the more likely they are to just accept the best solution they have found up to that point.

The Total Solution

Although I tried to neatly decouple the product or service from its provider, the separation is not always this clean. Often the two are enmeshed. For example, the product or service may be available from only one provider. In such "proprietary" cases, the provider, warts and all, must be considered as part of the solution. More commonly, the provider offers a number of value-added services or options that are not always available from others or that cannot be easily compared. Your visitor is thinking in terms of the total solution and is deciding based on that.

A total solution may involve the following elements:

- The base price
- The properly configured "out the door" price
- Additional costs such as shipping or installation
- Exchange and return policies
- Ease of setup and learning curve required
- Availability status and delivery date guarantees
- Service plans and options
- Ongoing costs to operate and maintain
- Convenient company physical locations
- Performance or level-of-service guarantees

Risk Reducers

Risk reducers are anything that lowers a visitor's anxiety. They help reassure the visitor that bad things are unlikely to happen:

Guarantees If I don't like it, I can get my money back.

Policies They have a no-hassle return policy.

Alternative transaction mechanisms I can also complete my transaction on the phone, by mail, or in person.

Trials and introductory offers If I don't like it, I can cancel before they charge my credit card.

Safe shopping symbols My personal information will not be stolen.

Privacy symbols I will not be spammed by this company, and my e-mail won't be sold to spammers.

Risk reducers need to be seen before the checkout process or conversion step itself, and as prominently as possible. Otherwise, the visitor may not feel comfortable enough to proceed. SmartBargains.com (www.smartbargains.com) lists a number of risk-reducing trust symbols on their website. Unfortunately, they are placed in the footer of the page (see highlighted area in Figure 4.6). Because this part of the page is well below the top of the page, they cannot be seen without scrolling. So the positive effect of displaying the trust symbols is significantly lower than it could be.

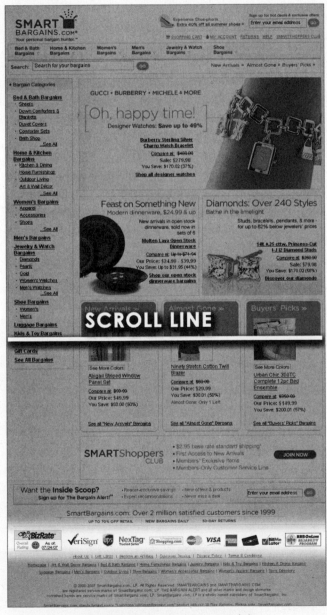

Figure 4.6 SmartBargains.com trust symbols

By contrast, PetSmart.com (www.petsmart.com) considers the ScanAlert HackerSafe trust mark so important that they chose to display it in the upper left corner—the most prominent and powerful position on any Web page (see Figure 4.7). This area is usually reserved for the company's logo. In this case, PetSmart compensated for the change by displaying their logo in a very large size and centered on the header. This instantly transmits a two-part message to the visitor: "We're safe to buy from—we're PetSmart."

Figure 4.7 PetSmart.com HackerSafe placement

If possible, the safe shopping and privacy symbols should be the leading ones in their category; otherwise, there is an additional momentary pause and possible confusion as the visitor evaluates the validity and credibility of the less-familiar trust symbol itself.

Validation and Credibility

Risk reducers lower your anxiety levels. It is also possible to raise you affinity level with validation and credibility indicators. These increase your affinity for the website or product. In effect, risk reducers make you feel "less-worse," while evidence of validation makes you feel "more-better." Both are based on transferring goodwill from other people or companies to yours. No one wants to be the fool who fell for a ruse and had to deal with the consequences. Validation tells people that others have previously done something similar and had a good outcome. In effect, they create social proof to back up your company's claims.

Examples of validation include:

- Industry or media awards (editor's choice, fastest-growing company)
- Media coverage (mentions in mainstream press, websites, or blogs)

- Inclusion in industry analyst reports

- Endorsements from individuals and associations

- Partnerships with other respected companies

- Studies and surveys (market share, customer satisfaction)

- Client lists and logos

- Case studies

- User testimonials and reviews

SiteTuners.com client SF Video specializes in large-scale DVD, CD, and video duplication. The company, whose landing page is illustrated in Figure 4.8, is well established and has worked with over 2,400 clients, including some of the top brands in the world. By adding a prominent area with client logos to their lead form, they were able to noticeably boost their form-fill conversion rate.

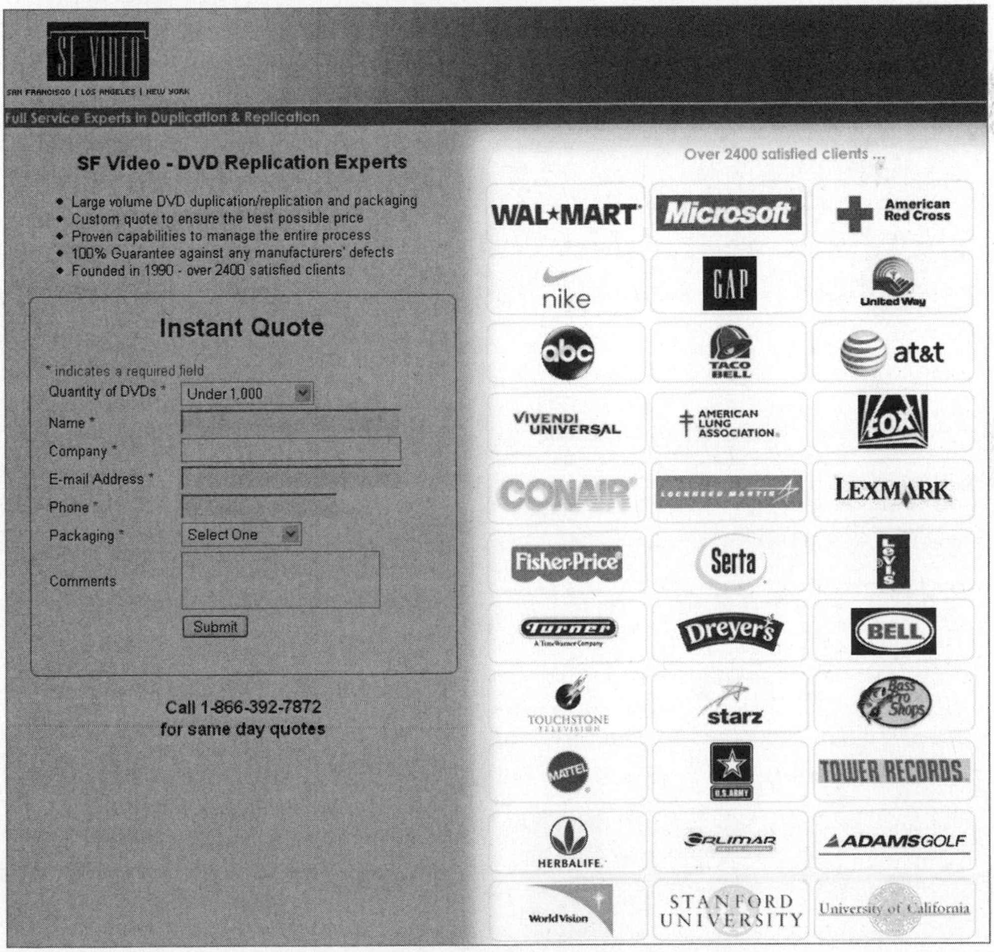

Figure 4.8 SF Video lead generation landing page with client logos

Transacting

Even if you have correctly done everything up to this point, remember that not everyone will act at this stage. They may not be able to afford your product. They may want to continue their search for alternatives. They may need the approval of another person (such as a coworker or spouse). They may not have the proper payment method, or the necessary supporting information to complete the transaction. Some may simply want to sleep on the decision before making it.

But let's assume that someone has finally built up enough desire to act. What is the best way to get that person to complete the transaction?

The Rules of Web Action

- Get out of the visitor's way.

- Make it easy for the visitor.

- Don't surprise the visitor.

Get Out of the Visitor's Way

The most criminal waste of attention at this point is focusing your visitors on unnecessary tasks or distractions. One of the most egregious is making them register before checking out.

In forced registration, visitors are required to give their e-mail address and create a password before buying something. The merchant does this ostensibly to help the consumer on subsequent visits. The checkout information, such as shipping address and payment method, is stored. On their next visit, they are asked to enter the e-mail and password, and the stored data is auto-populated in the checkout process forms for them. Figure 4.9 shows the first page of the checkout process at Overstock.com (www.overstock.com).

This registration requirement is particularly confusing. You are asked for your e-mail address first. Then you are asked if you are a new customer. Despite the fact that most people are likely to be new customers, the default radio button checked is the second choice: "No, I am a returning customer." If you investigate the alternative answer, "Yes, I am a new customer," you are confronted with the cryptic parenthetical remark "(You'll create a new password here.)". Where exactly is this "here"? There is no apparent place to click or enter the password.

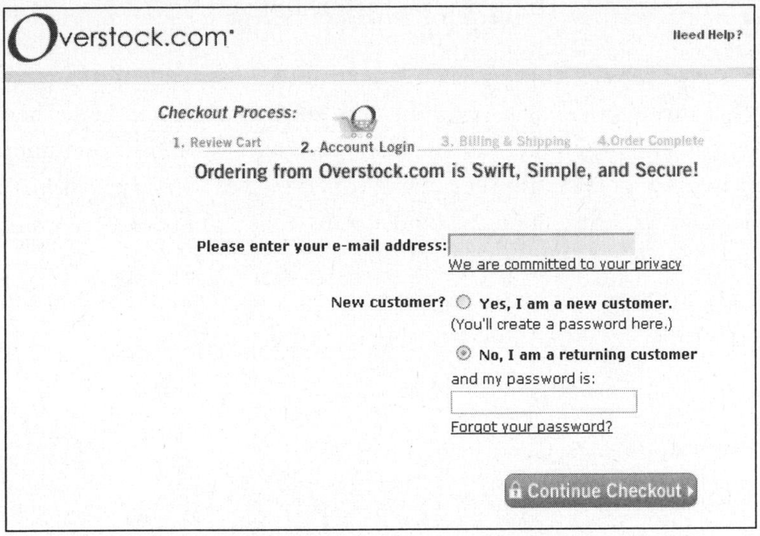

Figure 4.9 Overstock.com checkout process

If you actually select the "Yes, I am a new customer" radio button, then the form reconfigures as shown in Figure 4.10.

Figure 4.10 Overstock.com checkout process for new customers

Two new fields are created below the new customer radio selection, along with a checkbox for participation in e-mail special offers. The password entry field for returning customers disappears.

My guess is that software developers (instead of usability advocates) lead the way in creating this conceptual mess. It smacks of engineering if-then logic without any concern for the anxiety level created for the visitor. This process is confusing because it entwines data entry for new and returning customers. It also hides important information with no indication of how it can be revealed. When the form reconfigures, it is a total surprise to the visitor (violating the "Don't surprise the visitor" rule described below). It also creates unnecessary work for everyone by requiring a reconfirmation of the password. Only a few people will misspell the password that they had intended to enter. Even if they do, this can be easily dealt with by sending them an e-mail with a temporary password after their login attempt fails. Instead, extra data entry is forced on *all* potential customers.

Registration on your site may be a minor advantage to a small percentage of your visitors. But it is guaranteed to be an annoyance and hindrance to many more. If someone really wants the convenience of not having to frequently reenter their personal data, they can set up a central user authentication account (that works across multiple websites), or activate their Web browser's automatic form-fill capability. Many people may have no intention of transacting with you again and will not appreciate the extra work required to register. Others may object on privacy grounds to giving you their e-mail address since it is not an absolute requirement for completing an online transaction. Registration should never be forced and should be deemphasized in most cases. Even seemingly minor transactional friction such as filling out the e-mail and password may significantly lower your conversion rates. If you must have the registration and login options first, the alternative mock-up that I have created in Figure 4.11 illustrates a cleaner approach. Note the following differences from Overstock's actual version:

Self-selection As discussed in the previous chapter, it is important to clearly identify important user classes (in this case, new and returning customers) and to provide the correct tasks for each one.

Emphasis Most screen real estate supports new customers (usually the largest group by far). Within the new customer group, the main option is to proceed without registering.

Registration that is not forced New users can proceed immediately to the rest of the checkout process. The registration option describes the benefit of taking this step ("for faster future checkouts").

Visible choices There are no hidden context-sensitive parts on the page. What you see is what you get. This lowers visitor anxiety.

Minimal data entry The password for new customer registrations is entered only once.

An even better approach would be to remove the optional new customer registration requirement from this page altogether. The same information can be collected easily near the end of the checkout process. At that stage visitors have significantly more invested in the transaction. They are less likely to abandon the process and more likely to supply the requested additional information.

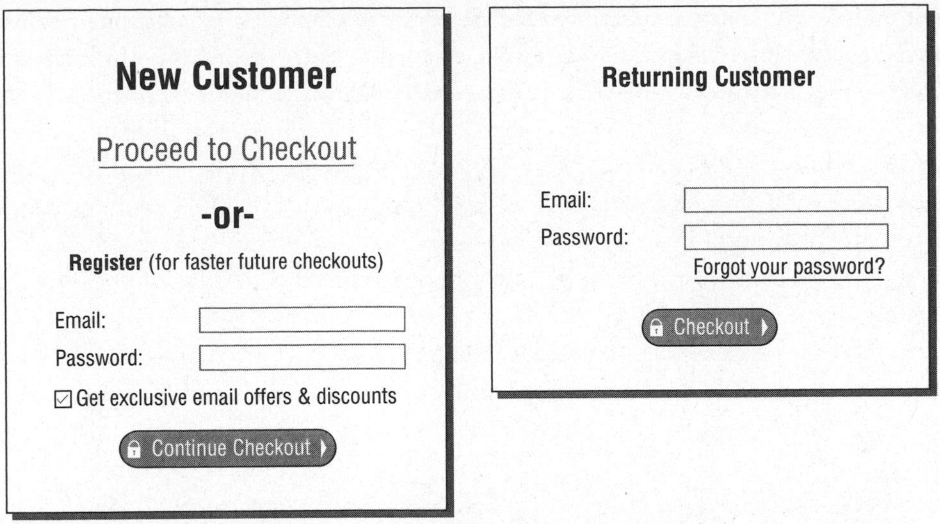

New Customer

Proceed to Checkout

-or-

Register (for faster future checkouts)

Email: [_____]
Password: [_____]
☑ Get exclusive email offers & discounts

🔒 Continue Checkout ▸

Returning Customer

Email: [_____]
Password: [_____]
Forgot your password?

🔒 Checkout ▸

Figure 4.11 Mock-up of alternative to the Overstock.com checkout process

Another common tactic during the transaction is to introduce last-minute up-sells, cross-sells, or special offers. This is fine if it is handled before the checkout step (e.g., by displaying accessories on a product detail page in an online catalog). However, during the checkout process such tactics should be carefully considered. Usually there is a trade-off between higher value per transaction and lower overall conversion rates. The method by which a secondary offer is presented greatly affects its potential impact. Efforts should be made to minimize disruption and surprise. The example from McAfee Inc. (www.mcafee.com) illustrates this point. After I started my checkout (with a single item in my cart), I was presented with the pop-up window shown in Figure 4.12. I was forced to deal with the up-sell offer presented before continuing the checkout.

Other examples involve coregistration (or "coreg" for short). This is a common online practice. During a transaction, you are invited (usually by simply checking a box) to participate in other (often unrelated) services or offers from co-marketing part-ners of the website. If you opt in, some of the information from your original transac-tion is then forwarded to the coreg partner for future promotional e-mails to you.

Many coreg programs are thinly disguised ways to gather and sell your e-mail to others for the purposes of e-mailing (and sometimes spamming) you. Since you are pig-gybacking the coregistration on your own transaction, ultimately the impact of this will rub off on your own brand and credibility. Your primary transaction presumably has a lot more value than the incremental money you can make from coregistrations. So you must be careful about the potential risks (such as lower conversion rates or damage to your reputation). It is rarely a good idea to transfer some of the trust that you have built up (enough to actually complete the desired conversion action) to another company. As suggested earlier, if you are considering up-sells or coregistration you should at least test the impact on your revenue per visitor.

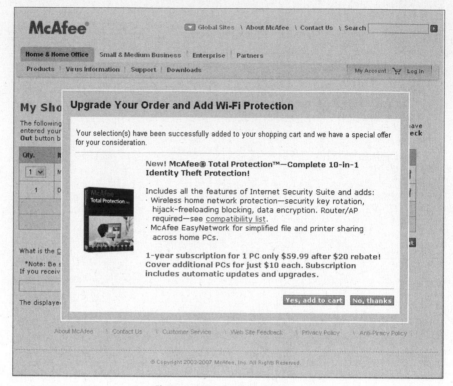

Figure 4.12 McAfee checkout pop-up

Make It Easy for the Visitor

One of the keys to making the user experience easier is to remove choice and simplify the transaction process. An easy way to do this is to change the navigation information available on the page. The main menu that is used during the earlier stages of the decision process is no longer applicable during the action stage.

The top of the home page for the Barnes & Noble website (www.bn.com) is shown in Figure 4.13. It includes many navigation options in the top header and the side column on the left of the page. Many of these links and search tools are necessary for the shopping process.

Figure 4.13 Barnes & Noble main site header and navigation

However, once a visitor starts the checkout process, the navigation is replaced with the simplified header shown here:

Only information relevant to the transaction is included in the new navigation. Everything else is removed.

If your landing page is designed for a single conversion action, you should not use the navigation or page structure from your main corporate website. You should remove the navigation completely, or limit it to specific information related to your conversion action. This is especially the case if you are paying for the traffic stream directly (e.g., via PPC or banner ad purchases). In such cases, I often recommend removing the navigation altogether. Sometimes you may still want to have your logo link back to your main site. But you should realize that this is a potential traffic leak, and that some people will wander off to your main site to never return. If you feel that your main site contains content that is necessary for the conversion action, you should copy it onto the landing page (or a supporting page on your stand-alone micro-site). Do *not* link off to the main site for such supporting information.

Forms should also be ruthlessly edited. A long and imposing form will turn many people away. The value of the incremental information gathered in a longer form will rarely outweigh the benefit of having many more people completing the process. Clarify forms with a headline or description. Shorten form label text as much as possible. Organize form fields into logical groups. Eliminate any strong horizontal visual separators in longer forms.

The most important part of form creation is minimizing the number and complexity of form input fields. As a start, you should eliminate all "optional" fields.

The Form Field Test: Is this information *absolutely necessary* to complete the *current transaction*?

You have to ask only for information that you need right now. Resist the temptation to ask for information that may not be needed at all or that can be collected later in the process (after you have established more trust with the visitor). It is good to avoid repeated data entry and have forms automatically uploaded into your sales force automation (SFA) or customer relationship management (CRM) systems. But do not insist on populating a complete record in these databases immediately. Such nice-to-have reasons do not meet the test above.

Along with the number of form fields, you should also shorten all descriptive labels, and explanatory text. It is also important to have a clear and concise form title. The title should describe the benefit that the visitor will accrue if they expend the effort to complete the form.

One of our partners, SEM firm Engine Ready, was running a large-scale PPC campaign for a client in the debt negotiation business. Their goal was to collect qualified leads for telephone follow-up. The conversion action was the completion of the landing page form shown in Figure 4.14.

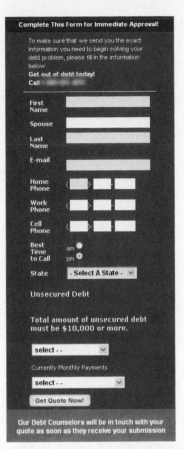

Figure 4.14 Original lead form for debt negotiation company

After discussions with the client, we determined that not all of the fields on the original form were absolutely required. Many of them could be collected during the follow-up phone call. At the conclusion of our test, we ended up with a number of changes to the landing page. Among them was the newly designed form shown in Figure 4.15.

Free Debt Consultation

First Name

Last Name

E-mail

Phone

State - Select A State -

Debt Amount select --

Get My Consultation

Figure 4.15 Simplified lead form for debt negotiation company

As you can see, it is radically stripped down (in terms of color, labels, and number of fields). As a result, it looks much less imposing and is more likely to be completed. The winning landing page in our test produced a 51% improvement in revenue per visitor over the original. The impact of this change was an estimated $48 million in additional annual revenue for the client.

Don't Surprise the Visitor

The McAfee up-sell pop-up and the Overstock reconfiguring form have something in common. They are examples of last-minute surprises. And surprises are the last thing that you want your visitors to experience at the delicate point when they have finally decided to act. In fact, you should work very hard to provide context and reassurance during this critical time.

Some examples of unwelcome surprises include:

- Introducing pop-ups
- Reconfiguring forms
- Making peripheral or unrelated special offers
- Including price increases, or extra terms and conditions
- Making changes in inventory availability or delivery dates during checkout
- Asking for unnecessary information
- Asking for information in a nonstandard order
- Not warning people about the supporting information that they will need to have on hand in order to complete the transaction
- Not specifying all acceptable payment methods up-front
- Using nonstandard or unclear text captions on your buttons

Many people already have an idea of how certain kinds of transactions should unfold. For example, when I buy from an online catalog I expect to put items in my shopping cart, review my selections, enter billing and shipping information, and see a confirmation page for my order. Other transactions are more customized. I may not have a well-formed expectation about what actions I will be expected to take, their order, or the supporting information that I am required to have. In any case, the website should always indicate my progress during the transaction. This provides me with context, and orients me by showing me where I am in the process.

InsWeb allows people to get insurance comparison quotes (www.insweb.com). When I started the search for homeowner's insurance, a tab-based navigation bar appeared at the top of the page (see Figure 4.16), showing me the steps in the quote process and my current position. The names on the tabs educated and reassured me about the upcoming steps. I was allowed go back at any point (by clicking on a preceding tab) and review or modify the information from the previous steps. An even clearer reassurance would have been provided by a "Back To Previous Page" link next to the "Continue" button near the bottom-right corner of each screen.

Figure 4.16 InsWeb page header tabs

Most transactions have a final point-of-no-return. Usually this involves clicking a button after filling out form information. It is critical to provide last-minute reassurances on the page where this point occurs.

Final reassurances include:

- A recap or review of the information provided to complete the transaction (items ordered, personal information, billing, and price)
- Details of the fulfillment process (e.g., service levels, delivery dates, contact methods, and time frames)
- Terms and conditions (the fine print)
- Spelling out exactly what will happen when the action is taken
- Validation and risk reducers (as discussed in the "Desire" section earlier)

The loan comparison site LendingTree.com (www.lendingtree.com) provides multiple loan quotes from financial institutions. After completing the multiple-page quoting process for a home equity loan, visitors are presented with the detailed terms and conditions before they act. The fine print states that the user's credit and employment history may be accessed, and that they agree to be contacted by the lenders via phone and e-mail. Unfortunately, the button text (see Figure 4.17) is the same as on the previous screens. Moreover, the text of the button is "Save and Continue >>"—implying that this is not the last step in the process. It would be much clearer to the visitor that the final action is about to happen if the button text on this page was unique and definitive (e.g., "Get My Quotes Now").

PRIVACY & SECURITY PROTECTED   << Back   **SAVE AND CONTINUE >>**

Figure 4.17 LendingTree.com final quote button

Let's take stock. You have reviewed the necessary background, and learned about landing pages, audiences, and the decision process. In the next part of the book you will learn how to uncover problems with your landing page, select tuning elements, understand the math behind landing page testing, and select the proper tuning method.

What and How to Tune

It does not matter how you mathematically find the best landing page design if the alternatives that you are testing do not "move the needle." In this part of the book you will learn how to diagnose potential problems with your landing pages, and to identify specific elements to test for creating the highest potential conversion rate improvements.

I will gently introduce you to the math of tuning, and the available methods for conducting tuning tests. There are hidden assumptions behind most tuning methods, and significant limitations to the kinds of answers that they can provide. What you do not know will definitely hurt you.

Part II consists of the following chapters:

Why Your Site
Is Not Perfect

5

There are in fact many methods for identifying landing page problems, and seeing why they are not meeting the needs of your Internet visitors. You just need the guts to lift the veil of denial, and to view these flaws and compromises objectively.

Chapter Contents

Your Baby Is Ugly

Imagine that you have been involved in designing landing pages for a long time. This typically involves holding fun brainstorming sessions, creating exciting graphical presentations of possible page designs, and writing persuasive offers and text copy.

Then comes the public unveiling. As the euphoria of the project starts to wear off, you inevitably start to see chinks in the armor of your beautiful and perfect creations: the text is too long, the intended audience is not identified clearly enough, there are no useful navigational cross-links if someone lands on a page deep within the site...

It gets worse.

Your dread may grow as objective evidence of poor design starts to mount: high shopping cart abandonment rates, extensive call-ins to the toll-free support number, high bounce rates on important pages, lower-than-expected conversion numbers.

Yet, in all of this gloom lies the way out of the mess too. After that, you'll see exactly why your landing pages are at cross-purposes with the way that people take in and process information. Based on your honest analysis you can prepare yourself for deciding exactly which elements to test.

Somewhere in the world is the world's worst doctor...
and someone has an appointment with her/him
tomorrow.

—Comedian George Carlin

The chilling thought above is brought to you by the deliciously twisted mind of master comedian George Carlin. What makes it so funny is that it is factually correct—there is somewhere by definition "the world's worst doctor." Of course, the consequences of being the world's worst landing page designer are not as severe. No one will die on the operating table. Your online marketing campaign will simply fail. If you are not the worst one, your campaign may simply bump along at a much smaller scale than it otherwise could. Besides, you can always go to your bosses and after throwing up your hands in frustration tell them all about how it is impossible to get cost-effective traffic to your site in the face of ever-increasing advertiser competition and rising prices.

The reality for most online marketers is this: you did not major in psychology, you have no formal training in usability, you have never taken a persuasive copywriting course, you do not understand test design or statistics, and you have rarely interacted with an actual user of our company's products or services. Yet most online marketers do not want to admit that they are doing a poor job at landing page design. They liken ourselves to the denizens of the mythical Lake Wobegon from Garrison Keillor's *Prairie Home Companion* where "the women are strong, the men are good-looking, and the children are all above-average."

The whole discipline of decision-making theory is based on the understanding that people have warped perceptions of themselves. They do not make rational decisions. People consistently overestimate their own skills, influence, and importance. In one survey, 80% of participants reported that they were above-average drivers...

You have to let go of your own professional ego structure long enough to let the following truth sink in:

Your Baby Is Ugly: Your landing page has significant and fundamental problems.

Stop. Now repeat this over and over until it starts to properly sink in.

Uncovering Problems

Instead of waiting only for good news, filter it out instead. Accentuate the negative. Focus on problems and things that are askew. The mind-set that I am describing is not some prescription to become a cynical person. It is actually a well-respected business approach called *managing by exception*. Assuming that you have set up your systems and procedures properly, you should have key indicators that tell you when things are going smoothly. During those times you should work on further strategic improvements to your business. Only if something goes wrong (as quickly flagged by your monitoring of key performance indicators) should your attention and resources be focused on the problem.

I do not mean to imply that if your online campaign is making money that you should be satisfied and smug. Unless every potential customer among your Internet visitors has already converted, you still have a lot of work to do.

The main point is to unflinchingly uncover and face problems, and not to duck or hide from them. This spirit of continuous problem solving and improvement is at the heart of some of the most successful businesses on the planet. It should be an example for all of us to follow.

Now that you are prepared to look for landing page problems, you will discover that there are a lot of places to turn.

Audience Role Modeling

Obvious problems with your site can be discovered by overlaying "The Matrix" (which I mentioned in Chapter 3, "Understanding Your Audience") onto it. Once you have identified all of your important user groups or roles, you can assign them to the important tasks that they may be trying to solve. For each task you need to make sure that the person is properly guided through the AIDA steps of the decision process (remember that discussion from Chapter 4, "Understanding the Decision Process"). If any of the roles, important tasks, or AIDA steps are missing, it is an indication of a potentially important problem.

I recently bought some teak patio furniture from Teak Warehouse (www .teakwarehouse.com). Take a look at their website in Figure 5.1. They are a worldwide supplier and distributor of teak outdoor furniture, with several retail locations throughout California.

Figure 5.1 The TeakWarehouse.com home page

The website is primarily aimed at the retail purchaser. However, Teak Warehouse is also a major supplier to the international market, supplying retailers, hotels, resorts, architects, landscapers, and designers in the Pacific region, Europe, and the United States from their manufacturing facilities in central Java, Indonesia.

The site is an example of nonfunctional *brochure ware*—it does not have any advantage over a corresponding printed brochure. There are no significant interactive features (other than, ironically enough, creating a printable "brochure" of items you are interested in buying).

When you overlay The Matrix, without even considering the AIDA steps within each task, it is clear that the site has obvious gaps and problems:

- Role 1: Retail buyer (partially supported)
  - Task 1: Research available products (browsing by category)
  - Task 2: Get product information (cannot determine pricing)
  - Task 3: Purchase (online checkout is not supported)
  - Task 4: Arrange for delivery (not supported)

- Role 2: Wholesale buyer (not well supported)
  - Task 5: Research available products (browsing by category)
  - Task 6: Get product information (cannot determine pricing)
  - Task 7: Get an online quote (not supported)
  - Task 8: Understand quantity discounts (not listed)
  - Task 9: Apply for credit and payment terms (not supported)
  - Task 10: Arrange for shipping (not supported)
  - Task 11: Arrange for local final assembly (not supported)

It is not difficult to identify key roles or mission-critical tasks for most websites. In this case, Teak Warehouse is definitely turning away business by disregarding important needs of their key audiences.

Web Analytics

As we discussed in Chapter 3, Web analytics software offers many powerful tools for analyzing your website and the behavior of your audience. Once historical data has been collected, you can mine it to discover problems that visitors had with your landing page. The following sections highlight how Web analytics features can be used to discover common problems.

Visitors

Web analytics can track the origin and capabilities of your audience in a very detailed manner. This includes geographic targeting, preferred languages, and browser technical capabilities.

Map

A map can show you the physical origin of your audience, and allows you to drill down to get the exact level of granularity that you need. If your service is national or international in scope, maps will show you the distribution of visitors across time zones and countries.

This information can be used to adjust customer service or business hours, or to create specialized content specifically for certain geographies. If your business covers a number of geographic areas, maps can help you to decide on the relative importance that you should assign to each in terms of emphasis and screen real estate (see Figure 5.2).

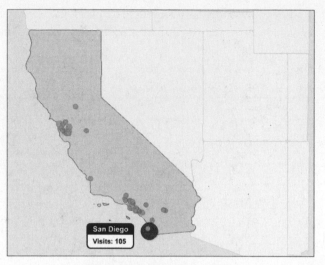

Figure 5.2 Web analytics map drilldown

Languages

If a significant number of your visitors originate in other countries, you can determine whether you are ignoring their needs. Additional native language and native culture–based content may be appropriate. This does not have to be a complete copy of your site in each applicable language. But if you intend to get conversions in other languages, at least the mission-critical tasks should be available in their native tongue.

Technical Capabilities

Analytics software records detailed information about the setup and capabilities of the visitor's computer and Web browser. This includes the operating system, browser type, screen resolution, Internet connection speeds, and support for various browser plug-in technologies such as Flash, Java, and JavaScript.

Screen resolution is perhaps the most important technical capability because it literally defines the visitor's window onto the Internet. This can range from a relative peephole to a veritable panorama. Your page should look ideal at the most common minimum resolution in use at the time. But it must also still look good at higher resolutions. People with outdated smaller screens are already used to having suboptimal Web browsing experiences. As long as very low resolution represents a small percentage, you should not bend over backward to accommodate everyone. As bigger computer displays become more common, the standard will shift, and your minimum resolution may need to be periodically adjusted.

The worst kinds of mistakes are ones that obviously disrupt the intended visual design. The home page for Vacation Palm Springs (www.vacationpalmsprings.com) shown in Figure 5.3 on a wide computer monitor has a darker vertical column in the open space on the right. This is the repetition of a background graphic image, which also served as the backdrop for the navigation column on the left of the page. It would not be exposed at lower resolutions, but is an obvious eyesore for visitors with larger monitors. This is an easily avoidable problem and is a painful (for the company) oversight by the designers of this site.

The top of the home page for Web superstore Amazon (www.amazon.com) shown in Figure 5.4 looks good at a 1024-pixel-wide minimum screen resolution. The highlighted paragraph describing the featured item at the top of the page looks visually reasonable, and the three featured product category images highlighted near the bottom of the page are displayed with appropriate spacing.

Figure 5.3 VacationPalmSprings.com (wider monitor view)

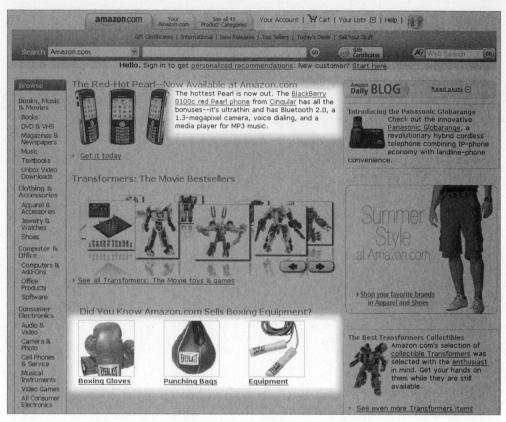

Figure 5.4 Amazon.com home page (typical monitor view)

Figure 5.5 shows how the top of the same page looks when displayed on my widescreen 1680 × 1050-pixel monitor.

The paragraph at the top of the page has now changed from a readable block to a long and narrow two-line entry that has less visual connection to the product image next to it. As you will see later in this chapter, lines of text of this length are much less readable. Large gaps have also appeared next to each of the three featured category images. It may be more appropriate to feature additional images in this available space, instead of having the space remain blank.

Stretching portions of the page design is a reasonable idea for dealing with different screen resolutions (and definitely preferable to a fixed-width design). But by itself it is not enough. It is also important to consider spatial relationships, proportions, and changes of emphasis at the different resolutions. These issues can be dealt with more elegantly since the screen resolution information is available.

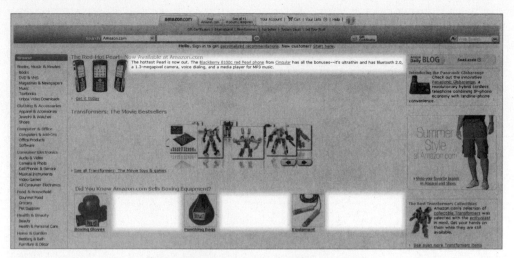

Figure 5.5 Amazon.com home page (wider monitor view)

Visible Browser Window

Another important consideration is what appears *above the fold*. This term originated in the newspaper industry and referred to the main content that could be seen on the top half of the front page (without flipping the paper or opening it). On the Web it describes the content seen on the page without horizontal or vertical scrolling. What appears above the fold is influenced not only by screen resolution, but also by the size of the current browser window (which may be smaller than the whole screen), various currently visible browser toolbars (which take up vertical space), and the default size of the text chosen in the browser (larger font sizes will push content further down the page).

Although long landing pages are no longer the absolute no-no that they were several years ago, key information should still generally be above the fold. This guarantees that visitors can see all-important choices as they make their decision to click away or to stay longer on your site.

While Internet users are accustomed to scrolling vertically, studies have shown that they universally despise horizontal scrolling. Under no circumstances should your page require horizontal scrolling at common screen resolutions.

Be very careful about anything requiring nonstandard browser plug-ins or technologies that are not widely supported. There are fewer experiences more annoying for the visitor than having to download a plug-in simply to see your landing page properly. At a minimum, always provide lower-tech alternatives, and never force visitors to download software that may be unfamiliar to them.

It goes almost without saying that you should optimize your pages, graphics, and media files to be an appropriate size. A surprisingly large number of Internet users still have slow connection speeds. The patience of Internet users is very short, and they will not generally wait for long downloads.

Likewise, your pages should be tested with common operating systems and browser versions. Like monitor screen sizes, this mix is always evolving and must be revisited periodically. Even small problems with coding style can cause obvious and unintended visual problems on some browsers.

New vs. Returning Visitors

With Web analytics, it is possible to identify not only the overall percentage of returning visitors, but also important details of their past interactions with your site. Most of the time the mechanism for tracking repeat visits involves the use of *cookies* (small files left on the visitor's hard disk by the browser software that can be used to identify visitors and personalize their experience on subsequent visits to the same or related website). There are different types of cookies, including first-party (those left by your website) and third-party (those left by other sites such as ad servers or some Web analytics programs). Recent research indicates that a significant and growing percentage of Web surfers regularly delete their cookies, thus destroying traces of their past visits to your site. This has the effect of understating the number of return visitors.

Since returning visitors have already been exposed to your message on their first visit, it may lose effectiveness on subsequent visits. Conversely, repeated exposure can actually strengthen your message. In any case, you need to consider if returnees are a significant audience segment for you. If so, you may consider showing different information or even a different offer to this group.

For example, returning visitors who have already acted once on your initial offer may not be eligible anymore, and should be presented with an appropriate follow-up offer instead. For e-commerce sites, returning buyers should be accorded special status. At a minimum this means recognizing them and acknowledging their return to your site. Additional business rules can be added to display certain promotions based on customer loyalty (such as the number of purchases or total spending to date).

Depth of Interaction

There are many ways to determine commitment and engagement. These include return visits and acting on various conversion call-to-actions. The depth of interaction helps to complete this information. It consists primarily of the length of visit (measured by average time spent on your site) and the depth of visit (measured by page views). These metrics are especially critical to websites that rely on advertising-supported, high-quality content.

If a significant number of your visitors display a high degree of commitment to your site, you should consider breaking them out as a separate highly interactive part of your audience and showing them different content. This may be done while they are still on your site by means of dynamic content presentation. For example, you may give them preferential and free access to premium content, or sweeten your call to action even more to move them out of the desire stage and into action.

Traffic Sources

Traffic sources come in four main types. Depending on your particular mix, you should consider the following issues.

Direct

Direct traffic is the result of people typing your company's URL directly into their Web browser. It is the combination of your event-driven publicity, offline marketing activities, and the strength of your brand. The common factor in all three traffic sources is that much of it will land on your home page.

If your company is mentioned in topical news stories or popular blogs, you may see surges or spikes in traffic to your site. If there is nothing compelling on the home page for these curious news hounds, they will never return.

Even if you specify a longer URL in your offline media advertising, many people will drop the additional information and just type in your main top-level domain for your company. For example, if you run TV commercials directing people to visit "xyz-company.com/tv," many will through laziness or carelessness shorten it to "xyz-company.com" and be lumped in with the rest of your home page visitors. It is better to reserve a completely separate domain name for such programs, so there is no confusion about the source.

As I have discussed previously, brands are very powerful. If people typed in your domain name directly, you are top-of-mind for their particular current need. They are aware of your company and have taken the proactive step of visiting it. Because of their familiarity with and affinity for your company, this kind of traffic is often the highest converting source that you will have. Unfortunately, they have landed on your home page. If a lot of your traffic is from this source, you should make special efforts to unclutter your home page and direct them to desired conversion actions.

Referred

Referred traffic comes from other websites that link to you. By examining your Web analytics reports, you can determine the top traffic sources. Since referred traffic comes from direct links, much of it can land on specific pages deep within your site. Review the specific landing pages to make sure that they function well as a starting point for a visitor and are not a dead-end with no relationship to your desired conversion goals.

You also need to take the time to visit each major referrer link and understand the context in which your site was last seen by the visitor. In some cases it will be favorable ("this company is the greatest thing since sliced bread"). In other cases, your link will be buried in a long list of competitor sites. It is also possible that the link will be there for the purpose of belittling your company. If you understand the mind-set of the visitors from important referral traffic sources, you can modify the landing page content (amplifying goodwill or neutralizing negative perceptions as appropriate).

Search

Many companies work very hard at SEO to get ranked near the top of organic search results for keywords that are important in their industries. Such rankings can guarantee a stream of "free" visitors to specific pages on your website. Depending on the keyword, the visitors may have a specific and actionable need, or a vague interest in your offerings.

As we will discuss in Chapter 11, "Avoiding the Pitfalls," there is often an inherent tension between getting high placement in search results and having a landing page that converts well. Search engine spiders prefer a lot of informational text centered on a coherent theme. But visitors who land on the page are often looking for something quick to click on and do not want to wade through a lot of text.

Often the most relevant page for a particular keyword is buried deep within your site. It was carefully designed to fit within the hierarchy of company information to serve a particular purpose. The path to it through your standard navigation may make perfect sense, and may provide the context necessary to understand the page's content. However, it has over time been plucked from obscurity by the search engine and given a lot more prominence. In effect, it now serves as an important entry point into your site.

But search keyword relevance does not mean that the page is effective in supporting your conversion goals. By examining the most popular organic searches and corresponding landing pages, you can modify their content to make them more actionable. They may have not been part of the mission-critical page set that you previously identified in Chapter 2, "Understanding Your Landing Pages." However, they may be important feeders for these pages. You should consider whether they effectively transport incoming visitors from important keywords to the intended conversion path. In other words, you may not be giving the visitor a clear trail to follow to get to your conversion task's front door.

Paid

Paid traffic (whether from PPC, banner ads, trusted feeds, or other sources) has several desirable characteristics. It can be controlled (turned on and off, or increased or decreased) depending on the circumstances. It can be targeted (the traffic from every PPC keyword can be sent to its own specialized landing page). Its value and profitability can be tracked (by campaign, keyword, and even the version of the ad copy used).

Yet many companies do not take full advantage of these capabilities. The main obstacles are improper traffic mapping and inappropriate landing page content.

In many cases, traffic is sent to the website home page instead of the more appropriate pages deeper in the site. Or the traffic is sent to the most relevant page on the corporate site but should instead be sent to a stand-alone landing page that does not have all of the navigation options and other distractions of the main website. The traffic mapping for all high-value keywords should be reviewed to make sure it is being sent to the best possible pages. You may have to create new and more specific landing pages to receive the traffic from these keywords.

By looking at Web analytics conversion reporting, you can also detect which paid traffic landing pages do not convert well and consider them as candidates for a test or redesign.

Content

Web analytics related to the content of your website can provide many important clues to uncover and prioritize potential problems:

Most visited content The popularity of a Web page helps you to understand whether it is getting the proper exposure. If a key page is not getting enough traffic, it may be necessary to move it to a more prominent location on your website, or to create more links to it from other popular pages.

Path analysis Path analysis allows you to see the sequences of pages that visitors use to traverse your site. They show you the most common flows of traffic. It may be possible to change the position of key conversion pages or links within the site to benefit from such drive-by visibility.

Top entry pages A list of the top entry pages shows you the point of first contact with your site. Generally, the more traffic that is hitting a landing page, the more attention that page deserves in terms of conversion tuning. Traffic levels can help you to prioritize which landing pages need to be fixed first.

Top exit pages Exit pages are the places where visitors leave your site. Each exit page can be viewed as a leaky bucket. If visitors exit your site, they probably did not find what they were looking for. In some cases, there is nothing that you can do about this. But for many of the visitors who left, you could have probably improved the page to provide more relevant information or better navigation. The total number of exits and the exit percentage of a page can be used to prioritize among problem pages.

The worst-case scenario is a popular entry page that is also a frequent exit page. The *bounce rate* is the percentage of entry page visitors who leave immediately without visiting any other site content. High bounce rates on high-traffic pages are a red flag indicating that those pages need attention.

Funnel analysis   Regardless of your visitors' initial wandering path on your website, they must often pass through a well-defined series of pages in order to convert. It is possible to see the efficiency of each step in this linear process. The funnel narrows as people drop off during each step. High drop-off percentages may signal that a particular step is especially problematic. If problems are uncovered, they may suggest breaking the process up into smaller and more manageable steps, or simplifying it. E-commerce shopping cart abandonment is a common example of this kind of funnel analysis.

Conversion goals   Web analytics software allows you to track conversion rates (CRs) for all of the important goals on your site. By comparing your CRs with analyst research for your industry, you can get a rough idea of whether your site efficiency is competitive or substandard.

Some Web analytics tools offer the ability to view reverse goal paths. These are the most common sequences of pages that visitors traversed on their way to completing a conversion goal. Unlike forward-looking funnel analysis, reverse goal paths look backward at the most popular points of origin for a conversion. By using these reports, you can discover unexpected ways that visitors are converting and evaluate the effectiveness of your desired conversion path.

A common Web analytics feature is the ability to overlay information on top of the clickable links on a Web page. This can be done with click information, or with other metrics. In the SiteTuners.com home page screenshot, illustrated in Figure 5.6, each link is overlaid with a small meter indicating the number of whitepaper downloads that ultimately resulted after a visitor first clicked on a particular link. As you can see from the highlighted areas (indicating the highest number of downloads), conversions came from a number of initial links. These links were not necessarily the most visible or prominent ones. Analyses like this can suggest improvements in the organization of information on a landing page (especially if it is your home page).

Onsite Search

Many sites offer an onsite search. It is viewed as a tactic for improving conversion rates and helping visitors directly find relevant information. But this is a two-edged sword. Research shows that many visitors will abandon a site if they do not find what they are looking for on the first page of results.

Onsite search can also be a source of information about what is *not* working. Many searches produce no matching results, indicating a mismatch between visitors' desires and expectations, and the ability of a site to provide relevant content.

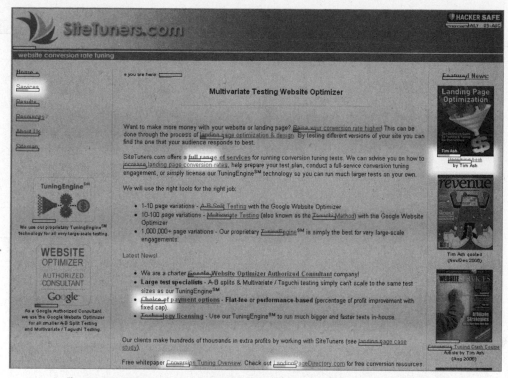

Figure 5.6 SiteTuners home page with Web analytics link overlay indicating whitepaper downloads

By taking a careful look at such empty search results, you can identify the type of information that is not effectively being found on your site. We once helped a client in the wine business to significantly improve their search function by returning proper results for common misspellings of wine brands and specific product names. By insisting that the visitor must be able to type in searches correctly, many sites are turning away business.

You can also auto-populate common empty search results with hand-picked search results pages. Alternatively, you can broaden the scope of the search to at least bring back close matches if exact results are not found.

If a search is very common it may be a candidate for inclusion in the site's permanent navigation. In other words, you may want to enshrine the search result with permanent visibility to help even more people find it (since a small minority of them will bother to use the search function).

Sophisticated onsite search from companies like SLI Systems (www.sli-systems .com) can actually adapt search results and even site navigation by monitoring search queries and click-throughs. They use historical data collected from all site visitors to serve up more popular results, thus improving the relevance of the user experience.

You may also want to consider using private-labeled search capabilities from major search vendors such as Google. This can often give much better results than a home-built system.

Usability Testing

Usability testing (as described in Chapter 3) allows you to test your design ideas on actual representative user of your website. It can be an effective means of uncovering disconnects between user's expectations and your designs. Usability testing companies can help you recruit appropriate subjects, conduct the tests, and deliver detailed findings.

But usability testing can often be done expensively and rather informally. After running as few as three subjects through your mission-critical conversion task, you can often uncover significant issues with your current landing page. All you need for this kind of informal approach is a quiet room, a mock-up of your proposed design (possibly just hand-drawn on paper), and a clear task statement (of what you want your subjects to accomplish).

There are several alternative protocols for the tester to get information from the subjects. SiteTuners.com has found an effective one to be asking subjects to narrate their internal thoughts as they attempt to complete the task. In this protocol, the testers are silent and simply observe or take written notes. Most marketers are shocked when first watching actual users struggle with the seemingly simple assigned task. Because they have been so close to the design of the pages, they are familiar with the conversion action and the page content. Because of this, they have a hard time putting themselves in the shoes of first-time visitors. After the initial shock has worn off, many marketers have a much higher degree of empathy for their audience and can see the landing page problems in a new light.

Usability Reviews

You do not always have to conduct full-scale usability testing. Hiring usability experts for a high-level review of your landing pages is often a terrific investment.

Usability experts have seen dozens or even hundreds of poor designs, and have learned to extract subtle commonalities. They can quickly focus on potential problems without even conducting a usability test.

Besides their testing expertise, usability experts also bring an outside perspective and a mandate to uncover problems. Often organizations that would be reluctant to take input from their own staff will listen to the advice of a hired expert.

Focus Groups

Focus groups, like usability tests, draw on people from the target audience. Via a moderated group discussion, insights can be gleaned about user needs, expectations, and attitudes. These findings can be compared to the proposed solution to determine if key elements are missing or are incorrect.

Of course, focus groups can be easily biased by their more outgoing and assertive participants, and the moderator's influence is important. But this is okay since the purpose of focus groups is to provide qualitative information that can serve as input into deciding what to test.

Eye-Tracking Studies

Eye-tracking studies have been used for many years to improve software, as well as the design of other visual systems such as aircraft cockpit instrumentation. This technology can literally show you what people are looking at, in what order, and for how long. The latest techniques can even monitor involuntary changes in your pupil dilation in order to determine how much attention your brain is devoting to the current object that you are focusing on.

Eye-tracking technology for website design testing has become cheaper, better, and less obtrusive over time. Recent versions of the hardware look similar to flat-screen monitors and do not require that any special gear be worn by the experimental participant. New software visualization techniques and analysis have also made the presentation of eye-tracking results more accessible for the mainstream online marketing audience. EyeTools Inc. (www.eyetools.com), illustrated in Figure 5.7, and Marketing Sherpa (www.marketingsherpa.com) have recently collaborated to conduct some pioneering work specifically on eye-tracking for landing page optimization.

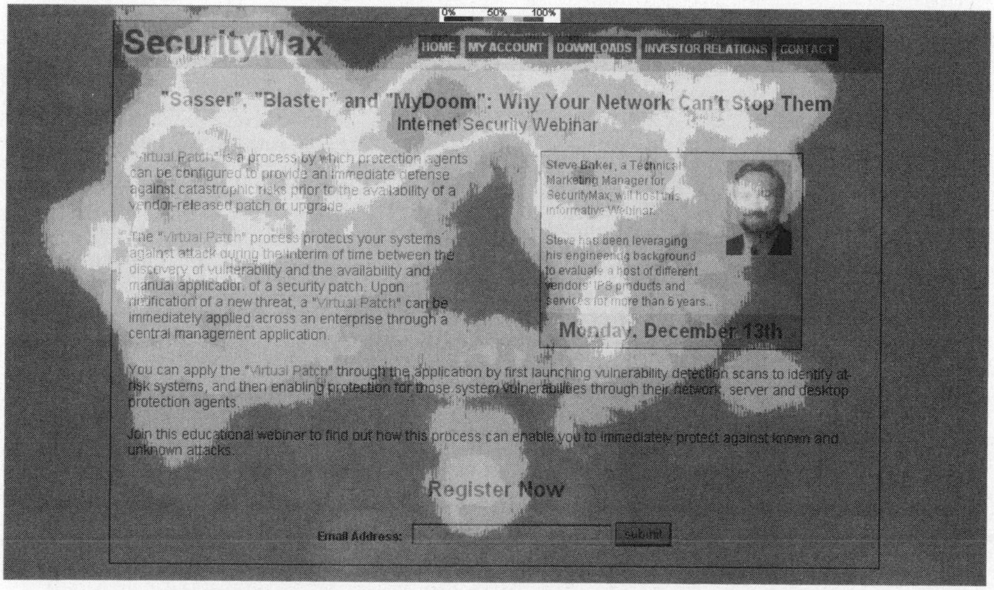

Figure 5.7 Landing page eye-tracking heat map from EyeTools and Marketing Sherpa

The EyeTools heat map is an aggregate of the eye movements of all test subjects looking at a particular landing page. "Hotter" areas show where subjects spent more of their time. Attempted and successful clicking can also be recorded. Before and after the tests, the subjects can also be asked specific open-ended questions or ones based on the commonly used *Likert scale* (strongly disagree, disagree, neither agree nor disagree, agree, strongly agree).

Eye-tracking is particularly useful in detecting problems in the earlier stages of the decision process (awareness and interest). If most test subjects do not look at the desired part of the page, they are not even aware that the conversion action is possible. In effect, for similar visitors to your site the conversion action does not exist. Such studies are an excellent source of problems regarding page layout, visual presentation of information and images, and emphasis.

Customer Service Reps

Customer service representatives deal with your website visitors' problems all day long. Of course, chat and phone support can proactively help users during key parts of the conversion process. But it would be best if human handholding was minimized. Most companies calculate the reps' contribution and value by focusing on call wait times, average call duration, and customer satisfaction. All of these measures assume that the website problems are here to stay, and that the only possible improvement is in how efficiently your company can deal with them.

However, customer service interactions can lead to valuable information about how to actually fix the underlying problems. Feedback can be collected in two ways: direct interviews or surveys of your reps, or a review of actual visitor interactions. Chat and phone call logs can be used to classify problems into categories. The prevalence of particular types of problems can be used as an indication of its severity. Such analysis can also point to where on your site the majority of problems originate.

A weakness of customer service–based feedback lies in the self-selecting audience. Only the most dissatisfied and assertive visitors will voice their complaints or escalate their resolution to a rep. This creates a bias toward late-stage issues (desire and action), while underestimating the problems with the earlier stages (awareness and interest). Early-stage visitors by definition do not have a lot of psychological investment in your company and are much less likely to contact you.

Surveys

A number of easy Web-based and telephone surveying methods and companies are available. Surveys among your target population can be a useful source for discovering additional problems with your site. People who have already completed your conversion action already would seem to be the best group to sample. However, you should generally avoid surveys and interviews of existing users. They are already biased because they have already made the decision to act on your offer. It is better to sample randomly among a pool of people from your intended target audience.

Forums and Blogs

Many industries have specific communities of interest and popular discussion forums. Even if your company is not a market leader that is mentioned directly in forum posts, you can still gain valuable insight into the concerns and problems of your target audience. Blogs and public comments about blog postings serve very much the same kind of communal discussion function. Such venues allow you to gauge the loyalty or frustration of people, their immediate needs, and attitudes toward your industry, company, or product.

Welcome to Your Brain

In the previous chapter I discussed the four stages of the AIDA decision-making model. I hope that the discussion made sense to you, and you found it rational, clear, and logical. If that is the case, you were probably using your higher-reasoning faculties at the time. But this is not the only mode in which your brain operates. Despite the fact that people can be very sophisticated and intelligent, we still carry a lot of our old evolutionary baggage with us.

A lot of the problems that we have with the Web in general (and landing pages in particular) are due to the limitations of our brains when trying to use this medium. There is a disconnect between how our brains evolved and how we are forced to use them on the Web. Much of the resulting friction stems from how we actually take in information, process it, learn, and make decisions. It is important for us to understand our own brains when designing better landing pages.

So let's take a moment to meet that very odd character: your brain...

Your Three Brains

According to Paul MacLean, the former chief of the Laboratory of the Brain and Behavior at the United States National Institute of Mental Health (NIMH), the older parts of the brain are still with us. MacLean developed a model of the brain based on its evolutionary development. According to his "triune brain theory" there are three distinct layers in the brain that evolved in turn to address new evolutionary needs. Although each layer dominates certain separate brain functions, all three layers also interact in significant ways. MacLean said that the three brains operate like "three interconnected biological computers, [each] with its own special intelligence, its own subjectivity, its own sense of time and space and its own memory."

The Reptilian Brain

The first to evolve was the reptilian brain (also known as the archipallium, basal brain, or primitive brain). It was called the "R-complex" by MacLean and includes the brain stem and cerebellum. This kind of brain is the high point of development among lizards, snakes, and other reptiles (hence the origin of its name). This brain is mainly responsible for physical survival and maintenance of the body (including, circulation, breathing, digestion, and movement). It is the brain that takes over in fight-or-flight situations, and is responsible for establishing home turf, reproduction, and social dominance. Since it is responsible for autonomic functions such as breathing and the heartbeat, it is active even in deep sleep states. The reptilian brain is the basic program that allows animals to function. The reptilian brain can be viewed as obsessive, compulsive, rigid, and automatic. It is not is adaptable or capable of change, and will repeat behaviors over and over—never learning from its mistakes.

The Limbic System

The second to evolve was the limbic system (also variously called the paleo-mammalian, intermediate, old mammalian, or mid-brain). It includes the hypothalamus, hippocampus, and amygdala. This type of brain is present in most mammals, and is dominant in more primitive ones. The limbic system is the seat of our primary centers of emotion, attention, and affective (emotion-charged) memories. The amygdala is critical in creating the link between emotions and events, while the hippocampus plays the dominant role in storing and recalling memories.

The limbic system is in the driver's seat when it comes to value judgments. It decides whether we like something or are repelled by it. Because of this, the limbic system tends to dominate behaviors that involve the avoidance of pain and the compulsive repetition of pleasure (including feeding, fighting, sex, fleeing, bonding, and caretaking). It also determines the amount of attention that we give to something, and is responsible for much of our spontaneous and creative behavior.

The limbic system is connected downward to the reptilian brain and upward to the neocortex. Because it links emotions and behavior, the limbic system often inhibits or overrides the reptilian brain's habitual and unchanging responses. Similarly, the more complex emotions of bonding, attachment, and protective loving feelings connect it to the neocortex through rich interconnections. According to MacLean, the limbic system decides how it feels about something, and the neocortex is often reduced to simply rationalizing that value judgment decision.

The Neocortex

The most recent brain to evolve is the neocortex (also called the cerebrum, cerebral cortex, neopallium, neomammalian brain, superior brain, or rational brain). It is composed of the two large hemispheres and some subcortical neuronal groups. This development is seen only in primates, and humans have by far the largest version (taking up more than two-thirds of total brain mass).

The neocortex contains specialized areas for controlling voluntary movement and processing sensory information. It is divided into two hemispheres (left and right), which control the opposite side of the body, respectively. There is some differentiation in function between the two. The left hemisphere is more linear, verbal and rational, while the right hemisphere is more spatial, artistic, musical, and abstract. Higher cognitive functions are all centered in this brain (including language, speech, and writing). It supports logical thinking and allows us to see ahead and plan for the future. MacLean called the neocortex the "mother of invention and father of abstract thought."

Putting It All Together

It is unclear exactly how and how much the three layers communicate (they are connected via an extensive two-way network of nerves). However, it is safe to assume that all three are active during most activities, with a particular one taking the lead in certain situations. The main point is that the neocortex does not dominate the lower levels. The limbic system often asserts its influence over higher mental functions. In times of extreme stress, even our reptilian brain can take over to accomplish seemingly superhuman tasks (such as lifting heavy cars under which people are trapped).

When we design landing pages for the Web, we must understand that we must often please the limbic system of our visitors. We are being judged on the emotional gut reactions that our pages evoke. Our mid-brain knows what it likes and what it doesn't. After-the-fact logical rationalizations by the neocortex are just that. At some level, the whole point of large-scale statistical landing page testing is to tap directly into this hidden limbic system decision maker and unmask it by seeing its emotionally based actions (unmediated by surveys, focus groups, or usability tests that require verbal skills and the ability to explain something).

Learning Modalities

There are three major ways to get information into your long-term memory. Research has shown that there are no significant differences in the prevalence of these learning styles between the sexes, or among different races.

- Visual (learning by seeing)
- Auditory (learning by hearing
- Kinesthetic (learning by doing)

Research in teaching has determined that most people have one predominant modality. Some have a more equal balance between two modalities, or even among all three. But there is no single optimal method for transmitting information. Depending on the specific person, different information presentation or teaching techniques will have different levels of effectiveness.

Effective Web persuasion requires a variety of methods that cover all three learning modalities. If people are aware of their preference they can often assimilate information more efficiently by favoring certain kinds of learning tactics and focusing on specific features of your website. So make it easy for them by providing different ways of interacting with your site when appropriate. This is especially important during the desire stage of the decision process, when people are learning about your products or services.

Try to use the following types of information to address each learning modality more effectively:

Visual Guided imagery, demonstration, color coding, diagrams, charts, graphs, photos, maps, video clips

Auditory Audio clips, oral instructions or presentations, poems, rhymes, word association, video clips, live telephone support

Kinesthetic Games and interactive activities, associating emotions with concepts, props or tangible examples, problem solving, role-playing

Keep in mind that this additional information should not be tacked on or gratuitous. But if there are key concepts that you want your audience to understand and remember, you should take the time to customize the experience for each modality and offer them the option of how they want to take in that information. For example, let's assume that you have a template for a product detail page in an e-commerce catalog. You may provide detailed specs and diagrams for your visual learners, a video clip overview of the product's main features and benefits for auditory learners, and a customization wizard (which lets the visitor pick colors and other options) that allows the kinesthetic learner to explore, construct, and interact with the product.

Constraints and Conventions

When visitors come to your website, they are not a blank slate. They carry with them all of the physical and brain machinery that I discussed earlier. They also carry the sum total of their life experiences to date. This includes attitudes, irrational fears, and conscious beliefs, as well as unconscious assumptions.

Our beliefs and assumptions have an enormous impact on how we behave. If I have just gotten a static electricity shock from a doorknob, I am going to be more consciously aware of other doorknobs, and approach them with apprehension, based on the belief that another shock is possible. If I believe that the earth is flat (as most people did just a few centuries ago), I would not try to circumnavigate the globe, and would be afraid of exploring based on the logical fear of falling off the edge.

Most of your visitors already have enormous experience with the Internet. Even recent or casual users have probably logged hundreds of hours interacting with websites. Out of that experience they have constructed a mental model (also called a schema) of how the Web works.

Part of that mental model includes constraints (things that can't be done) and conventions (an understanding of how things are commonly done).

A convention is a cultural constraint, one that has evolved over time. Conventions are not arbitrary: they evolve, they require a community of practice. They are slow to be adopted, and once adopted, slow to go away. So although the word implies voluntary choice, the reality is that they are real constraints upon our behavior. Use them with respect. Violate them only with great risk.

—Usability guru Don Norman

The model may not be exact or correct. For example, a disturbingly high percentage of people will type a URL into the Google search window instead of into their browser's address window. But this does not matter. As far as you should be concerned, the model is set in stone and not likely to change anytime soon.

In his excellent book *Don't Make Me Think* (New Riders Publishing, 2000) author Steve Krug suggests that you should have a firm grounding in common Web design conventions and use them whenever possible. They make things easier for your visitors, and lessen the mental load and attention required for them to interact with your landing page.

Examples of powerful Web conventions include:

- The company logo and home link appear near the upper-left corner.
- The navigation menu is on the left side of the page.
- The e-commerce shopping cart link is near the upper-right corner of the page.
- Blue underlined text is a hyperlink.
- Bright animated rectangular graphics are advertisements.

Usability Basics

Common sense is not so common.

—Voltaire, *Dictionnaire Philosophique* (1764)

Much of this section should make perfect sense in the context of what I have discussed earlier. The question is: have you used common sense on your landing page? Review your site to make sure that you have followed these guidelines. If you have not, flag any deviations as the basis for constructing possible alternatives to be tested.

Some of the overall goals of usability are:

- Decrease the time required to finish tasks
- Reduce the number of mistakes
- Shorten learning time
- Improve satisfaction with your site

When we are considering usability for landing pages, we should always take into account the following picture of our visitor's typical mind-set and behavior:

- The visitor has extreme impatience.
- The visitor's commitment level to your website is low.
- Text is scanned, not read.
- The visitor has a short fixation on more prominent items of interest.
- The visitor will pay attention to certain kinds of pictures.
- The visitor's typical desired next action is to click on something.

Information Architecture

Information architecture defines the way that information is organized on your website. This is typically hierarchical in nature (and looks like an extended outline on your sitemap page). However, it is important to remember that the Web is a hyperlink medium. People do not necessarily follow orderly or linear progressions (like they would when reading this book, for instance). They jump around and follow their nose. For this reason, some websites provide multiple navigation schemes to support their visitors' mental maps.

In general, your site navigation should:

- Be easy to understand (and grouped into logical units)
- Be visible (not require scrolling to find key navigation)
- Support the visitor's task (and not your company's organization)
- Be consistent throughout the site (except when the context for the task changes)
- Use clear and distinct labels (so people know what to expect on the next page)
- Provide context (visitors need to know where they are in your site)
- Be tolerant of mistakes (allow visitors to easily reverse their last action and get back to their previous state)

Accessibility

Accessibility is closely related to the awareness stage of the decision process. If I cannot find something on your landing page, it might as well not exist at all. Accessibility has to do with how information is organized, how much emphasis is assigned to items, and how easy the information is to access.

Availability Do visitors know what their options are by visually inspecting the page? Is your navigation prominent enough, consistent, and placed in a conventional location?

Feedback When users take an action, do they get immediate feedback? Does the page change when they click on or mouse over important content?

Organization Is your information architecture clear, consistent, and based on appropriate visitor roles and tasks? Is it organized into a small number of digestible "chunks"? Is it easy to skim and scan?

Fault tolerance Do you anticipate common user errors or refuse to deal with them because only "illogical" people would make them? Do you suggest meaningful or helpful alternatives when the visitor has reached an apparent dead-end? Does your site support the easy reversal of unintended actions by the user? Are your error messages supportive or alienating?

Affinity Does your intended audience like your site? Do they feel comfortable or anxious during their visit? Do they consider you professional and credible? Are your visual look-and-feel and editorial tone appropriate for your audience? Remember, these questions are answered automatically by the visitor's limbic system and cannot be fooled or reasoned with. Their initial gut impression of your site will influence their motivation to continue, trust, confidence in the information that you provide, perception of the ease of use, and overall satisfaction.

Legibility Is your font easy to read? Is it the right size for your intended audience? Do text and background colors clash, or assault the senses? Are too many fonts, sizes, and colors used throughout the page?

Since most of our Web experiences are currently based on reading, legibility requires special attention. The following Web legibility guidelines should be followed:

Font styles Use *sans serif* fonts such as Arial, Helvetica, or Geneva. Do not use *serif* (with small lines at the end of characters) fonts such as Times Roman, Courier, or Palatino. At typical monitor resolutions (which are a lot lower than printed materials), serif fonts are harder to read.

Font sizes Use 10–12 point fonts for most body text. Larger and smaller fonts reduce reading speed. Consider increasing your font size by a couple of points if you are targeting an older audience, and make sure that you allow sufficient spacing between lines as well.

Font consistency Do not use a wide range of font styles, colors, or sizes.

Underlines Do not use underlines in regular text. Underlines are by very strong convention expected only on hyperlinks. If you must emphasize text, consider other methods (different size, bolding, italics, different text color different background color).

Justification Do not justify paragraphs of text to create equal-length lines. The jagged ends of unjustified lines have been shown to help people position themselves in the text and increase reading speed and comprehension. Always use left-justified text. Do not center body text—especially bullet lists of varying line lengths.

All-caps Avoid using text in all capital letters. It has been shown to be harder to read.

Line length Blocks of text over 50 characters wide are harder to read. Consider putting in forced carriage returns (also called "hard breaks") in your paragraphs to make sure that your lines do not become too long when displayed on wider computer screens.

Contrast High contrast between text and background increases legibility. For reflected light sources like books, black text on white background is best. Projected light sources like computer monitors are actually best with light text against a dark background. The light emitted by the light-colored pixels on the screen interferes with your ability to pick out the passive dark pixels of the text itself. However, there is such a long-term bias from the printing world regarding dark text on light backgrounds that you should use it whenever possible.

Link text Blue underlined links are a de-facto standard (as is the purple color for previously visited links). Do not change these defaults unless you have a very compelling reason.

Text background colors and images White backgrounds for body text are a strong convention. Navigation and header background colors should also be relatively light to enhance legibility. Do not use high-contrast graphical images as background for text.

Language

> *How Users Read on the Web:*
> *They don't.*
> —Web usability expert Jakob Nielsen

Even though the words above were written in 1997, they still hold true. Jakob Nielsen's pioneering work in this area has been confirmed by a lot of subsequent research. The vast majority of Internet users do not read a Web page word by word. They scan it and focus on individual words, phrases, or sentences. They are often seeing your company for the first time, and do not know how much trust to place in your information. They are used to being assaulted with promotional messages and will tune out most of your attempts to overtly market to them. They are task-oriented and are on your site to get something specific accomplished.

Most of the adaptations that you need to make to your writing have a single purpose: to reduce the visitor's cognitive load. Instead of being forced to pay attention to how the information is presented, they can devote more focus to getting their intended task accomplished. By getting out of their way, you empower them to be faster, more efficient, and effective. This will lead to higher conversion rates for you, and higher satisfaction for them.

To increase the odds of a favorable outcome you need to consider the following areas of your writing:

- Structure
- Tone
- Format

Let's take a look at each in turn.

Structure

The preferred structure for most Web writing is the *inverted pyramid*. It uses the principle of primacy (ordering) to control saliency (importance). In this style of writing, you put your conclusions and key points first. Less important and supporting information should be placed last. This is critical since most readers will choose not to read very far.

Most of this is probably not earth-shaking insight in the world of newspaper writing. Newspaper editors have a similar audience makeup: casual visitors who scan for information that competes for their attention, and consider the source as a transient and disposable resource. Because of this they have developed a very similar model. Headline size and prominent positioning indicate the importance of articles. The lead paragraph summarizes the whole story, and supporting detail is buried further down (or by following text hyperlink jumps to other pages).

Get to the point and let them decide if your content is relevant enough for them to stick around. By writing in this way you maximize the chances that they will come away with the information that you consider most valuable. The same structure should be used for creating online audio or video clips for your site.

Remember that the visitor may have arrived from any number of different inbound links and may not have a lot of context about your page. Use clear and prominent page titles to tell them why each page is important.

Make sure that you only have one main idea per paragraph. If you bury a second idea lower in a block of text, it will probably be missed as the reader jumps down to scan the lead-in text of the subsequent paragraph.

The inverted pyramid approach should be used when creating bullet lists or lists of navigational links—put the important ones on top.

Keep your pages short. This will allow them to be digested in small, bite-sized chunks that correspond to a Web user's attention span. There is evidence to show that significantly shorter text results in higher retention and recall of information, and is more likely to lead to conversion actions. Your page should only contain important information for its topic and level of detail. You can move longer supporting text to other pages, and create links for the dedicated reader.

However, at SiteTuners.com we have run across an occasional exception to the shorter-is-better guideline. Some single-product consumer websites have very long direct response pitch letters that outperform significantly shorter alternatives. They draw the reader in and encourage them to spend a lot of time on the page. After a certain point the visitor's attention investment gets high enough to build momentum toward the conversion action. This is not to say that long sales letter pages cannot be made better. There is definitely a lot of bloat and deadwood on the ones that we routinely test and improve.

Tone

As I discussed earlier, the reality for most Internet surfers is that they are constantly subjected to a barrage of promotional messages and advertising. As a basic defense mechanism, they have learned to tune out most hype. Perhaps you do have to be somewhat crass to get them to your landing page. For whatever reason, they have ended up there. But as I advised in the "Keys to Creating Awareness" section in Chapter 4, you should now stop screaming at your visitors. You are no longer (for the moment) competing for their attention with other websites. So you need to change the focus to the task that they are trying to accomplish.

Your visitors detest *marketese*. Unfortunately, your landing page was probably written in this kind of over-the-top promotional style. It usually involves a lot of boasting and unsubstantiated claims. If your company is the "world's leading provider" of something, you are in good company. A recent search on Google turned up 8.58 million matching results for this phrase. Your claims are probably not true anyway, but even if they are you can use different language to make your point.

Marketese may be (barely) acceptable in your press releases when you are trying to puff up your company and accomplishments. But on your landing page it spells disaster. Marketese requires work on the part of your visitor. It saps their energy and attention, and forces them to spend time separating the content from the fluff. It also results in much longer word counts. You are missing an enormous opportunity by not creating a hype-free zone on your landing page.

How to Avoid Writing in "Marketese"
- Do not use any adjectives.
- Provide only objective information.
- Focus on the needs of your audience.

Save your visitors the aggravation and only tell them what they want to hear. Your editorial tone should have the following attributes:

Factual Writing factually will take a little work. It is difficult to stop making subjective statements. You may catch yourself lapsing into marketese at unexpected moments. But stick with it. You will be amazed at how much more effective your writing will be. Remember, your visitor is not looking to be entertained, and certainly not to be marketed to. They are there to deal with a specific need or problem that they have. The best kind of information you can give them is objective in nature.

Task-oriented Task-oriented writing is focused on the roles, tasks, and AIDA steps that are required to move your visitors through the conversion action. You should organize your text in the order that the visitor is likely to need it. For example, a big-ticket consumer product site might lay out the following high-level steps for the buying process: research, compare, customize, purchase. Once you have built The Matrix for your landing page, it should be clear where the gaps are.

Precise It is critical to be clear in Web writing. The audience can be very diverse and can bring a variety of cultural backgrounds to their interpretation of your language. Be careful about your exact choice of words. Never try to be funny or clever. Do not use puns, metaphors, or colloquial expressions.

This is doubly true for link text or button text. Your visitors need to have a clear understanding of exactly what will happen when they take the action of clicking on something. Text links should describe the content on the target page. Unhelpful link labels such as "click here" are a wasted opportunity to focus the visitor's awareness on an important available option. Also, link text is used by search engines to help people find information. If you use good link text, then you will be helping your own cause.

Buttons should accurately describe the intended action. For example, many e-commerce sites mistakenly put "Buy It Now!" buttons next to products when the actual action is "Add to cart." Another common mistake is to use the label "Order Now" when you really mean "Proceed to Checkout." This causes unnecessary stress and anxiety for visitors as they try to figure out the threat or opportunity presented by your button. It is always best to remove the hesitation and assure them that taking the next step is a small and safe action.

Use unambiguous standard language for all button labels. The screenshot above shows the search box in the header of the PetCareRx website (www.petcarerx.com). The author was probably trying to be clever by using the word "Fetch" superimposed on picture of a bone. Unfortunately, it has a negative effect, and creates doubt and confusion surrounding an important e-commerce site feature. The visitor is first forced to decide if the bone is a button. They then have to think about whether "fetch" is equivalent to the "search" function that they are looking for. The end result is a guaranteed to be a significant and ongoing reduction in sales.

Concise Become a word miser. Ask yourself, "How can I make this even shorter? Do I really need to communicate this at all?" Brevity has several advantages. It increases absorption and recall of information. It shortens the time that visitors spend reading it—minimizing the likelihood of increased frustration and impatience. It supports the goals of inverted pyramid writing, and the scannable text requirements described in the next section.

Format

Since people don't read the Web, the format of your writing should support their opportunistic scanning behavior. Use the following guidelines to help you write scannable text:

- Write in fragments or short sentences (don't worry about grammatical correctness if you have made yourself clear).
- Use digits instead of words to write out numbers (e.g. "47" instead of "forty seven")
- Highlight important information-carrying words (do not highlight whole sentences; stick to 2- or 3-word phrases).
- Use clear, emphasized titles for page headings and important subheads.
- Use ordinary language (avoid industry jargon and acronyms that are not widely understood).
- Use active voice, and action verbs.
- Use bullet lists instead of paragraphs.
- Keep lists between three and seven items (the limit of human short-term memory "chunking").
- Do not use more than two levels for lists or headings.

- Use descriptive link text (describing the information on the target page).
- Use supporting links to maintain present supplemental information and "see also" cross-referenced information.

Visual Design

Visual design is critical to the success of your landing pages. It makes a powerful first impression and is responsible for many visitors leaving your site within the first few seconds of arriving. Upon arrival your visitors have not had a chance to scan or digest most of your text message. They are mainly reacting emotionally to your page design. As I previously mentioned, you can't fool or argue with the limbic system. If it does not like something, there is no appeal.

Most of us can tell instantly whether a landing page appeals to us or repels us. We can tell if the page is "cheesy" and unprofessional. This determination is made based on the page structure, color scheme, font variety, graphics and images, and the degree of visual clutter on the page.

Use the following guidelines to improve your visual design.

Page Layout

The main quality that your page design has to have is coherence. It must be well organized and hang together as a single unit. It is helpful to use a grid design to create your preliminary layout. Design the page around the visitor's task and the conversion action.

Give the proper visual prominence to important elements. However, be careful not to give too much prominence. Some people take this to an extreme, and subscribe to the "I'll make it so big they can't possibly miss it" school of thought. Unfortunately, large and obvious graphical elements can be largely ignored by most visitors (especially if they are surrounded by too much whitespace). This well-documented phenomenon is called *banner blindness*. Too much visual distinction can cause the item to be perceived as an ad and ignored. If you intend to make prominent items very salient, always provide identical text links below them, and in the main navigation areas of the page.

The balance of your design is created at this early stage and should be carefully preserved. The page should be simple and uncluttered and include enough whitespace for the eye to rest. Group like items together. Unless advertising is your primary source of revenue, seriously consider whether you should show any banner ads. Banner ads are visually bold and may destroy the relative emphasis and coherence of the other page elements. In the end, the drop in conversion may end up costing you more money than the banner ads bring in.

Use high-quality production graphics and images. Do not mix different visual styles (such as photos and clip-art cartoons). Make sure that all of your image file sizes are small enough to load quickly. The only exception to this is the product "click to enlarge" close-up. These images should be as large as possible while still fitting on a reasonably sized monitor.

Be wary of introducing any kind of horizontal rules or separator into your design. Rules, or even abrupt changes in background color, serve to stop the eye from going further. In effect they say, "This is the end of something" and discourage further exploration. This is also true of too much whitespace because it reduces scannability.

Never make the user scroll to find critical information like transactional buttons or important navigation links. Even if they are appropriate near the bottom of the page, include another copy somewhere above the fold.

Frames are composite pages created like a photo collage from several individual Web pages. Unless your landing page absolutely depends on the use of frames, they should be avoided. Frames have several significant practical problems and break the fundamental navigation paradigm of the Web because they pull in only portions of the final visual page (which often make no sense when seen outside of the original context). Basically just say no to frames.

Graphics

Images on your landing page are a powerful two-edged sword. They can support your key messages and desired actions. Or they can serve as major distractions or interruptions for your visitor. Their effect depends mainly on their purpose and how they are perceived.

The best images support your visitor's task:

- Relate to the content on the page
- Illustrate key concepts (not simply used as window dressing)
- Show product views or details
- Contain pictures of friendly real people (not models)
- Have clear composition and tight cropping

However, images can also be ignored or have a negative effect:

- Generic images or stock art (unrelated to the topic of the page)
- Clearly fake, staged, contrived, or slick images
- Bright flashy images that look like advertisements

Visitors will look at images of other people—they can't help it. This can be useful in two tactical situations. Important text or calls to action can be displayed as a caption immediately below the graphic. This guarantees that the caption text will get more exposure. Similarly, if only the top of your picture is visible above the fold, your visitors will be encouraged to scroll.

Animation is almost universally annoying and should be generally avoided. If animation is required to illustrate a concept, the user should be given the affirmative option of watching it, and should not have it forced upon them. Similarly, Flash technology should be used only if there is a compelling need for it that would significantly improve the user experience.

Color

Color has a strong emotional impact on people and can dramatically alter moods and attitudes. This is also true on the Web. So you should use color sparingly and conservatively. This applies not only to individual colors, but also to palettes of complementary colors chosen for the landing page's visual theme. Make sure that your colors look unified, professional, and appropriate for your target audiences.

Do not use inverse color schemes with dark backgrounds and light text colors. Most Web browsers cannot print such pages very well. Stick to common color conventions. Use white (or very light) colors for text background areas (wild background patterns make it harder to read). Use colored text sparingly, and always use blue underlined text for links (and do not use blue for any other text).

This chapter has allowed you to see your landing page through new eyes. Undoubtedly many problems have surfaced. In the next chapter I will help you address them by deciding which page elements to tune.

Selecting Elements
to Tune

If I had a nickel for every time someone asked me, "What page elements should I test?" I would be a wealthy man by now. The answer to that question is, of course, "It depends." It depends on a lot of factors that are unique to your industry, audience, traffic levels, and particular landing page.

I wish that I could provide tactical prescriptions that would hold up for everyone—like the doctor who, regardless of your malady, orders you to take two aspirin and call back in the morning. But there is no such thing as the right answer in landing page testing. The best I can do is to offer some perspective on selecting promising tuning elements, and to cover testing themes that have consistently produced solid results.

6

Chapter Contents

How to Think About Test Elements

If you did your homework after reading the previous chapter ("Why Your Site Is Not Perfect"), you should have come up with a long list of potential problems and concerns about your site. These issues probably ranged from tactical problems, to fundamental mismatches between your visitor's goals and your landing page.

So how do you decide which ones are worthy of testing? The following filters will help you to separate the wheat from the chaff.

Breadth of Impact

The Pareto Principle, also commonly known as the "80/20 Rule," has been applied to a wide range of disciplines and observations. It predicts that a vital few (20%) of something are responsible for the vast majority (80%) of the results. If you apply this notion to landing page optimization, it follows that fixing a few fundamental problems will result in securing the majority of the available conversion rate improvement. Conversely, it also implies that some of the elements that you decide to test will not affect conversion rate at all.

So how do you determine what is vital and what is trivial? In general this can be hard to do, but you can follow the guideline of looking for the widest potential impact. This can be done at a number of different levels, as you'll see next.

Most Important Conversion Actions

In many cases, you will have more than one desired conversion action. You should concentrate on improving or emphasizing the one that results in the biggest financial rewards. For example, if you offer three different service levels, you probably know which ones your audience already prefers and their relative revenue value. By fixing or emphasizing the most popular one, you stand to gain the most. If your least popular plan only accounted for 1% of sales, even doubling its conversion rate would not have a dramatic impact on your overall revenues.

Biggest Possible Audience

Often companies have multiple landing pages for specific online marketing campaigns. You should examine which ones have the highest traffic levels and result in the highest number of conversions. Give first priority to the pages that are generating the most revenue.

Many companies only focus on obviously underperforming landing pages. Of course, shoring up your weaknesses is a valid approach to improving your business. However, you should not let it blind you to the opportunities hidden away in your best-performing pages. Just because they are generating a lot of revenue does not mean they are optimized or performing as well as they could be. By improving your top pages even more, you can usually unlock a lot of value.

Most Popular Paths Through Your Site

Web analytics software shows you the most popular paths (flows of traffic) through your site. Some of these packages even show you the reverse goal paths—the common sequences of pages that led the visitor to the conversion action.

Analyzing paths can be a somewhat complex business involving several interacting factors. You need to know where traffic lands on your site. In the case of main-site landing pages, the traffic may land on several types of pages on your site. For example, for an e-commerce catalog, you may have significant traffic hitting your home page, category pages, brand pages, search results pages, and product detail pages. The mix will depend on your particular business.

Do not pay attention only to the size of the landing page traffic flows because not all traffic has equal value. For example, your home page may have a high percentage of type-in traffic. This may mean that you have a strong brand and people are proactively seeking out your company, with a correspondingly higher likelihood of conversion. Conversely, most of your home page traffic may be from your successful SEO efforts. Unfortunately, the traffic may be coming primarily from generic keywords. In such cases, the large number of visitors may hide the fact that they are disinterested "tire kickers" who are much less likely to convert.

A lot of traffic (especially from paid campaigns) lands on pages that are deep within your site. This *deep linking* is intentional and is used to present the most relevant information possible. Deep linking is common in PPC campaigns, where the intent of searchers can be inferred from their keyword. Those who use generic keywords are sent to your home page, while those showing more specific intent or knowledge about their needs are taken directly to particular information or to product detail pages. The conversion likelihood of the deep-linked traffic is usually significantly higher because of visitors' later position in the decision process, and the targeted information that they see on the landing page.

You can combine all these factors into a single metric for estimating the magnitude of the potential losses for each type of landing page within your site. Multiply the revenue per visitor for a particular type of landing page by the number of visitors who land on it. This will give you a revenue estimate for the traffic source. Multiply that number by the bounce rate (the percentage of visitors who immediately exit without viewing another page). This will give you a rough sense of the potential lost revenue. You can now rank-order your pages and focus on the ones with the largest lost revenues first.

Actually, things can get a little more complicated in the real world. Sometimes a page can serve as both a landing page and as a link in the conversion path from other pages upstream of it. In such cases, the lost revenue calculation can be extended to include not only its bounce rate but also its abandonment (or drop-off) rate for traffic that is simply passing through it. But the basic idea is still the same—to estimate the value of the dollars draining out of your leaky conversion bucket.

Let's take a look at a specific example. Assume that you run a site for generating real estate agent buyer leads. You get paid a fixed amount for each visitor that you deliver to a local real estate agent's home page. Your only traffic source is a national PPC campaign on popular search engines. You use a mix of general and specific keywords (e.g., "buying a house," "california home listings," "san diego real estate"). Depending on the specificity of the keyword, the traffic is landed on the home page, a state-specific page, or a local community page. If searchers land on the national page, they must select a state page and then a particular local community page before taking the desired conversion action (clicking over to a local real estate agent's website). Similarly, those landing on state pages must first click on a local page, and then on the paid link.

The three types of pages have the following characteristics:

National page

> NV = 1,000,000 landing page visitors per month
>
> NB = 50% bounce rate (for traffic landing on this page)
>
> NR = $0.20 revenue per visitor

State pages

> SV = 500,000 landing page visitors per month
>
> SB = 40% bounce rate (for traffic landing on this page)
>
> SR = $0.30 revenue per visitor
>
> SA = 35% abandonment rate (for through traffic)

Local pages

> LV = 200,000 landing page visitors per month
>
> LB = 35% bounce rate (for traffic landing on this page)
>
> LR = $0.50 revenue per visitor
>
> LA = 30% abandonment rate (for through traffic)

Based on these figures, we can calculate the potential lost revenues for each page as follows:

National page

> $= NV \times NR \times NB$ (national bounce loss)
>
> $= \$100,000$

State pages

$\quad$ = SV × SR × SB (state bounce loss)

$\quad$ + NV × NR × (1 - NB) × SA (national abandonment loss)

$\quad$ = \$95,000

Local pages

$\quad$ = LV × LR × LB (local bounce loss)

$\quad$ + SV × SR × (1 - SB) × LA (state abandonment loss)

$\quad$ + NV × NR × (1 - NB) × (1 - SA) × (LA national abandonment loss)

$\quad$ = \$83,000

As you can see, the lost revenue of each page is surprisingly close, especially given the significant differences in direct traffic levels. Because the state and local pages act as conduits for upstream traffic, their value is enhanced significantly.

As I discussed in "The Myth of Perfect Conversion" section in the first chapter, you will not be able to convert all your visitors under any circumstances. So the lost revenue calculation is an upper limit on the actual performance improvement and should serve only as a rough guide for prioritizing the pages to test first.

Most Prominent Parts of the Page

All page elements are not created equal. A visitor's scanning behavior changes based on the specific task at hand. During e-commerce comparison shopping, visitors may inspect all items on a particular search results page with roughly equal attention until they find the right one. When reading articles or a column of search results, visitors will scan the material starting from the upper-left corner and focusing with decreasing attention to each new subheading or entry in the list.

But there are common general considerations. Eye-tracking and other behavioral studies have consistently shown that people pay inordinate amounts of attention to the information near the upper-left corner of a page when they are trying to get oriented. They look for important content in the central portion of the visible page and typically ignore information in the upper-right and lower-left corners. Placing items above the fold is critical for the awareness stage of the decision process (since you can't click on a link that you do not even know exists). But there is some evidence to indicate that that the fold is not at the actual visible limit of the browser window. People start tuning out when they get about two-thirds of the way down the screen. In fact, many people would rather scroll something up into the middle of their screen to examine it than look down to the bottom of the page.

Granularity

The granularity of your test elements is the level of detail at which you will make changes to your design. At one extreme, you can use specific and fine localized variations (such as changing button colors or text font sizes). At the other extreme, you can create coarse and fundamental changes that incorporate dozens of smaller individual design alternatives. It is not uncommon to completely redesign your whole landing page and test it head-to-head against your original.

In between is a continuum of possible scales at which you can test proposed changes. Sometimes these design alternatives can be nested within one another. For example, you may change the text of the call-to-action button on your form, change all of the text labels on the form input fields as well, or also change the size of the form and its position on the page.

As you will see in the next chapter, "The Math of Tuning," the size of your test will be constrained by the traffic to your landing page and its data rate (the number of conversion actions per unit time). In Chapter 8, "Tuning Methods," you will also understand the limitations on the total number of alternative designs possible for each particular tuning method. Changing the granularity of your tests allows you to include all or most of your important ideas while still fitting into a reasonable test size. Reducing search space size is done by combining several individual changes into a single larger variable for testing.

At SiteTuners.com we use our proprietary TuningEngine technology to routinely run large-scale tests involving millions of possible versions of a landing page. When this kind of test size is available, it makes sense to get very granular on most of the changes that you are considering. With other testing methods or low data rates, you will be forced to consolidate your test size. At that point, you have to decide if you want to focus on fine granularity changes or combining several of them into larger tuning elements.

The advantage of fine granularity changes is that they are quick and easy to implement. For example, you may want to consider different headlines for your page. It would not take long to come up with some reasonable alternatives, set up a test, and start collecting data. By continuously running back-to-back fine-granularity tests, you can often make significant conversion improvements. By their nature, these kinds of small incremental tests do not require a lot of work or emotional investment, and are ideal for this kind of champion-challenger continuous testing.

Wholesale page redesigns are sometimes the only option when you want to consider many potential changes but do not have the data rate or time to run a series of finer-granularity tests. Such redesigns are also the only way to deal with landing pages that have low coherency (see the next section). The main drawback of whole-page redesigns is the time and effort that goes into creating them. Since you don't know if the new design will outperform the original, you are taking a gamble that your larger up-front investment will pay off. I have also heard online marketers argue that complete redesigns deny them so-called "learnings" about which individual elements contributed the most to the improved performance. As you will see in the "Variable

Interactions" section in the next chapter, I am highly dubious of this kind of thinking. It is based on the flawed assumption that the individual elements are completely independent of one another, when in fact they are often highly dependent on the context in which they are presented.

There is no inherent advantage to testing fine or coarse granularity changes. In a fine granularity test, one of SiteTuners.com's business-to-business clients used a "Free Quote Request" headline for their lead capture form. We proposed changing this single element of the landing page to "Instant Quote" and saw the form-fill conversion rate skyrocket by 58%. For SiteTuners.com client Power Options, we were asked to improve the sign-up rate for a free trial of stock option research software (see the case study under the "Delayed Conversions" section in Chapter 11, "Avoiding the Pitfalls," for additional information). We concluded that the only viable option, because of the low data rate and fundamental issues with the original page design, was to test complete redesigns of the page. We tested the two whole-page alternative redesigns against the original in a three-way head-to-head test. Both of the new designs significantly outperformed the original, with the winning one resulting in 75% higher revenue per visitor after completion of the free trial.

Granularity does not have to be uniform among the elements that you are testing. I frequently devote more attention to key elements of the landing page. For example, I may have different call-to-action button colors (complementing the rest of the page or contrasting), formats (a button only, or a button with a text link under it), and text (several alternative variations). For less important or visible parts of the page (e.g., the footer), I may only test one alternative that includes several concurrent changes that might improve performance.

Sweep

Closely related to the granularity of a tuning element is the notion of sweep. Do your alternative testing element ideas represent radically different outside-the-box thinking? Or are they a tame incremental change that is unlikely to produce significant changes in visitor behavior?

> *Efficiency is doing things right; effectiveness is doing the right things.*
> —Business management guru Peter F. Drucker

You have a choice. You can continue to refine your landing page within the current framework of its design, messaging, and intention in an evolutionary manner. Or you can test extreme and radical revolutionary alternatives that can fail miserably, or produce unexpected levels of breakthrough performance. There is no correct answer. The level of iconoclasm in your testing depends on your company's culture of risk tolerance and business objectives.

Coherency

You can put lipstick on a pig, but it's still a pig.
—Common saying

Coherency is an overall sense of your design "hanging together." It is a congruity and harmonious consistency in the relation of all landing page parts to the whole. It is clear to most Internet surfers within a split second of clicking on a link whether the destination page has coherency.

It is also clear when coherency is lacking. Visitors respond to incoherent pages with a variety of gut reactions, and none of them are flattering. In the extreme, such pages can be experienced as tacky, cheesy, bewildering, or obnoxious. Unfortunately, you have probably seen hundreds of examples before.

Who you are screams so loudly in my face, I can't hear a word you are saying.
—Ralph Waldo Emerson

Low-coherency landing pages affect visitors on an emotional level, and no amount of logic will convince them to linger on them. And that may be a pity, because the content may be relevant to their needs. But they can't get past the cognitive dissonance of the inconsistent presentation to even focus on the intended message. Incoherent and unprofessional pages also give most consumers a low confidence in the product.

Review the "Usability Basics" section of the preceding chapter to make sure that everything works smoothly together. The visual design of the page is particularly important. This includes consistent color palettes; professional graphics in the same visual style; consistent font sizes, colors, and families; and the amount and layout of the writing.

Coherency is an emergent property of the unified whole. All of the supporting elements that contribute to it must work together. Because of this, I often suggest that the coherency-related elements all be grouped into a single unified look-and-field test element that governs the visual experience of your landing pages. As I mentioned in the previous section, the need for high coherency is an excellent reason to consider whole-page redesigns (especially in low data rate environments). This allows you to fix all known visual problems in one shot. Often the details of good coherence have already been formally codified in your company's visual design brief document. Much of the actual implementation can be encapsulated in HTML Cascading Style Sheets.

Conversely, if fine-granularity elements are used, the tester can unwittingly decrease the coherency of the landing page. This happens in two primary ways: mixing, and unexpected juxtaposition.

Let's assume that all of the elements you decide to test on your original page have significant problems—that is, of course, the reason you chose them in the first place. You spend considerable time writing your test plan document and coming up with better alternatives for each of the original elements, and you succeed. Each of the new elements is *in isolation* indeed better than its original counterpart. In fact, when they are all collected together in a highly coherent new whole they become even more synergistic and powerful.

Unfortunately, if you are running a typical multivariate test, the new elements will be mixed and matched at random with other elements that were part of your original design. When this kind of mixing occurs, the new elements may actually suffer by their combination with poor-quality original elements. They will be judged not on their own merits, but by the company that they keep. In such cases the new elements will look worse than they really are. They may even seem worse than their original counterparts due to the fact that the mixing produced a wider range of quality differences on the page. In other words, the original design elements may have been mediocre, but they were all roughly equally mediocre. The introduction of a new element into this mix actually brought the quality difference into even sharper contrast, thus making the overall design seem worse.

Unexpected juxtaposition can be another source of decreased coherency. Since all elements are shuffled randomly in the testing process, it is critical to consider in advance how nearby combinations of elements may appear, and to anticipate potential problems.

For example, let's assume that you have landing page that includes a call-to-action button, long descriptive text, and a second call-to-action button with different text. Your test plan contains alternatives for the last two elements. In your brainstorming, you decide that since most people won't read the long descriptive text, the alternative is to remove it altogether (a reasonable variant to test). You also figure that having a consistent call-to-action is important for the strength of your messaging, and decide to test a copy of the first call-to-action as an alternative to the second one (also a reasonable course of action in isolation).

However, based on this test plan, a quarter of your audience will see a version of the page that includes two back-to-back copies of the first call-to-action button (without any intervening text). Most visitors will think that your landing page is broken, or that your Web designer accidentally inserted an extra copy of the button. In either case, they will probably have a negative reaction to it. So both the removal of the descriptive text and the repetition of the first call-to-action in the second one will be penalized. This example was fairly obvious, but this type of test design mistake is common among inexperienced testers.

Audience Segmentation

There are two different outlooks on whether to segment your audience for testing. One group of online marketers insists that you should test for the winning combination of elements separately for each traffic source. The other suggests that you aggregate all of your available acquisition traffic together for purposes of testing. Actually, both are correct depending on the main focus of your testing:

Content and offer focus If you are primarily focused on tuning elements of your offer (such as price, promotions, or service levels), the traffic source can become important. If you know something about the demographics and psychographics of your online campaigns, you may want to test different elements (such as sales copy or details of your incentive) for each major traffic source. Similarly, if you are attracting visitors with diverse needs to specially themed landing pages, the page content should be tailored to the intended audience segment. It is important to note that you should still have a high enough data rate within each segment to conduct the necessary testing. Depending on the scale of your traffic, it is possible that you will only be able to do this on your largest campaigns, or not at all.

Function and usability focus If your focus is on more fundamental functional and usability issues, there is probably little difference across your online channels. For example, fixing the clunky checkout process on your e-commerce site will positively impact all of your visitors. In such cases, it is best to combine all traffic in order to be able to conduct larger or faster tests. In effect, you are tuning for the best possible performance across your most representative and realistic mix of traffic.

The two approaches can be combined. For example, let's assume that your visitors land on a large number of landing pages that all share a common structure. You can first tune across all traffic sources to fix your functional and usability issues with the page template, and then tune the message and content of the pages for each specific audience.

Longevity

Another key consideration is the longevity of the elements that you are considering. The value of a landing page change depends on how well it will hold up into the future. Changes to time-sensitive promotions or special offers may cause a significant conversion improvement, but they will be short-lived. By contrast, changes that fix underlying usability or coherency problems will continue to provide benefits for the whole time that the improved site design remains in use (possibly for many months or even years).

You should test both types of elements, but even smaller less-dramatic conversion rate improvements to elements with high longevity will translate into substantial profits over time.

More transient elements need to be retested more frequently to make sure that they retain their effectiveness, or rotated to account for seasonal factors. Additional issues for testing highly seasonal elements are discussed in the "Seasonality" section in Chapter 11.

Baggage

Many of the ideas for possible tuning elements that you come up with in your brainstorming may be much better than the corresponding originals. However, some of them may have attendant baggage. In other words, it may not be possible to test them through the efforts of you or your team alone. They may require resources or cooperation from others that may not be available to you for a number of reasons:

Turf Elements that you may want to test are controlled and jealously guarded by others (e.g., your advertising agency, webmaster, or I.T.).

Skill set You need unavailable outside experts to help create certain elements (e.g., usability reviewers or professional graphic designers).

Resources A significant amount of money or staff time is required to implement the elements (e.g., Web design, copywriting of new content, or programming).

Approval The approval process to make certain changes is bureaucratic, time-consuming, and onerous (e.g., legal reviews).

Schedule The creation of certain elements would introduce long delays (e.g., programming functional changes to data-driven websites).

Such practical considerations should definitely be a part of your decision making. If you feel that you have plenty of other ideas that may yield significant conversion rate improvements, you may want to eliminate the problematic elements from your current test plan. You can always include them in a follow-up test once you have established a track record of success. However, if the changes are important enough, you may want to push them through anyway, despite the political cost and effort involved. Please see "The Company Politics of Tuning" section in Chapter 9, "Assembling the Team and Getting Buy-In."

Selecting Elements to Tune

Not all things on your landing page matter. As I discussed earlier, the Pareto Principle (also known as the "Rule of 80/20") suggests that a few key changes to your page will result in the biggest conversion rate improvement. This implies that there are a large number of trivial changes that will not help at all. Since you don't know ahead of time which those are, you must resign yourself to the fact that not all of your testing ideas will pan out. In fact, some of your elements may already be great performers, and your proposed alternatives will actually drag down conversion rates during the test.

One key thought to keep in mind: "Your mileage may vary." Do not automatically copy recent changes that your competitors have incorporated in their sites. They may not know what is best, or their audience may respond differently than yours. The only way to be sure is to test on your own audience. There have been classic cases where the market leader in an industry actually had a much worse site design than their smaller challenger. Testing allowed that challenger to take and hold the lead.

The phrase "Fiddling while Rome burns" refers to the (probably false) account of Roman emperor Nero playing music and singing during the fire of 64 C.E., which he was purportedly responsible for setting. Whether or not that story is true, the phrase has come to symbolize people who occupy themselves with unimportant matters and neglect priorities during a crisis. Landing page testing can be likened to hospital emergency room triage—you have to prioritize the most critical issues first. There is no point fixing some superficial or tactical problem when something more fundamental undermines its effectiveness.

You have to use your current landing page as a starting point. No one can tell you where your biggest deficiencies currently are. However, they usually fall into the following closely related classes of problems.

Page Structure

Page structure is closely related to both coherency and emphasis (see the "Emphasis" section later in this chapter). It defines how the real estate on your page is organized and used. By changing the sizes and positions of various page sections, you can also dramatically impact the emphasis that key areas receive.

If you have a number of similar landing pages for specific content topics, you may not have enough traffic on a particular one to conduct a landing page test. However, it is often possible to combine traffic from all of your pages and test the elements related to their common page structure.

Typical page structure testing elements include:

- Size and contents of page header
- Size and contents of page footer
- Size and location of page navigation
- Placement of trust symbols and credibility logos
- Separation of page shell and navigation from page content
- Size and location of forms or other calls-to-action
- Mirror images (swapping) of key page sections (e.g., a form located to the left of the text or to the right)
- Vertical stacking versus horizontal arrays of page sections
- Single versus multiple columns

The location of your navigation is closely tied to the number of columns on your page. In general, try to use vertical menus because horizontal menus take up more-valuable vertical screen real estate. Since people do not like to read wide text blocks, vertical menus also enhance readability by making the page content narrower on widescreen monitors.

Information Architecture

As you may recall from the previous chapter, information architecture defines the way that information is organized on your website. It should basically create an accurate mental map of how your site works, and how the visitor can interact with it.

Typical information architecture–related test elements include:

- Self-selecting by role or by task
- Clear and distinct descriptive link text and choices
- Sensible and prominent page titles
- Breadcrumbs or other context ("you are here")
- Consistent placement of all page elements
- Navigation (organization of menu options)
- Number of available choices presented
- Alternative navigation methods
- Cross-linking to other key information
- Availability and format of on-site search
- Ability to avoid, minimize, reverse, or easily correct mistakes (e.g., on-page error checking, context-sensitive form fields)

Presentation

Presentation mainly has to do with the *format* in which you deliver your message. Although it is a close cousin of both page structure and emphasis, it has its own distinct flavor.

Typical presentation testing elements include:

- Degree of detail (e.g., full text, or links to supporting information)
- Writing format (inverted pyramid versus traditional prose)
- Choice of input elements (e.g., radio buttons or pulldown lists)
- Action format (e.g., buttons, text links, or both)
- Editorial tone of your writing
- Use of alternative formats and modalities (e.g., charts, figures, audio clips, video, presentations, demos)

Emphasis

Emphasis is about the *relative* importance that you place on something. Resist the temptation to pump up the volume on everything, since this just annoys your visitor. In fact, there is evidence that obvious and obnoxious visual elements are automatically tuned out by some people (so-called *banner blindness*). Instead, try to selectively focus attention on the key elements on your page, and de-emphasize everything else.

Typical emphasis testing elements include:

- Amount of screen real estate devoted to an item
- Use of relevant images (e.g., specific product or believable people)
- Image captions
- Font sizes and font families (e.g., headline sizes)
- Font emphasis (e.g., italics, bolding, underlines, background colors, text colors, capitalization)
- Background color blocks or background images
- Call-to-action button shapes, sizes, visual styles, and effects (e.g., beveling, borders, and drop shadows)
- Visual separators (e.g., horizontal rules)
- Use of whitespace and visual isolation to focus on important items
- Removal of distracting secondary information

Tuning Multiple-Page Flows

Most of the attention so far in this chapter has been on individual landing pages. However, there are many online campaigns that require a visitor to pass through a series of pages before converting. Tuning multiple-page sequences of pages ("flows" hereafter) has its own unique challenges.

It is common in linear flows (such as registrations or checkouts) to ask for the least invasive and personal information first. By starting with small and innocuous sharing, your visitors are drawn in smoothly and painlessly. By the time you ask for the bigger commitments (like entering credit card payment information), they already have a lot of investment in the process and are much more likely to continue.

A common testing element is the granularity of the steps in the flow. In some cases (if you have a smaller amount of information on your conversion form), you may want to squeeze all of the input fields onto one page. The conversion action can then be labeled as "instant one-step" or something similar implying expediency and immediate gratification. Another approach is to break up the process into multiple pages. Each page can then contain a small and non-threatening micro-action that is easily completed by visitors on their way to the ultimate goal.

In general, flows should exhibit certain characteristics, which I'll cover in the following sections.

Systematic

I have already discussed roles, tasks, and the AIDA stages of the decision process at length. The Matrix framework provides a systematic view of *who* needs to accomplish *what* on your site, and makes sure that visitors have the *proper support* at every step along the way. When identifying problems with your current site in the previous chapter, you should have noted any missing or incomplete parts of The Matrix for your campaign. Now is the time to rectify the situation.

Imagine that you are trying to get your visitors to cross a rickety rope bridge across a wide chasm. This analogy is not too much of a stretch. In terms of attention spans on the Web you are requiring a significant commitment on the part of your visitors. If you do not put in place a series of solid and reasonably spaced planks, most people (except for a very determined few) will not make it across to the conversion goal on the other side.

You should consider testing changes to your site that will fill in the missing pieces. Sometimes this will require creating significant new content (such as wizards, demos, or video presentations), but often you will only need to reorganize content that already exists, and put it into the language of your visitor (instead of your company).

Connected

Even if all of the cells in your Matrix have been properly filled in, this is not enough. There must be strong and obvious connections between adjacent ones in order to maintain or increase the visitor's psychological momentum toward the conversion goal.

Researchers Peter Pirolli and Stuart Card at the Palo Alto Research Center (formerly known as Xerox PARC) have worked for many years on their *information foraging theory*. It describes how people hunt for information on the Web much like wild animals in search of their prey. They follow *information scent* in order to determine if they are getting closer to their goal. They will keep clicking on additional links if they feel that the scent is getting stronger. Otherwise, they might simply give up and start foraging in some other location (your competitor's website, for example).

The information scent is conveyed by clues in their immediate environment. Mostly these are in the form of links on the page. So devote particular attention to the connections between pages:

- Make in-content and navigation link text clear and objective.
- Describe exactly what visitors will see on the destination page.
- Match the title on the destination page with the inbound link text used.
- Do not use cute language, made-up words, or industry jargon in link text.

- Do not use generic link labels such as "click here."

- Restrict your link text to scannable short phrases (do not create links out of long sentences).

- Lead people to more specific information with each click (as they try to zero in on their goal).

- Provide feedback about visitors' current context, and their position in the big picture (I'll discuss this topic further in the next section).

Your visitors' process may have started off of your site (unless they typed in your URL directly). In such cases, the landing page should match their expectations (e.g., in terms of the search term they typed in). Echo the search term (or inbound link text) on your page, or take visitors to the most relevant starting page possible (if you are using PPC to drive traffic). This helps them to bypass all of the more generic information near the top of your site, and deep-links them closer to their intended goal.

If you are using graphical buttons to advance visitors through a process, follow the language conventions listed earlier for button labels. In addition, consider augmenting your buttons with identical text links just below. Some people will overlook larger graphics, but will respond to the humble text link. Get rid of nonessential buttons like the common form "Reset." If you absolutely *must* have more than one button, follow proper conventions (e.g., the button on the left should represent the primary desired action, with the others serving as exceptions). You can also use different button colors or sizes to indicate relative importance or to shift the visual focus.

Flexible

Unfortunately, even a well-connected and systematic Matrix is not enough. In reality, many of your visitors will not follow an orderly progression along the neat and well-marked little paths that you have laid out. They may jump around, they may back up, or they may leave and return much later (after forgetting most of their previous interactions with your site).

The Stranded Parachutist

Imagine that your website visitor is a parachutist who was blown off course in the middle of the night. He crash-lands and breaks through the roof of your house, and lands in the middle of a particular room. He is completely disoriented and knows nothing about his surroundings. There are several closed doors leading out of the room.

What have you done to prepare for these kinds of unexpected guests? Have you left enough clues and markers to quickly guide them to their goal with a minimum of confusion, disorientation, and frustration?

Many visitors will not even arrive at your front door. They will enter on pages deep within your site that were never designed as starting points for your conversion process (e.g., previously bookmarked pages, links in blogs, or from organic search results).

You can do several things to prepare for the random entry points and unpredictable visitor behavior:

Provide context It is important to provide consistent global navigation on your site. In addition, you should provide "you are here" information via breadcrumbs. Alternatively, you can include a map showing progress and the current step in a linear process. Provide cross-links to important pages in your conversion process from all deep-linked content pages that might serve as entry points into your site.

Be flexible Allow visitors to wander off of the conversion path and look around. Always let them back up or easily undo actions that they have recently taken. Include obvious cross-links to return them to various points in the conversion path.

Save visitor state Use cookies or other tracking methods to record your visitors' behavior. If they have previously filled in some information on a particular page, always save and repopulate it upon their return. If you normally collect information in a linear fashion, try to piece it together opportunistically instead. Sometimes the order in which it is entered is not important; as long as you end up with all of the required information by the end of the conversion action, you should not insist that it be collected in a predetermined particular sequence. Yes, this is a bit more of a pain from a programming standpoint, but it is your visitors who are buying your product, not your software developers.

Timeless Testing Themes

I have spoken many times on the topic of "Landing Page Testing and Tuning" at various *Search Engine Strategies* conferences. On the discussion panel we have had speakers from several testing companies. Despite our differences in focus and approach, we were able to identify certain commonalities with regard to what leads to consistent conversion improvements. These are not specific prescriptions, but rather promising areas and directions for your own testing explorations. Not surprisingly, all of the testing themes that I discuss next are directly related to the AIDA decision process stages described in Chapter 4.

Less Is More

Although the general idea of uncluttering is powerful throughout the decision process, this testing theme has an especially powerful impact on improving visitor awareness. If visitors do not recognize quickly that you have something in which they might be interested, they will leave your site immediately. In Figure 6.1 you can see a Web analytics report showing distribution of visit lengths to a site. The bars show a general bell-curve shape with the peak at 61–180 seconds. This amount of time spent on a non-news site is impressive. However, the long bar at the top indicates that over 55%

of visitors punched out within 10 seconds. These short-timers are the ones who are likely to have "bounced" and not clicked on any other links from their original landing page. They represent a significant lost opportunity.

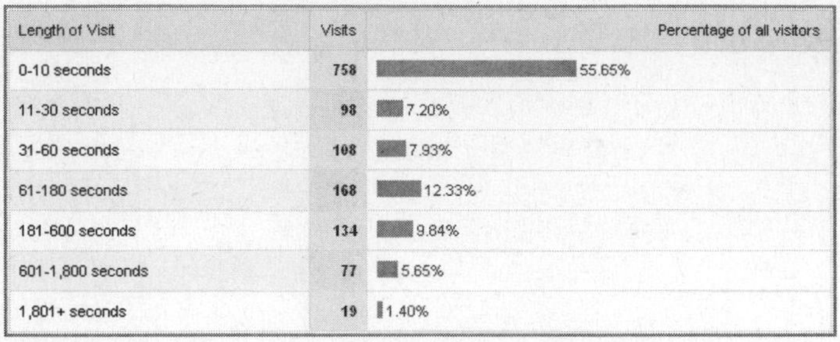

Length of Visit	Visits	Percentage of all visitors
0-10 seconds	758	55.65%
11-30 seconds	98	7.20%
31-60 seconds	108	7.93%
61-180 seconds	168	12.33%
181-600 seconds	134	9.84%
601-1,800 seconds	77	5.65%
1,801+ seconds	19	1.40%

Figure 6.1 Web analytics report on length of visit

Within this problem lies the opportunity for clearing away the clutter and significantly increasing the number of people who have meaningful interactions with your site.

Less is more applies to a whole range of test elements:

- Fewer and smaller graphics
- Shorter bulleted text
- Reduced number of choices and links

"Less Is More" Is an Exercise in Editing: Instead of creating alternatives to the original page's elements, you should consider doing away with them altogether.

Cut until you can't stand it any more, and then cut some more. You will be surprised at how little content is needed on a well-designed landing page. Don't be afraid to try radically stripped-down alternative test elements.

Case Study—RealAge.com

SiteTuners.com client RealAge.com has developed a unique test that determines the biological age of your body based on how well you have maintained it. It has received widespread exposure and has been featured in several newspaper and talk and news shows. The whole business depends on the number of people who sign up for the free RealAge Test. RealAge had already tested a number of ideas to improve the efficiency of the sign-up process, and thought that they were doing well because of their high (double-digit) conversion rate. SiteTuners.com's goal was to improve the conversion rate of the sign-up process even more.

Case Study—RealAge.com *(Continued)*

We identified several variables that might improve performance, among them the page header, navigation bar, headlines, sales copy, call-to-action, graphics, and button format. For each variable, the original version was included in the test, along with one or more alternatives. The variables and values tested resulted in 552,960 unique recipes (versions of the site). Because of the size of the test, the engagement was conducted with SiteTuners.com's proprietary *Tuning Engine* technology.

At the end of the test, the best alternative champion design was run head-to-head against the original baseline and showed a 40% lift in conversion rate. The bottom-line impact of this change on RealAge was significant.

If you compare the before and after screenshots in Figures 6.2 and 6.3, you will note that the two pages still basically look the same.

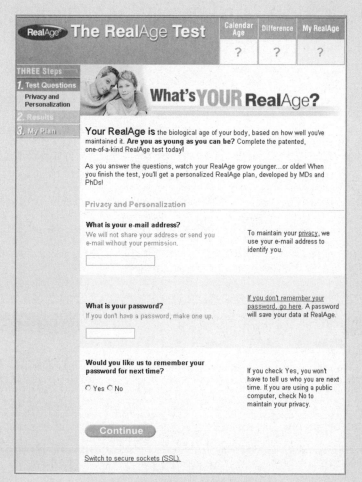

Figure 6.2 RealAge.com "before" landing page

Continued

Case Study—RealAge.com *(Continued)*

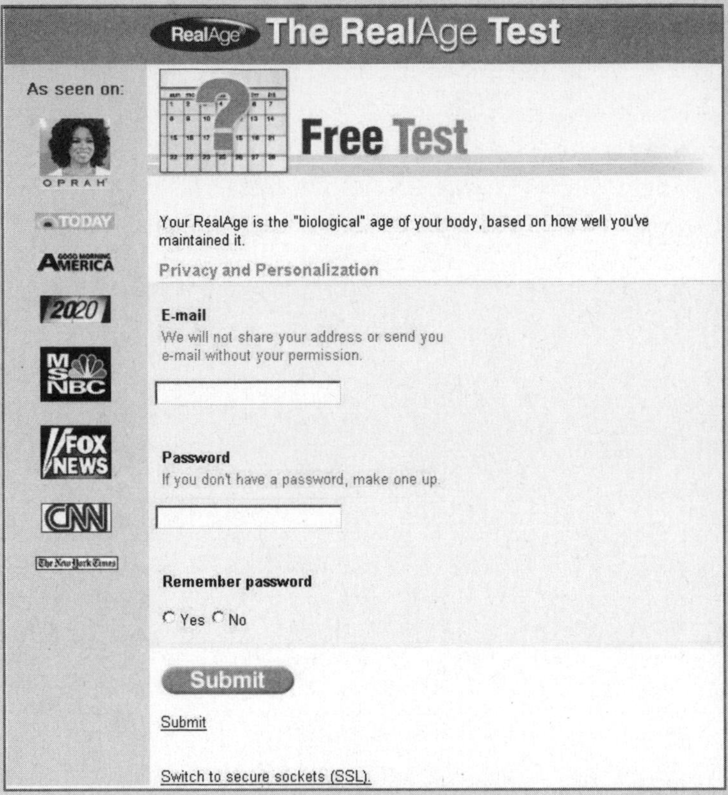

Figure 6.3 RealAge.com "after" landing page

However, upon careful inspection, you will note that many simplified page elements ended up in the final solution:

- Smaller and simpler header graphic
- Removal of left navigation menu
- Shorter headline
- Different graphic (calendar with question mark instead of photo of a couple)
- Shorter lead-in sales copy
- Shorter question labels
- Removal of question explanation text
- Single background color for questions (instead of alternating for each question)

Personalize It

Personalization builds desire and affinity for your particular solution. As I discussed in Chapter 4, "Understanding the Decision Process," customization can be a powerful conversion tool. Personalization can be tested using a wide array of available tactics. Some examples include:

- Echo the keywords that visitors used to find your landing page as the page title
- Pre-populate your search box with the text of the keywords that visitors used to find your landing page
- Present localized content by using geo-targeting information
- Do not require people to log in if they have been there before
- Fill in checkout information for returning e-commerce buyers
- Customize content by visitor role once someone has self-selected
- Allow visitors to configure your product or service offering
- Display deeper or richer content to those who have shown enough commitment (based on page views or time on your site)
- Show last-minute special offers via exit pop-ups to visitors who are about to leave your site without converting
- Follow up by phone or e-mail if someone abandons your registration process partway
- Proactively initiate a live chat session if your visitor is clearly struggling with something on your site

Of course, you have to be careful to use personalization properly. It can be very effective. However, if your tactics are unexpected they can backfire and become off-putting in a "big brother" sort of way.

Some of the suggested testing elements above require the use of a content management system and multiple session tracking, or even tie-ins to your customer relationship management (CRM) or sales force automation (SFA) systems. New segmentation, targeting, and business trigger capabilities are also becoming increasingly commonly in Web authoring tools. But even without these, many personalization tuning elements can be implemented with the use of simple cookies and information extracted from the visitor's browser environment settings.

Test the Offer

Ultimately, it is your offer that gets a visitor to act. However, when considering specific testing elements there are a lot of ways that you can influence someone:

- The primary offer
- The total solution surrounding the offer (as discussed previously in Chapter 4)
- Headline
- Sales copy
- Images chosen
- Call-to-action text and graphical format
- Repetition of the call-to-action in multiple screen locations and formats
- Offer context (e.g., by bracketing the desired action in a bronze/silver/gold set of options)
- Limited availability or other scarceness indicators (e.g., deadlines, remaining inventory)

Pricing is also a vital part of the offer and will be discussed in more detail in the next section.

Price Testing

Technically, testing price is simply a component of the offer. But because of its powerful influence on purchase conversions, and other particular qualities, it deserves a separate closer look. The price testing that I am discussing applies only to a single item. Tuning catalogs of items is a much harder problem.

The advantage of price testing on the Web is that you have several desirable conditions:

- Large numbers of new prospects who have not been exposed to your company before

- Ability to easily modify pricing displayed to a particular visitor
- Ability to hold all other factors constant
- End-to-end tracking and immediate recording of the sale

However, a host of possible issues make price testing potentially problematic even on the Web:

- Seasonality
- Changing supply-demand imbalances
- Product obsolescence
- Degree of commoditization
- Reactions of your competitors

Because of this shifting environment, it is important to regularly re-test your price to detect any significant changes. Although I refer to product pricing in the following sections, the same applies to services pricing as well. True price testing is still something of a "Wild West" situation in practice. Hopefully the following summary will give you a framework for how to approach it.

Qualitative Methods

There is a whole industry around pricing and profit optimization. Most companies in this field are consultants and have an array of qualitative methods to determine the correct price.

Some common approaches and considerations include:

- Expert judgments
- Primary research
- Benchmarking
- Internal data analysis
- User or sales prospect focus groups
- Product lifecycle

Pricing consultants have radically different methodologies and approaches. Some are more evidence-based, while others prefer more intuitive "soft" considerations.

Quantitative Methods

At the end of the day, whatever pricing you come up with via qualitative approaches, you would still have to test the predicted best price point on your actual visitors. This section gives you an overview of common methods that can be used on your landing page.

Price Testing Basics

All of the website elements that I have discussed so far in this book have something in common: they are *discrete variables*. In other words, they involve distinct choices.

Should you have a red button, a blue one, or a green one? Should you use our current page headline or a new one? Should you offer free shipping with product purchase—or not?

Focusing only on discrete variables overlooks an important class of variables that can also dramatically improve conversion rates. *Continuous variables* can theoretically be set to an infinite number of different values. One of the most important continuous variables is the price of a product. Price can be varied over a wide range in one-cent increments. There is no way to properly *guess* the exact value that will give you the highest profits.

A typical price/profit curve for a single product looks like an inverted "U" shape (see Figure 6.4). At the lower end, your profits will be zero because you have no profit margin left. In other words, the price of the product equals your cost to produce and deliver it. At this point, it does not matter how many people buy—there is no profit to be made. At the higher end, your profits will also approach zero because the price will be too high, and you will not have any customers.

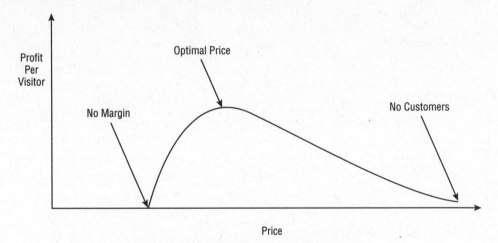

Figure 6.4 Typical profit curve as a function of product price

Of course, the exact shape of the profit curve will vary widely depending on your specific situation. It may have a flat top and gentler fall-off at the shoulders. Setting the wrong price can have disastrous consequences for the success of your product or service. Your goal should be to set the price at (or near) the profit sweet spot at the top of the curve.

There are several common approaches to finding the right price:

Spot Testing

Most companies treat price as a discrete variable. If you try to test price as a discrete variable (e.g., you test three distinct prices—your current price, a specific lower price, and a specific higher price), you are only getting information about the *exact* prices you choose to test. You will know which one of the tested prices is better. But you will not know if *any* of them are at the exact profit optimum point. In other words, you may very well be leaving money on the table. The only advantage to this approach is that it works with your existing (discrete variable) landing page optimization tools. If your only alternative is not to test price at all, then you should use spot testing—a little bit of something is better than a whole lot of nothing.

The situation is even more difficult with up-sells. Because of the strong variable interactions between the base product and the up-sell, it becomes very difficult to test reasonable combinations of the base product price and the up-sell price by using spot tests (see the last section in this chapter for an alternative method).

Walking The Price Curve

As I mentioned above, the typical single product profit curve looks like an inverted "U" shape. Many companies conduct informal price testing by "walking" this curve. They change the price and measure the resulting performance. If it improves, they incrementally change the price again in the same direction (either raising it more or lowering it more depending on the circumstances). Eventually they will overshoot the top of the curve and experience a decline in profits. At that point they back up to the previous price and lock that in as their winner.

This approach has significant drawbacks. First, it can be very time consuming. Depending on the size of the price change increment that you choose, you may have to run several back-to-back tests. The lost opportunity cost of being at suboptimal pricing for the length of these tests can be significant. Second, there is no clear way to decide on how to calculate your price change increment. Some companies use a fixed amount, others use a percentage of the current price. Regardless of the approach, if you choose incorrectly, you will either require many tests (as mentioned above), or not find the top of the profit curve because your increment is too large. Third, pricing changes are done sequentially. Once a change is made, everyone sees the new price. As I describe in the "Biased Samples" section of Chapter 7, "The Math Of Tuning," sequential sampling should be used as a last resort. You don't know what other outside factors have impacted price across all of your tests (seasonality, traffic changes, or external events such as competitor price changes or company announcements).

Price Elasticity Modeling

It is possible to build a model of the predicted sales conversion rate as a function of price. Such price elasticity models are constructed using a variety of mathematical approaches, and include different assumptions at their core. But the basic idea is the same. If you can predict what percentage of people will buy your product at a given price, and you know your costs at any price point, you should be able to calculate your profit per visitor for all prices.

SiteTuners.com has developed a proprietary PriceTuning methodology for determining the exact shape of the profit curve based on the actual behavior of website visitors.

Example: Single Product Price Elasticity Model

At SiteTuners.com we normally bracket the current price with a higher and lower value. The original price and the two bracket prices are shown randomly to new visitors. If the profit maximum falls between the two bracket values, we can create a model for all of the intermediate prices. From this we can determine where the top of the profit curve lies. We then conduct a head-to-head test of the original price against predicted best to verify results.

Figure 6.5 shows the results of an actual client engagement. The original e-book product price was $20. Even though fewer units were sold at the profit optimum price of $47, it was actually 37% higher in terms of revenue (and profit) per visitor.

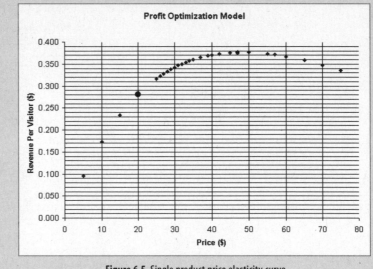

Figure 6.5 Single product price elasticity curve

It is possible that your current price is already close to the profit optimum, especially if the top of the profit curve is pretty flat across a wide range of prices. Since the model also predicts the conversion rate at a given price, you can consciously make the trade-off between higher market share and perceived exclusivity in such cases. In other words, you can choose a lower price and more customers, or a higher price and fewer customers while still maintaining a near-optimal profitability per visitor.

Price elasticity modeling also works for a product with a single up-sell option. Within this configuration you need to determine the revenue-per-visitor optimal pricing for both the base product and the up-sell. The up-sell can be displayed in parallel (shown side-by-side on the same page) or serially (shown on a subsequent page once someone has decided to buy the base product).

Parallel and serial presentations can result in radically different pricing models. Parallel presentations tend to show stronger influences between the base product and up-sell since they appear near each other on the same page. Serial models are more independent, since the visitor has already decided to "open their wallet" for the base product, and is then presented with the up-sell. Because of this it is best to independently find the best price settings for the parallel and serial models, and then pick the one that produces the highest profit per visitor.

Example: Single Product Plus Up-sell Price Elasticity Models

In Figure 6.6, the optimal pricing for the base product alone would have suggested a $36 price point. However, when taking the value of the up-sell into account at different base prices, the best price point for the base product turned out to be $28. If left uncorrected, this mistake would have cost the client approximately 5 cents in profit for every visitor (a very large sum considering the traffic to their landing page).

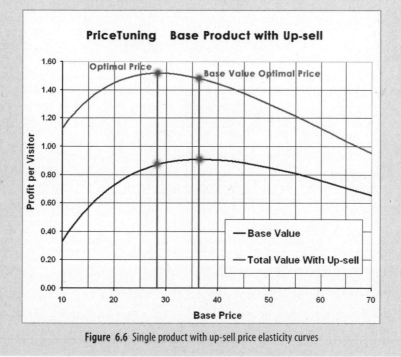

Figure 6.6 Single product with up-sell price elasticity curves

In the next chapter, we will switch gears and start looking at the "math" involved in tuning. So buckle up, and let's go!

The Math of Tuning

In the previous chapter you learned how to select elements for landing page tests. My focus was on how to pick elements that would have the greatest impact on your landing page performance. I am sure that you can't wait to get started.

But how do you interpret the results of your test? In order to understand the power and limitation of tuning methods, you first need to understand the basics of the underlying math.

Chapter Contents

Just Grin and Bear It

In this chapter we have to take a side trip into the wonderful land of mathematics. I know that many online marketers may have gotten into the field to *avoid* math. Nevertheless, you need to understand this material, because Internet marketing is about results. And results are about the numbers. Unfortunately, if you do not run your tests properly, or incorrectly analyze or interpret the results, you may come to erroneous or unsupported conclusions.

In this chapter, I will try to walk a tightrope. If you are already well versed in mathematics (or are actually an advanced statistician), I apologize in advance. You will probably find this chapter too elementary. In addition, you may think that I have oversimplified, garbled, or misrepresented the content. But my goal is to make sure that everyone has at least an understanding of the math of testing. So just grin and bear it.

If, on the other hand, you are not comfortable with even basic math, I also apologize in advance. I will try to summarize only the key concepts that you need to know, and keep formulas and numbers to a minimum. But, you can't properly conduct landing page tuning tests without understanding this background. I also guarantee that it will make the next chapter, "Tuning Methods," much easier to understand. So just grin and bear it.

Lies, Damn Lies, and Statistics

There are three kinds of numbers: lies, damned lies, and statistics.

—Mark Twain, quoting Benjamin Disraeli

The statistics branch of mathematics has a poor reputation among the public. Much of modern science and economics is based on it in a fundamental way. So is public policy. Since public policy is a matter of priorities and heated debate about the allocation of government budgets, statistics has gotten pulled into the fray to support or undermine various political positions. Unscrupulous or ignorant people have corrupted it for their own purposes.

While there is nothing wrong with statistics itself, there are many common misuses of it. In this section, I have surveyed these along with some implications for landing page tuning.

As additional background I recommend the book *Rival Hypotheses: Alternative Interpretations of Data Based Conclusions* by Schuyler W. Huck. This book presents one hundred short vignettes describing the results of various social sciences experiments as reported in popular media. After each story, the authors dissect the possible experimental problems that may cast doubt on, or completely invalidate, the reported results.

Throwing Away Part of the Data

Statistical studies are based on a confidence level in the answer (commonly 95%). If you conduct a large number of experiments, even two identical effects can seem different based simply on a statistical streak. For example, if you flipped a coin five times you might be surprised to see it come up heads every time, and might even suspect that it could be loaded. However, this is exactly the result that we would expect based simply on random chance about 3% of the time. So if this experiment was repeated one hundred times, a series of all-heads would be expected to come up about three times.

Unscrupulous people might rerun the experiment many times, and report a single all-heads result as proof that the coin was loaded. By discarding the remaining experiments that did not support their desired conclusion, they are misrepresenting the results.

As you will see in Chapter 8, "Tuning Methods," there are sometimes valid (or at least practical) reasons to hold out some of the data that you collect during a landing page test. But do not "cherry-pick" and only look for data that supports your conclusions.

Biased Samples

Statistics assumes that a random selection of test subjects was drawn from the population in question. However, samples can be biased by oversampling or undersampling from particular groups. In extreme cases, no representatives are drawn from a particular subset of the population.

For example, online or call-in polls are often skewed by definition. They represent self-selecting groups of people who are motivated enough to answer the polls. This usually implies that they have a strong opinion and want to express it. So these types of polls tend to produce more polarized results with a disproportionately large percentage of extreme views (at the expense of the more moderate outlook of the silent majority).

Traffic Filtering

In landing page testing, you generally want to get as wide a range of traffic sources as possible. That way, they are more likely to be representative of your visitor population as a whole. However, as I mentioned in Chapter 3, "Understanding Your Audience," you generally want traffic sources that are recurring, controllable, and stable. If your traffic does not have these characteristics, it may be very hard to tune. For this reason, you may want to remove unstable sources (such as some of your larger but highly variable affiliates) from your testing mix. You should also generally remove nonrecurring e-mail traffic.

Data Collection Method

So let's assume that you have picked appropriate filters for your traffic and are selecting the largest possible stable group among your population of visitors. If you have implemented your test properly, then each new visitor should be assigned at random to see one of the alternative versions of your landing page. However, even this sample may not be completely random because of technology considerations.

For example, SiteTuners.com's TuningEngine technology requires visitors to have JavaScript turned on in their Web browser, and to have them accept *first-party cookies* (small files left on their hard disk by your website containing information about their visit, which can be used to customize and personalize their experience upon return visits). If a visitor does not meet these technical criteria, they are not included in the test and are simply shown the original landing page.

Based on current Web usage statistics, our technical requirements disqualify fewer than 5% of Internet users. When our test is completed, we are forced to make some assumptions about how these people will react to our new page design. We assume that they will act like the other 95% that we are able to track. But this may not be true. Since they have JavaScript or first-party cookies turned off, they may represent a small, self-selecting group of people who are more cautious, technically savvy, or concerned with privacy. Such people may indeed behave differently than the rest of the population. As a practical matter, this does not change our recommendations very much. Since the missing 5% represents such a small segment, even a significant difference in their behavior will be overwhelmed by the much larger conversion rate improvements that we usually uncover. However, it is important to be aware of such technical sampling issues.

Sequential Testing

Another type of sampling bias can be introduced by sequential testing. For example, you may test your original design for a month, and then replace it with another one during the following month. It is hard to reach any kind of conclusions after this kind of experiment. Any number of external factors may have changed between the two testing periods. For example, there may have been a holiday with common family vacations, some major breaking news affected your industry, or you made a major public relations announcement. The point is, you are comparing apples to oranges. In landing page testing you should always try to collect data from your original version and your tested alternatives in *parallel*. This will allow you to control for (or at least detect and factor in) any changes in the external environment. Only use sequential testing as a last resort.

Short Data Collection

Even if you run your tests by splitting the available traffic and showing different versions of your site design in parallel, you may still run into biased sampling issues related to short data collection periods. Experiments involving very high data collection data rates may be especially prone to this.

For example, let's assume that you are testing two alternative versions of your page and are measuring click-throughs to a particular target page as your conversion action. Because of the high traffic to your landing page, you collect about 10,000 conversion actions in the first hour of your test. This data shows you that one of your versions outperforms the other to a very high level of statistical confidence. Many people would conclude the test at this point and immediately install the best performer as the new landing page.

But what if I were to tell you that the data was collected in the middle of the night? You might correctly conclude that people visiting your site during the day are a different population, or at least that they behave differently then. The same is true of weekday (accessing the Internet from work) versus weekend traffic (accessing the Internet from home). I suggest that regardless of your data rate you collect data for at least a one-week period (or multiple whole-week increments if your data rate is low). This will allow you to get rid of the short-term biases discussed earlier. Of course, this does not address the question of longer-term seasonality (which will be covered in more detail in the "Seasonality" section of Chapter 11).

Overgeneralization

Overgeneralization is the erroneous extension of your test conclusions to a setting where the original results no longer apply. For example, let's say that I set up an experiment to count the ants in my kitchen and tracked it for a full week during a record cold spell in the wintertime. My finding was that there were no ants in my kitchen at all during the study period. However, it would probably be incorrect to assume that the same would hold true during a heat wave in the summer. Often the overgeneralization is not made by the original researcher, but rather by those who subsequently summarize or cite the results.

A common overgeneralization in landing page testing is to assume that traffic sources that were not part of your original test will behave in the same way as the tested population. For example, if you see a particular effect with your PPC traffic, you should not assume that it will hold up when you expose the new landing page to your in-house e-mail list.

Loaded Questions

The answers that people give in surveys can be manipulated to skew the results in a certain direction. This is done by asking the question in a certain way, or preceding it with information that will support the desired answer.

For example, imagine a survey that is polling about support for a salary raise for local firefighters. Depending on which side of the issue the pollster was on, you might imagine two different questions:

- Given the chronic neglect of city streets and the rising crime rate due to the understaffing of our police force, do you support a raise for our firefighters at this time?

- After considering the extraordinary risks that firefighters face every day to protect your family and property, do you support a raise for our firefighters at this time?

In normal surveying, loaded questions and the context for how the information is presented can be a problem. But in landing page testing, we stand this whole premise on its head. We *want* to create loaded landing page content. In fact, our whole goal is to see what our audience responds to best. A cynic might even say that landing page testing is the scientific and systematic discovery of the best audience manipulations available to you.

False Causality

Correlation does not imply causation.
—Common scientific saying

This phrase does not use the word "imply" in its common sense (i.e., to suggest). The scientific sense of *implies* (taken from formal logic) can be better translated as *requires*. The phrase refers to a common error that people make. They assume that since two effects are related or occur together, one causes the other. This is not necessarily the case. There may be a third previously unrecognized lurking variable (also called a confounding variable, or confounding factor) that causes the other two.

For example, if I told you that the vast majority of car accidents occur within five miles of people's residence, you might be tempted to start taking the bus instead of driving. But it would be wrong to conclude that accidents are caused by the proximity to your home. There is a third confounding variable that could explain both: people do the vast majority of their driving close to home, and accidents are directly related to the time spent driving.

In landing page optimization, many people insist on extracting so-called "learnings" from their test results. Hindsight is used to rationalize why a particular landing page version had a higher conversion rate. For example, I may test two call-to-action buttons: orange and green. If the green one performs better, I may be tempted to conclude that my audience likes the color green more than orange. In fact, there may be another explanation: the contrast of the button color with the main color theme of the page. If my page was predominantly orange themed, the orange call-to-action button would seem muted and may get lost in a scene composed of similar colors. The green button color may stick out and seem more prominent because of its contrast, and not the actual color used.

There may also be more subtle issues relating to other design changes that were also made at the same time. For example, the green button may have been a different size, or perhaps it used a different color for the call-to-action text. It may have been these look-and-feel factors rather than the button color that increased the propensity of people to act.

Trying to rationalize results after the test is a dangerous activity because it may cause you to inappropriately fixate on elements of your design that had nothing to do with the performance improvement. You should try to restrain yourself from engaging in this kind of after-the-fact myth construction.

You Are Here

Let's go back to the roots of the statistics underlying landing page testing. Within the vast field of mathematics, I will guide you down to the specific subset that you will need to understand. Along the way, I will point out the specific relationship to landing page optimization. And since landing page testing is often a messy business, I will also flag where real-world considerations and issues deviate from the theoretical framework. This drill-down is a quick overview. You may need to do some additional background reading in the areas of probability and statistics.

Probability Theory

Probability theory is a branch of mathematics that deals with the description and analysis of random events. The key building blocks of this framework are as follows:

Random variables A *random variable* is a quantity whose value is random or unpredictable, and to which we can assign a probability distribution function. The *probability distribution function* determines the set of possible values that can be assigned to the random variable, along with their likelihood. The total of all possible outcomes' likelihood must by definition equal one (i.e., one of the possible outcomes must happen, and its value will be assigned to the random variable).

Let's use a fair gaming die as an example. The top face of the die can take on one of six possible outcomes (i.e., 1,2,3,4,5,6). The probability distribution function is uniform (i.e., there is an equal one-in-six chance of any value between 1 and 6 coming up). When you sum up all of the possible probabilities, they add up to exactly one.

Stochastic processes There are two kinds of processes considered in probability theory: deterministic and stochastic. A *deterministic process* will go along a set path depending on its starting conditions. In other words, if you know where it starts, you can exactly compute where it will end up at some point in the future.

A *stochastic process* (also called a random process) is more difficult to understand. You cannot tell exactly where it will end up, but you know (based on its probability distribution function) that certain outcomes are more likely. In the simplest case, a stochastic process can be described as a sequence of samples from random variables. If these samples can be associated with particular points in time, it is a *time series* (a series of data points that were measured at successive times).

In our die example, the stochastic process is the repeated roll of the die. Each roll will produce a random variable outcome (one of the six possible values), and successive rolls are independent of each other (what was rolled on the previous attempt has no influence on the likelihood of any particular number coming up on the next roll).

Events An *event* in probability theory is a set of all possible outcomes to which a probability is assigned (also called the sample set). In the simplest case, the set of possible outcomes is finite. Each of the basic possible outcomes is called an elementary event, but more complex events can be constructed by selecting larger groupings of elementary events (a proper subset of the sample space).

In our die example, the elementary events are individual possible values of a die roll. But we can also construct other events and assign the proper probabilities to them (e.g., an even roll of the die—with a probability of one-half—or a roll with a value greater than 4—with a probability of one-third).

Probability Applied to Landing Page Testing

So how does all of this apply to landing page optimization?

The random variables are the visits to your site from the traffic sources that you have selected for the test. As I have already mentioned, the audience itself may be subject to sampling bias. The probability distribution function is pretty simple in most cases. You are counting whether or not the conversion happened as a result of the visit. You are assuming that there is some underlying and fixed probability of the conversion happening, and that the only other possible outcome is that the conversion does not happen (that is, a visit is a Bernoulli random variable that can result in conversion, or not).

As an example, let's assume that the actual conversion rate for a landing page is 2%. So there is a small chance that the conversion will happen (2%), and a much larger chance that it will not (98%) for any particular visitor. As you can see, the sum of the two possible outcome probabilities exactly equals 1 (2% + 98% = 100%) as required.

The stochastic process is the flow of visitors from the traffic sources used for the test. Key assumptions about the process are that the behavior of the visitors does not change over time, and that the population from which visitors are drawn remains the same. Unfortunately, both of these are routinely violated to a greater or lesser extent in the real world. The behavior of visitors changes due to seasonal factors, or with changing sophistication and knowledge levels about your products or industry. The population itself changes based on your current marketing mix. Most businesses are constantly adjusting and tweaking their traffic sources (e.g., by changing PPC bid prices and the resulting keyword mix that their audience arrives from). The result is that your time series, which is supposed to return a steady stream of yes or no answers (based on a fixed probability of a conversion), actually has a changing probability of conversion. In mathematical terms, your time series is *nonstationary* and changes its behavior over time.

The independence of the random variables in the stochastic process is also a critical theoretical requirement. However, the behavior on each visit is not necessarily independent. A person may come back to your landing page a number of times, and their current behavior would obviously be influenced by their previous visits. You might also have a bug or an overload condition where the actions of some users influence the actions that other users can take. For this reason it is best to use a fresh stream of visitors (with a minimal percentage of repeat visitors if possible) for your landing page test audience. Repeat visitors are by definition biased because they have *voluntarily chosen* to return to your site, and are not seeing it for the first time *at random*. This is also a reason to avoid using landing page testing with an audience consisting of your in-house e-mail list. The people on the list are biased because they have self-selected to receive ongoing messages from you, and because they have already been exposed to previous communications.

The event itself can also be more complicated than the simple did-the-visitor-convert determination. In an e-commerce catalog, it is important to know not only whether a sale happened, but also its value. If you were to tune only for higher conversion rate, you could achieve that by pushing low-margin and low-cost products that people are more likely to buy. But this would not necessarily result in the highest profits. Many of our engagements at SiteTuners.com involve tuning for the highest possible revenue per visitor (or profit per visitor after considering the variable costs of the conversion action). For these kinds of situations, you need to consider real-valued random variables and their cumulative distribution functions. That discussion is more involved and is beyond the scope of this book.

Law of Large Numbers

The *law of large numbers* states that if a random variable with an underlying probability (p) is observed repeatedly during independent experiments, the ratio of the *observed* frequency of that event to the total number of experiments will converge to p.

Let's continue with our die rolling example. The law of large numbers guarantees that if we roll the die enough times, the percentage of sixes rolled will approach exactly 1/6 of the total number of rolls (i.e., its expected percentage in the probability distribution function). An intuitive way of understanding this is that over the long run, any streaks of rolling non-sixes will eventually be counteracted by streaks of rolling extra sixes.

The exciting thing about this law is that it ties something that you can *observe* (the actual conversion percentage in our test) to the unknown underlying *actual* conversion rate of your landing page. It guarantees the stable long-term results of the random visitor events.

However, before you start celebrating, it is important to realize that this law is based on a *very* large number of samples, and only guarantees that you will over the long term *eventually* come close to the actual conversion rate. In reality, your knowledge of the actual conversion rate will accumulate slowly.

Moreover, the law of large numbers does not guarantee that you will converge to the correct answer with a small amount of data. In fact, it almost guarantees that over a short period of time, your estimate of conversion rate will be incorrect. Short-term streaks can and do cause conversion rates to significantly deviate from the true value.

The best way to look at this situation is to keep in mind that collecting more data allows you to make increasingly more accurate estimates of the true underlying conversion rate. However, your estimate will always be subject to some error; moreover, you can only know approximate bounds on the size of this error.

The Normal Distribution

The *Gaussian*, or *normal*, distribution (also called the *bell curve* because of its characteristic shape) occurs commonly in observations about science and nature. The exact shape and position of the bell curve is defined by two parameters: the position of its center point, and how wide it is. The bell curve can be tall and almost needle-like, or a wide low smudge (as shown in Figure 7.1).

Mean (μ) The *mean* is the sum of all of the random variables divided by the number of random variables observed. It also commonly called the "average" value.

Variance (σ^2) The *variance* shows how spread out or scattered the values are around the mean. If they are tightly clustered, then the variance is lower. If they are very spread out, then the variance is higher.

Standard deviation (σ) A standard deviation is defined as the square root of the variance. It is often more useful than the variance itself since it is directly comparable to the underlying measurement.

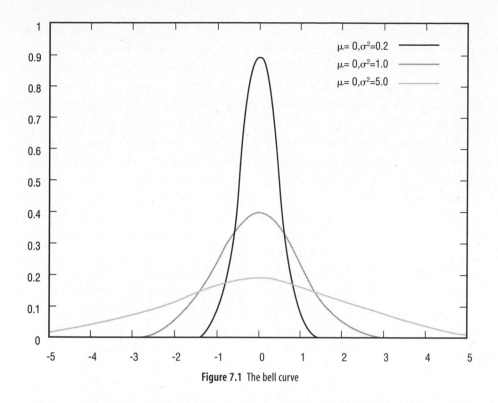

Figure 7.1 The bell curve

The *unit* normal distribution is a special case of the more general Gaussian distribution. Basically, a particular Gaussian distribution can be standardized (by moving its mean to zero and magnifying or shrinking it so that it has standard deviation equal to 1). Normalizing a particular bell curve allows us to easily compare its properties to those of other bell curves. The area contained under any normal distribution is always one by definition.

The 68-95-99.7 rule (also called the *empirical rule*) tells us that for a normal distribution almost all values lie within three standard deviations of the mean (see Figure 7.2).

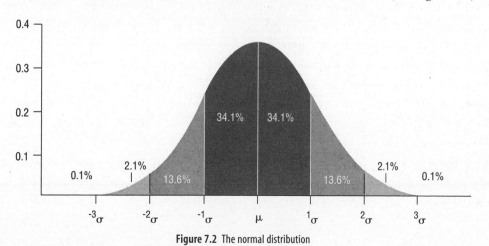

Figure 7.2 The normal distribution

About 68% of the values are within one standard deviation of the mean ($\mu \pm \sigma$). About 95% of the values are within two standard deviations of the mean ($\mu \pm 2\sigma$). About 99.7% of the values lie within three standard deviations of the mean ($\mu \pm 3\sigma$). For many scientific and engineering purposes, the 95% confidence limit is commonly used as the dividing line for making decisions. In other words, if your answer falls into the plus or minus two standard deviation band around a predicted value, it is considered to be consistent with the prediction.

The Central Limit Theorem

The *Central Limit Theorem* tells us that regardless of the distribution that the original random variables were drawn from, if that distribution has a finite variance their *average* will tend to conform to the normal distribution. This is the case across a wide range of real processes, including data collection in landing page testing.

The Central Limit Theorem assures us that the conversion rate estimate that we observe for a particular landing page design will look like a normal distribution. This allows us to estimate the probable range of values for the actual underlying conversion rate. The more data we collect, the tighter our estimate will become.

Statistical Methods

One of the common questions answered by statistics is whether there is a relationship between some predictors (independent variables) and the response or resulting effects (the dependent variables). Often, our experiments can be arranged so that when we detect such a relationship, we can say that changes in the independent variables *caused* the changes in the dependent variables. There are two main types of statistical studies:

Experimental studies In *experimental studies* you first take measurements of the environment that you are studying. You then change the environment in a preplanned way and see if the changes have resulted in a different outcome than before.

Landing page testing is a form of experimental study. The environment that you are changing is the design of your landing page. The outcome that you are measuring is typically the conversion rate. As I mentioned earlier, landing page testing and tuning is usually done in parallel, and not sequentially. This means that you should split your available traffic and randomly alternate the version of your landing page shown to each new visitor. A portion of your test traffic should always see the original version of the page. This will eliminate many of the problems with sequential testing.

Observational studies Observational studies, by contrast, do not involve any manipulation or changes to the environment in question. You simply gather the data and then analyze it for any interesting correlations between your independent and dependent variables.

For example, you may be running PPC marketing programs on two different search engines. You collect data for a month on the total number of clicks from each campaign and the resulting number of conversions. You can then see if the conversion rate between the two traffic sources is truly different or possibly due to chance.

The basic steps of any scientific experiment are well known. I have summarized them next with notes on their applicability to landing page tuning. Chapter 10, "Developing Your Action Plan," covers these steps and all of the other required landing page testing activities in more detail.

Plan the research Determine the landing page to tune, your traffic sources for the test, and the traffic levels available. Understand and try to correct for or eliminate any sampling biases among your population.

Design the experiment Create a written test plan that explicitly lays out the alternative landing page elements that you intend to test (your independent variables). Define the performance measurement that you will be trying to improve (typically the conversion rate for a key process on the landing page).

Collect the data You will need to collect the number of visits or impressions for your test pages as well as the number and value of any conversions.

Summarize the data Use descriptive statistics (see next section) to summarize your findings. Hide unnecessary levels of detail.

Draw conclusions Use inferential statistics (see next section) to see what information can be gleaned from your data sample about the underlying population of visitors on your landing page. Normally this would involve statistical tests to see if any of your alternative landing page designs are better than the original.

Present the results Document and present the results of your experiment. This can be a casual e-mail or a detailed formal report, depending on your circumstances and purpose.

Applied Statistics

Statistical theory (also known as *mathematical statistics*) is based on probability theory and mathematical analysis, and is used to understand the theoretical basis of statistics. Applied statistics falls into two basic types:

Descriptive statistics *Descriptive statistics* is used to summarize or describe a collection of data. This can be done numerically or graphically. Basic numerical descriptions include the mean, median, mode, variance, and standard deviation. Graphical summaries include various kinds of graphs and charts.

Inferential statistics *Inferential statistics* is used to reach conclusions that go beyond the specific data that you have collected. In effect, you are trying to infer the behavior of the larger process or population from which you drew your test sample. Examples of possible inferences include answers to yes-or-no questions (hypothesis testing), as well as other techniques like Analysis of Variance (ANOVA), regression analysis, and many other multivariate methods such as cluster analysis, multidimensional scaling, and factor analysis.

Both types of applied statistics are commonly used in landing page testing and tuning. Unfortunately, descriptive statistics are often viewed as a substitute for the proper inferential tests, and are used to make decisions. Remember, descriptive statistics only summarize or describe the data that you have observed. They do not tell you anything about the meaning or implications of your observations. Proper hypothesis testing must be done to see if differences in your data are likely to be due to random chance or are truly significant.

Have I Found Something Better?

Landing page optimization is based on statistics, and statistics is based in turn on probability theory. And probability theory is concerned with the study of random events. But a lot of people might object that the behavior of your landing page visitors is not "random." Your visitors are not as simple as the roll of a die. They visit your landing page for a reason, and act (or fail to act) based on their own internal motivations.

So what does probability mean in this context?

Let's conduct a little thought experiment. Imagine that I am about to flip a fair coin. It has the potential to be in one of two states (heads or tails). What would you estimate the probability of it coming up heads to be? Fifty percent, right? So would I.

Now imagine that I have flipped the coin and covered up the result after catching it in my hand. The process of flipping is now complete, and the coin has taken on one particular state. Now what would you estimate the probability of it coming up heads to be? Fifty percent again, right? I would agree because neither of us knows any more than before the coin was flipped.

Now imagine if I peeked at the coin without letting you see it. What would you estimate the probability of it coming up heads to be? Still 50%, right? How about me? I would no longer agree with you. Having seen the outcome of the flip event I would declare that the probability of coming up heads is either zero or 100% (depending on what I have seen).

How can we experience the same event and come to two different conclusions? Who is correct? The answer is—both of us. We are basing our answers on different available information. Not having seen the outcome of the flip, you must assume that the coin can still come up heads. In effect, for you the coin has not been flipped, but rather remains in a state of pre-flipped potential. I on the other hand know more, so my answer is different. So probability can be viewed as simply taking the best guess given the available information. The more information you have, the more accurate your guess will become.

Let's look at this in the context of the simplest type of landing page optimization. Let's assume that you have a constant flow of visitors to your landing page from a steady and unchanging traffic source. You decide to test two versions of your page design, and split your traffic evenly and randomly between them.

In statistical terminology, you have two stochastic processes (experiences with your landing pages), with their own random variables (visitors drawn from the same population), and their own measurable binary events (either visitors convert or they do not). The true probability of conversion for each page is not known, but must be between zero and one. This true probability of conversion is what we call the conversion rate and we assume that it is fixed.

From the law of large numbers you know as you sample a very large number of visitors, the measured conversion rate will approach the true probability of conversion. From the Central Limit Theorem you also know that the chances of the actual value falling within three standard deviations of your observed mean are very high (99.7%), and that the width of the normal distribution will continue to narrow (depending only on the amount of data that you have collected). Basically, measured conversion rates will wander within ever narrower ranges as they get closer and closer to their true respective conversion rates. By seeing the amount of overlap between the two bell curves representing the normal distributions of the conversion rate, you can determine the likelihood of one version of the page being better than the other.

One of the most common questions in inferential statistics is to see if two samples are really different or if they could have been drawn from the same underlying population as a result of random chance alone. You can compare the average performance between two groups by using a t-test computation. In landing page testing, this kind of analysis would allow you to compare the difference in conversion rate between two versions of your site design. Let's suppose that your new version had a higher conversion rate than the original. The t-test would tell you if this difference was likely due to random chance or if the two were actually different.

There is a whole family of related t-test formulas based on the circumstances. The appropriate one for head-to-head landing page optimization tests is the *unpaired one-tailed equal-variance t-test*. The test produces a single number as its output. The higher this number is, the higher the statistical certainty that the two outcomes being measured are truly different. Lest you be scared by the imposing name of the test, let me assure you that it is very easy to compute and requires only basic spreadsheet formulas.

How Sure Do I Need to Be?

Online marketers often make the mistake of looking only at the descriptive statistics for their test and neglect to even do basic inferential statistics to see if their answers are due simply to random chance. They often do not have the knowledge or discipline to specify the desired confidence in their answer ahead of time, and to patiently collect enough data until that level of confidence is reached.

There are three common issues associated with lack of statistical confidence.

Collecting Insufficient Data

Early in an experiment when you have only collected a relatively small amount of data, the measured conversion rates may fluctuate wildly. If the first visitor for one of the page designs happens to convert, for instance, your measured conversion rate is 100%. It is tempting to draw conclusions during this early period, but doing so commonly leads to error. Just as you would not conclude a coin could never come up tails after seeing it come up heads just three times, you should not pick a page design before collecting enough data.

What many people forget is that there can (and should) be short-term streaks that significantly skew the conversion rates in low data situations. Remember, the laws of probability only guarantee the accuracy and stability of results for very large sample sizes. For smaller sample sizes, a lot of slop and uncertainty remain.

The way to deal with this is to decide on your desired confidence level ahead of time. How sure do you want to be in your answer—90%, 95%, 99%, even higher? This completely depends on your business goals and the consequences of being wrong. If a lot of money is involved, you should probably insist on higher confidence levels.

Let's consider the simplest example. You are trying to decide whether version A or B is best. You have split your traffic equally to test both options and have gotten 90 conversions on A, and 100 conversions on B. Is B really better than A? Many people would answer yes since 100 is obviously higher than 90. But the statistical reality is not so clear-cut.

Confidence in your answer can be expressed by means of a *Z-score*, which is easy to calculate in cases like this. The Z-score tells you how many standard deviations away from the observed mean your data is. In other words, it is the same as the number of standard deviations in the test's normal distribution. The Z-score therefore follows the 68-95-99.7 rule that I discussed earlier. Z=1 means that you are 67% sure of your answer, Z=2 means 95.28% sure, and Z=3 means 99.74% sure.

Pick an appropriate confidence level, and then wait to collect enough data to reach it.

Let's pick a 95% confidence level for our earlier example. This means that you want to be right 19 out of 20 times. So you will need to collect enough data to get a Z-score of 2 or more.

The calculation of the Z-score depends on the standard deviation (σ). For conversion rates that are less than 30%, this formula is fairly accurate:

$$\sigma = \sqrt{(\text{Conversions})}$$

In our example for B, the standard deviation would be calculated as follows:

$$\sigma = \sqrt{(100)} = 10$$

So we are 67% sure (Z=1) that the real value of B is between 90 and 110 (100 plus or minus 10). In other words, there is a one out of three chance that A is actually bigger than the lower end of the estimated range, and we may just be seeing a lucky streak for B.

Similarly at our current data amounts we are 95% sure (Z=2) that the real value of B is between 80 and 120 (100 plus or minus 20). So there is a good chance that the 90 conversions on A are actually better than the bottom end estimate of 80 for B.

Confidence levels are often illustrated with a graph. The *error bars* on the quantity being measured represent the range of possible values (the confidence interval) that would be include results within the selected confidence level. Figure 7.3 shows 95% confidence error bars (represented by the dashed lines) for our example. As you can see, the bottom of B's error bars is higher than the top of A's error bars. This implies that A might actually be higher than B, despite B's current streak of good luck in the current sample.

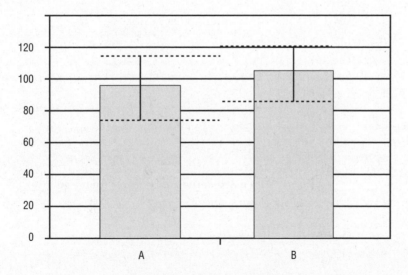

Figure 7.3 Confidence error bars (little data)

If we wanted to be 95% sure that B is better than A, we would need to collect much more data. In our example, this level of confidence would be reached when A had 1,350 conversions and B had 1,500 conversions. Note that even though the ratio between A and B remains the same, the standard deviations have gotten much smaller, thus raising the Z-score. As you can see from Figure 7.4, the confidence error bars have now "uncrossed," so you can be 95% confident that B actually is better than A.

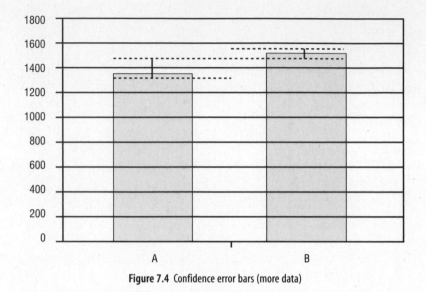

Figure 7.4 Confidence error bars (more data)

All of this may all seem a little intimidating at first, but the math for these calculations can easily be programmed into a spreadsheet formula. After that, you just plug in the current test numbers and see if your desired confidence level has been reached yet. Believe me; this is preferable to making wrong decisions one-third of the time as you might have done in this section's example.

Confusing Significance with Importance

In the preceding section I discussed how people often want to believe that large effects are statistically significant when they do not have enough data to support such a conclusion. Because of their lack of statistical literacy, many people also make the converse mistake—they believe that just because they have found something statistically significant, it is also practically important.

The word "significant" in statistical terms means only that you have high enough confidence in your answer. It does not mean that the effect found in your test is large or important. If you collect a large enough data sample, even tiny differences can be found to be statistically significant. Most people would probably not get excited if the difference between two landing page versions on which they collected test data for a long time turned out to be extremely small (yet significant to the required confidence level).

Even if you reach a high level of statistical confidence, you may not have found an effect that is interesting in practical terms.

Understanding the Results

The *null hypothesis* in probability and statistics is the starting assumption that nothing other than random chance is operating to create the observed effect that you see in a particular set of data. Basically it assumes that the measured effects are the same across the independent conditions being tested. There are no differences or relationships between these independent variables and the dependent outcomes—equal until proven otherwise.

The null hypothesis is *rejected* if your data set is unlikely to have been produced by chance. The significance of the results is described by the confidence level that was defined by the test (as described by the acceptable error "alpha-level"). For example, it is harder to reject the null hypothesis at 99% confidence (alpha 0.01) than at 95% confidence (alpha 0.05).

Even if the null hypothesis is rejected at a certain confidence level, no alternative hypothesis is proven thereby. The only conclusion you can draw is that some effect is going on. But you do not know its cause. If the experiment was designed properly, the only things that changed were the experimental conditions. So it is logical to attribute a causal effect to them.

However, as I have already discussed, there are often subtle and gross sampling bias and test design errors in landing page optimization, and the documented effects can also be attributed to these. Under such conditions you can only strictly state that there is a high degree of correlation between the tested changes and the corresponding outcomes, but not true causality. Having said that, online marketing is an applied discipline that has to earn its keep, so don't let such considerations dissuade you from using statistics to run your tests. I just feel obliged to point out the specific deviations from the pure underlying math.

What if the null hypothesis is not rejected? This simply means that you did not find any statistically significant differences. That is not the same as stating that there was no difference. Remember, accepting the null hypothesis merely means that the observed differences *might* have been due simply to random chance, not that they *must* have been. Statistics cannot prove that there was no difference between two test conditions. The absence of evidence for a difference does not provide any evidence for the notion that no difference exists.

How Much Better Is It?

Internet marketing produces a detailed and quantifiable view of your online campaign activities. As I discussed earlier, most of numbers produced fall under the general category of descriptive statistics. Descriptive statistics produces summaries and graphs of your data that can be used for making decisions. The descriptive information has to do with the value of a particular quantity as well as its variability (how scattered it is). Unfortunately, most people focus only on the measured average value and completely ignore the variability. This is a major problem that continues to persist because people confuse the precision of the *observed effects* (the ability to measure conversions during the test), with the precision of the describing the *underlying system* (the ability to draw conclusions and make predictions about your landing page visitor population as a whole). You should not generally quote the observed improvement as a certainty. Even though you've observed an exactly computable conversion rate improvement percentage, you don't know what it really is for your visitor population as a whole.

> Exact measurement of observable effects does not imply that you know anything about the underlying process.

By itself, the mean of an observed value can be misleading, especially at small sample sizes. The situation gets even murkier if you are trying to model two separate means (each with its own variance). The situation gets downright ugly if you are trying to compute a ratio of such numbers. Yet this is exactly what is required to estimate a percentage improvement between two landing page versions.

Figure 7.5 shows the results of a small landing page test conducted by the e-zine Marketing Experiments Journal (www.marketingexperiments.com).

Page Layout Optimization Micro-Test		
Metric	Page A	Page B
Unique Visitors	2478	2384
Orders	36	65
Conversion Rate	1.45%	2.73%

✓ **What You Need To UNDERSTAND:** Conversion of Page B (one column) was 88% better than that of Page A (two columns).

Figure 7.5 Summary and conclusions from a Marketing Experiments Journal landing page test

Based on a sample size of 36 conversions for page A and 65 conversions for page B, you are told to conclude that the conversion rate improvement is 88%. Indeed, I would probably be happy with such a result. But let's take a closer look.

Let's assume that you want a 95% confidence in your answer. This corresponds to a Z-score of 2, meaning that the number must fall within two standard deviations of the observed mean. If you compute the 95% confidence interval numbers on the number of conversions for both landing pages, you will find the following:

Page A: 36 ± 12 (the interval from 24 to 48)

Page B: 65 ± 16 (the interval from 49 to 81)

Let's take a look at the best case scenario:

Conversions: A = 24, B = 81

Conversion rates: A = 0.97%, B = 3.40%

Conversion rate improvement: 251%

Now let's take a look at the worst case scenario:

Conversions: A = 48, B = 49

Conversion rates: A = 1.94%, B = 2.06%

Conversion rate improvement: 6.2%

There is some rationale for reporting the conversion rate improvement based on the ratio of the means. Since more of the mass of the normal distributions lies close to the mean, the actual numbers are more likely to be near it. However, this should not be used as a reason to abandon the use of error bars or confidence intervals. Both the 6.2% and 251% conversion rate improvements are within the realm of possibility based on the confidence level that you had selected. There is a huge range of possible outcomes simply because the sample size is so small.

> To focus only on the observed improvement and to report it as a certain quantity is problematic, especially for small sample sizes.

Marketing Experiments Journal typically provides solid online marketing education and conducts well-designed landing page tests. All online marketing educators are walking a fine line (myself included). We are trying to get at least a basic level of mathematical literacy across to our audiences. However, if the going gets too rough, many online marketers will just tune out and give up on the math altogether. I am somewhat torn. On the one hand, "half a loaf is better than none" and it is good to use some kind of statistical benchmarks. On the other hand, "a little knowledge is a dangerous thing" and can be easily misapplied during landing page optimization.

At SiteTuners.com we have also been guilty of oversimplifying. We often report public case study results as a simple percentage improvement. However, in our defense the amount of data collected in a typical SiteTuners.com test is very high, and the consequent error bars are narrow. We also provide detailed statistical reporting and analyses of the results to our clients.

The bottom line is this: take the time and care to properly collect and analyze your data. When faced with uncertain measurements (basically all of the time), display them with error bars or confidence ranges.

How Long Should My Test Run?

I am often asked how long a landing page optimization test should last. The answer depends on the following factors:

- The data rate (number of conversions per day)
- Size of improvements found (percentage improvement)

- Size of your test (number of alternative designs)
- The confidence in your answer (how sure you need to be)

I have already covered the last factor in the "How Sure Do I Need to Be?" section. Let's take a look at the other ones next.

Data Rate

The data rate describes how quickly you collect data during your test. Many people are familiar with common metrics of Web traffic such as the number of page views or the number of unique visitors. The volume of traffic for landing page optimization tests is best measured in the number of conversion actions per day (and not the number of unique visitors).

Another way of thinking about this is that conversions are very scarce and are the limiting factor. Unique visitors are relatively plentiful and do not tell you anything by themselves. You are simply splitting them up randomly and showing them different versions of the landing page. Websites with low conversion rates require more visitors to reach valid statistical conclusions.

A significant portion of your testing bandwidth (typically 15–50% depending on your circumstances) should also be directed to the original or *control* version of your website. This allows you to compare the performance of alternative recipes against a known baseline, even if that baseline continues to move around due to seasonal factors.

Probabilistic tests yield results slowly and require a lot of conversions to find the best results. In Chapter 8, I will give some guidelines for minimum data rates that are appropriate for different tuning methods.

So what can you do if your data rate is too low and there are no additional traffic sources available?

You can decrease the size of your test. As discussed in the previous chapter, this can be done by decreasing the granularity of your test elements. In the simplest case, you may have to run a simple head-to-head test of your original page and one alternative version. The coarsest possible level is to do a comprehensive redesign of your landing page (with all of your best alternative design ideas included in it).

Another strategy is to measure different conversion actions. Sometimes, more plentiful measurable actions occur *upstream* of your current one. Since there are more of them, these intermediate actions can be used to bulk up your data rate. For example, your e-commerce catalog may have too few sales, and your shopping cart abandonment rate is 90%. This implies that you have ten times as many shopping cart "puts" as sales. This allows you to tune the main catalog experience up to the point that a visitor puts an item in their cart. If you assume that the shopping cart abandonment rate does not change, you can assign 10% of the average sale value on your site to each shopping cart put. You can then run your test and count the more numerous puts as the conversion action.

Size of Improvements Found

If you managed to uncover a clearly superior version of your landing page, the performance improvement would quickly become apparent. Often, an initial round of changes will fix some of the obvious problems and improve performance significantly. This will leave you with more subtle improvements in subsequent tuning tests. The cumulative impact of several small improvements (in the 1–5% range) can still be very significant. However, it can take much longer to be able to validate these smaller effects to the desired confidence level. Since you do not know the size of the possible improvements ahead of time, the length of the time required for the tuning test may vary significantly.

Of course, the amount of data collected also influences whether the difference found is considered significant. Table 7.1 shows the size of effects that can be reliably identified (to a 95% confidence level) at various sample sizes.

▶ **Table 7.1** Size of Improvements and Sample Sizes Required to Identify Them at a 95% Confidence Level

Sample Size	Size of Improvement
100	20%
1,000	6.3%
10,000	2%
100,000	0.63%

As you can see, resolving small effects requires a lot more data.

You typically know your available data rate, and need to decide on an acceptable length of data collection for your test. Let's assume that you have about 500 conversions per month and are willing to spend two months on data collection. As a rough guide based on Table 7.1, you will be able to identify 6.3% improvement effects in your head-to-head test. Any found improvements smaller than that will be deemed inconclusive.

Size of Your Test

The size of your test can be measured by the size of the search space that you are considering. The search space is the whole universe of alternative designs possible in your test. A simple head-to-head test has a search space size of 2 (the original, and the alternative landing page version that you are testing). If you are testing multiple elements on the page, you need to multiply together the number of alternative versions for each one. For example, if you are testing three headlines, four offers, and six button colors, then there are 72 possible versions ($3 \times 4 \times 6 = 72$) in your test. As you increase the total number of elements and the number of alternatives for each one, the possible number of versions grows very quickly (geometrically).

The amount of data required to reach conclusions scales with the size of your search space. As you will see in Chapter 8, many testing approaches cannot practically be used in tests beyond a few dozen total recipes because they would require too much time to reach a reasonable confidence level. Since you can control the size of your search space, it is usually scaled to your data rate and the tuning method that you have chosen in order to complete in the allotted amount of time while still finding reasonable size effects.

Variable Interactions

A player who makes a team great is much more valuable than a great player.
—UCLA Coach John Wooden

When professional basketball players were allowed to play in the Olympic Games, the United States assembled a "dream team" from the ranks of top NBA superstars. The expectation was that this high-powered assembly of top talent would walk all over their competition. However, the United States lost in the gold-medal match to Yugoslavia.

How could this have happened? Clearly the individual U.S. players were superior to their Yugoslav counterparts. But the Yugoslav squad had trained together and was used to playing by the slightly different rules of Olympic basketball. By contrast, the U.S. team was assembled shortly before the games and had not practiced very much. They had not "jelled" as a team. Similarly, some of the landing page elements that you may be testing may be superstars *individually*. But you should be looking for the *combination* of variables that performs best when presented together.

What is a *variable interaction*? Simply put, it is when the setting for one variable in your test positively or negatively influences the setting of another variable. If they have no effect on each other, they are said to be *independent*. In a *positive interaction*, two (or more) variables create a synergistic effect (yielding results that are greater than the sum of the parts). In a *negative interaction*, two (or more) variables undercut each other and cancel out some of the individual effects.

Let's look at a simple example. Let's assume that you are an auto dealer who sells both Ferrari and Volvos. Your goal is to sell cars and you want to test two different headlines and two different accompanying pictures. So there are a total of four possible versions based on your two variables.

If you believe that there are no interactions, then you must also believe that there is a "best" headline regardless of the accompanying picture, and that there is a "best" picture regardless of the headline used.

Clearly this is not the case. Each variable depends on the *context* in which it is seen. Figure 7.6 has a strong positive interaction (connecting the speed and power in the picture with the word "Fast" in the headline).

Figure 7.6 Example ad: Picture A, Headline A

Figure 7.7 has a strongly negative interaction (making you think about the consequences of fast driving—"speed kills").

Figure 7.7 Example ad: Picture B, Headline A

Figure 7.8 has a mildly positive interaction (supporting the notion that you can go fast and still be safe).

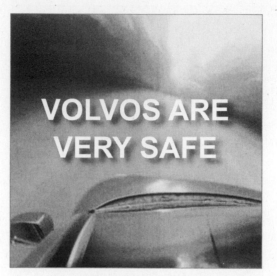

Figure 7.8 Example ad: Picture A, Headline B

Figure 7.9 has a positive interaction (playing on the fear of accidents and highlighting Volvo's longstanding safety record).

Figure 7.9 Example ad: Picture B, Headline B

So it's not the picture, and it's not the headline that determines the performance of the ad. It is their particular *combination*.

In online marketing, we *want* interactions. We want the picture to reinforce the headline, and the sales copy, and the offer, and the call-to-action... Similarly, we want to detect any parts of the landing page that are working at cross-purposes and undercutting the performance of other page elements. Our goal should be to find the best performing *group* of landing page elements.

As you will see in Chapter 8, some tuning methods (such as A-B split testing and many forms of fractional factorial multivariate testing) assume that there *are absolutely no interactions* among your variables (that they are completely independent of each other).

Obviously for online marketing this is an absurd assumption. Very strong interaction effects (often involving more than two variables) definitely exist, and in SiteTuners.com's experience are pretty common. So while you may be able to get some positive results by ignoring interactions, you will not be getting the *best* results.

So where can you look for interactions? In general, there is no way to guarantee that any subset of your testing elements does not interact. However, you should consider elements that are in physical proximity, or that are otherwise confounded with each other. For example, let's assume that you are testing a form and have chosen to test the call-to-action button color and text. Although these may seem independent, that is not the case. They both combine to create the specific presentation of the call-to-action, and you should test for possible interactions.

Similarly, if you are testing different headlines followed by different sales copy, you should expect interactions. The headline is supposed to draw the visitor into reading further. If there is a disconnect between the headline and the following text, you can expect negative interactions. If they reinforce each other, you should expect positive synergies. So far I have primarily focused on interactions between two test elements. In fact, there are often strong interactions among several variables on a landing page. I will revisit this topic again in the "Variable Interactions" section of Chapter 11, "Avoiding the Pitfalls."

In the next chapter, you will learn how to apply your general understanding of statistics to the common tuning methods available for landing page optimization. You will explore the strengths and weaknesses of each method, as well as their hidden assumptions.

Tuning Methods

If the only tool you have is a hammer,
then every problem will start to look
like a nail.
—Common proverb

Each tuning method has its own advantages, limi-
tations, and hidden assumptions. The one that
you choose will greatly influence the granularity
of your test elements, the size of your test, the
ability to uncover important variable interactions,
and the quality of your results.

In this chapter I will introduce common testing
terminology and test design issues. You will also
learn how to choose the tuning method that is
right for your test.

Chapter Contents
Introduction to Tuning
Common Tuning Issues
Overview of Tuning Methods
A-B Split Testing
Multivariate Testing

Introduction to Tuning

Before I discuss common testing methods, you need to understand some common concepts and definitions used in landing page testing. Members of the testing community refer to the same concepts but use different language to describe them. I will note such cases as appropriate, and will use the terminology interchangeably for the remainder of this book.

As I discussed in the previous chapter, the primary objective of landing page testing is to predict the behavior of your audience given the specific content on the landing page that they see. You will collect a limited sample of data during your test, summarize and describe it (descriptive statistics), and predict how people from the same traffic sources will act when interacting with the page (inferential statistics). In other words, the ultimate goal is to find the best possible version of the landing page among all of the variations that you are testing.

Input and Output Variables

A landing page test has two basic components: a set of *input variables* (also called "independent variables") that you can control and manipulate, and one or more *output variables* (or "dependent variables") that you measure and observe. Note that what I mean by "independent variables" here is not the same as in the discussion of variable interactions in the previous chapter. Independent variables as discussed here are simply the tuning elements that you have chosen for your test.

Variable

The word *variable* (when used by itself) means a tuning element that you have selected. As I mentioned in Chapter 6, "Selecting Elements to Tune," variables can be of any granularity or coarseness. For example, a variable might be the headline of your landing page, or a whole-page redesign. In multivariate testing, a variable is also commonly referred to as a *factor*.

In a multivariate test, you will have more than one variable. To distinguish among them I will use the following notation: a capital "V" followed by the number that you have assigned to a particular variable. For example, let's assume that you have a simple landing page with a headline, some sales copy test, and a call-to-action on a button (see Figure 8.1). You might decide to test alternatives to each of these page elements and name them as follows:

V1 = Headline
V2 = Sales copy
V3 = Button text
V4 = Button color

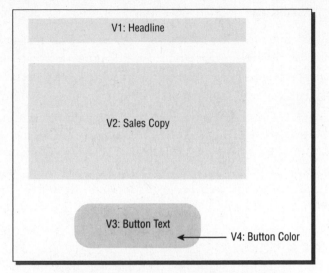

Figure 8.1 Sample landing page layout with variable locations

Note that the variables do not necessarily define a unique physical location on the page. In fact, V3 (the button text) and V4 (the button color) actually occupy the same space. Nor do they have to be localized. For example, I can choose a variable to test a larger font size (for improved readability) versus an existing smaller one. In this case, the font size change would take effect throughout my whole landing page and would overlap with other variables (such as the actual text on the page) that I might also be testing.

Value

A value is a particular *state* that a variable can take on.

When traditional multivariate testing is used in other fields, variable values are often *continuous* (which means they can vary smoothly across a range). This allows you to predict the behavior at interpolated values of the variable (in between the places where you actually sample). For example, if I know that the output of a car engine at 1000 RPM (revolutions-per-minute) is 100 horsepower, and at 2000 RPM is 200 horsepower, I can interpolate between these two values to estimate that the output should be 150 horsepower at 1500 RPM.

In landing page tuning, variable values are almost always *discrete* (distinct from each other, and countable). For example, a button color might be green, blue, or red. I will number the possible choices by successive lowercase letters. By convention, the letter *a* represents the original version of the variable (as seen on your baseline pretest landing page). The letter is combined with the variable name to exactly specify the value of a particular variable. If V4 is our button color, an example assignment might look as follows:

V4a = green button (the original)

V4b = blue button

V4c = red button

Unlike continuous variables, measuring the effect of discrete variable values does not give us any information about the other possible values. Continuing our example from earlier, even if we had measured the average conversion rates with the green and blue buttons, we would not have any information about the performance of the red one.

Branching Factor

The total number of possible values for a discrete variable is called its *branching factor*. For discrete variables, the branching factor must be at least 2 (the original version and one alternative). As I will discuss later in this chapter, some experimental designs require that the branching factor be the same for all variables in the test.

In the button color example, V4 has a branching factor of 3 (because it can take on the values signified by a-green, b-blue, and c-red).

In traditional multivariate testing, the number of values for a variable is called the *level of the factor*. Each value is also called a *level* because historically it was drawn from continuous variables. For example, if your variable only has two values, they might be signified by "low" and "high" (or "-1" and "+1").

Recipe

A *recipe* is a unique combination of variable values in your test. It is a sequential listing of the specific values that each variable takes on in the specific version of the landing page.

For example, let's assume that you had set the following variable values from my previous example for a particular landing page in your test: V1b, V2c, V3a, V4a. The recipe could be abbreviated as *bcaa*.

Each recipe is unique. By convention, the recipe with all *a*'s is the original or *baseline* recipe to which all others will be compared.

Search Space Size

The number of unique recipes in your test is your *search space size*. It can generally be computed by multiplying together all of the branching factors of the variables in your test (for a possible exception to this rule, please see the next section, "Test Construction").

In my earlier example, let's assume that there are three headlines, four versions of the sales copy, four calls-to-action, and three button colors (and "BF" stands for the branching factor for a particular variable).

Search space size

$= BF_{V1} \times BF_{V2} \times BF_{V3} \times BF_{V4}$

$= 3 \times 4 \times 4 \times 3$

$= 144$

This example is a small one. As you can see, if you have more variables, and higher branching factors for each one, the search space size will grow very rapidly. If the search space size is large, it can quickly exceed the practical limits of common tuning methods such as A-B split testing, fractional factorial parametric, and full factorial parametric testing.

Test Construction

There are two primary types of multivariate test designs: unconstrained designs and constrained designs. Let's discuss these further.

Unconstrained Designs

Unconstrained design test variables can be created and displayed independently of each other on your landing page. For instance, if all variables can be displayed in separate locations on your landing page, they are usually unconstrained. Most basic landing page tests involve unconstrained designs.

This does not mean that there are no variable interactions among variables in unconstrained designs. Some variables may interact with each other. In my previous example, the call-to-action text on the button can obviously interact with the button color. Imagine that the button text says "go." On a green button this makes sense. However, the same text displayed on the red button would be confusing since people commonly associate red with word "stop." So you should look for possible interactions among all the possible variable value combinations of V3 and V4, but your choices of the exact wording of the alternative calls-to-action text can probably be considered independently of your choices about alternative button colors.

Constrained Designs

Constrained designs involve conditional rules for constructing certain recipes. In other words, some of the allowed values for a particular variable are *contingent* on the setting of others, or can exist only under certain conditions. Under such circumstances, take special care to properly define and structure your variables. You may also have to make sure that you sample appropriately during your test and do not accidentally create improper recipes for presentation to your visitors.

Let's consider a simple example. Assume that you have a two-page registration form. You want to test an alternative design for the second page, but you also want to consider a design where all of the form fields are moved onto the first page (i.e., there's no need for a second page at all).

One possible test construction approach is as follows:

V1—first page contents

    a—original first page

    b—extended first page (containing all original first and second page fields)

V2—second page contents

    a—original second page

    b—alternative second page design

    c—no second page (all content moved to V1b first page)

Under this *unspecified constraint* approach, you will need to keep track of the fact that V1b and V1c can only appear together, and enforce it through rules that are external to the variable definition itself.

Another common solution is to *flatten* the constrained variables and create a single variable containing values for each allowable design.

V1—registration process

    a—original first and second pages

    b—original first page and alternative second page

    c—extended one page (containing all original first and second page fields)

As a real-life example of a constrained design, ScanAlert, the creators of the HACKER SAFE website trustmark, has partnered with SiteTuners to offer free multivariate testing of the trustmark to qualifying potential prospects and current customers of HACKER SAFE. The goal of this testing is to find the biggest conversion rate improvement possible due to adding the trustmark. We do this by testing all possible HACKER SAFE logos (currently six) in multiple positions on the client's landing page (up to four). We test against the original landing page, which does not contain the trustmark.

Obviously, if the trustmark is not present on the landing page, the specific logo chosen and its position becomes meaningless. To run these tests, SiteTuners has chosen the *specified constraint* test construction approach. In other words, we reserve one variable specifically for the constrained condition, and a placeholder variable value for it in all other appropriate variables:

V1—trustmark presence (branching factor = 2)

    a—no trustmark

    b—trustmark

V2—trustmark logo (branching factor = 7)

    a—no logo (placeholder for constraint in V1)

    b—red-horizontal logo

    c—red-vertical logo

    d—black-horizontal logo

    e—black-vertical logo

    f—white-horizontal logo

    g—white-vertical logo

V3—trustmark location (branching factor = 5)

    a—no location (placeholder for constraint in V1)

    b—location #1

    c—location #2

    d—location #3

    e—location #4

Based on the branching factors here, you might assume that this test has 70 distinct recipes ($2 \times 7 \times 5$). However, it only has 25 (one original plus 24 trustmark logo and position combinations). Besides the baseline recipe (specified by *aaa*), no other recipes are allowed to contain any *a*'s.

Common Tuning Issues

Regardless of the tuning method that you choose, there are some general issues that impact all landing page tests.

Measuring and Counting

What exactly are you trying to optimize? This might seem like a simple question, but it deserves a second look. How you measure and record data during your test will have a profound impact on the results (and your test's basic validity). You may also have to use different math in order to analyze the data that you have collected.

Fixed Value vs. Variable Value

In many cases, your conversion actions all have the same estimated or actual revenue value (e.g., form-fills, downloads, registrations, click-throughs). For tests involving a single action with the same value, you can simply count the number of conversions, and use basic statistical tests (such as the *t*-test described in the last chapter) to analyze the significance of your results.

However, if your conversion actions have a variable value, you must take this into account. For example, if you have an e-commerce catalog, you may sell items at widely varying prices. If your test variables have an effect on the average sales price, you must take this into account along with the conversion rate. If you do not, it is possible that any improvements in conversion rate might be diminished or actually canceled out by decreases in your average sales price. In such cases, you should measure the revenue per visitor. This will provide you with a normalized measure that takes into account the conversion rate and the average value of the transaction. By using revenue per visitor, you can determine whether a shift to a higher or lower average transaction value is actually a net benefit to your business.

Depending on your profit margin on different items (or categories of products), you may also have to consider the profit margin on each item. For example, it is very easy to shift your product mix toward selling low margin or "loss leader" items in the hopes that your clients will eventually buy more from you (either during the same transaction or in subsequent ones). Such sales can increase your conversion rate, and even improve your overall sales (i.e., they may increase your revenue per visitor). However, this may devastate your profitability.

In this case, use available information about the wholesale price of the individual product. You can then calculate the *gross margin contribution* by subtracting the cost of the product or service from the sales price. Although gross margin contribution is not technically your profit, it is closely related and I will use the two terms interchangeably. Instead of using revenue per visitor, you can use the more accurate profit per visitor measure for your test. If individual product margins are not available, you can often estimate them at the category level. For example, if you know that your cost of goods sold for a particular product category is 60%, you can assign a value corresponding to 40% of the sales revenue to the relevant transactions. If all of your product categories have similar profit margins, you can bypass this complexity and continue to record the simpler revenue per visitor.

Single Goal vs. Multiple Goals

If you have a single conversion goal, and it has a fixed value, you should be able to use simple counting as described earlier. If you have multiple conversion goals, you must use revenue per visitor (or profit per visitor) even if each type of conversion action has a fixed value.

For example, imagine that you run a lead-generation campaign. Visitors have the option of completing your online form (a $20 value), or calling your toll-free number and providing the same information over the telephone (a $40 value based on the higher conversion rate of this more-motivated self-selecting audience segment). One of the variables that you are considering testing is the prominence of the toll-free number on the landing page. A smaller one will presumably lower the proportion of phone leads, while a more prominent one would increase it. To properly handle this trade-off, you should record each conversion action and its accompanying value for each landing page recipe. You can then use a revenue-per-visitor-based analysis to find the best recipe.

You also need to be clear about whether you are dealing with saturating goals versus accumulating goals. A *saturating goal* is one for which you receive no additional credit after it has been completed. For instance, in a lead-generation business, once the lead is generated and you get paid for it, you can't get credit for generating the same lead a second time even if the same person fills out the form again. Product sales is an example of an *accumulating goal*, where selling more product to the same person adds up additional revenues (and usually profit). These need to be handled differently.

Note that all of the metrics that you are trying to optimize are *normalized*. In other words, they are a ratio that divides one quantity by another. In all of my previous examples, the item that you normalize by has been the unique visitor (e.g., conversion rate per visitor, revenue per visitor, and profit per visitor). In reality, things are more complicated. You will need to decide whether to normalize on a per-view, per-visit, or per-visitor basis. The correct choice is very important here. For most landing page optimization tests, it is appropriate to normalize per new visitor (i.e., per each first-time view), but this is not a given.

Maintaining Consistency

In most cases, you will want to maintain consistency of experience for visitors during their interaction with your test pages. For example, if you are testing the look and feel of a website, you would not want visitors to see an ever-changing presentation of the pages as they click around your site. A common way to stabilize your users' experience is to record the recipe that they were shown and store it in a cookie on their computer. The cookie should be a "first party" cookie (originating from your website). The vast majority of people on the Internet currently allow such cookies. This will make it possible for you to present consistent information throughout their initial visit and during return visits.

Be aware that many people delete their cookies on a regular basis. If someone does this and then returns to your landing page, you may not know that they have been there before, and you may treat them like a new visitor (i.e., showing them a new re-randomized recipe instead of the same one that they originally saw). This is less of a problem with tests that have an immediate call-to-action. But it can be significant if you have a large "tail" of stragglers who convert long after their initial visit. The consequence of a significant percentage of delayed conversions is that you will be undercounting return visitors, and then counting them again as new visitors.

One solution is to use multiple methods for tracking and counting your visitors. But there are limitations to all Internet tracking approaches (as evidenced by the varying numbers produced by different Web analytics software packages on the same website). You will never count all of your website visitors accurately. The requirements of landing page test tracking are generally not as stringent as those of Web analytics. As long as the sample that you collect is not too biased (due to classes of visitors that it underrepresents, or by the distortions created by your tracking and counting method), you should generally be okay. The main requirement is that you collect data consistently, and compare apples to apples.

However, in some tests you may want to treat someone as a new visitor during every return visit. In those cases, reset their cookie and assign a new recipe to them. It is also possible to do this based on elapsed time between visits. For example, you may assume that if they have not converted within a day, they have forgotten about their previous experience and can be shown a new version of your page. Deliberately reusing your return visitors is sometimes done and often does not produce any negative effects. But be aware that it technically breaks the assumption of randomness required by the underlying statistical theory (i.e., the behavior of each visitor is supposed to be fresh, and not dependent on previous interactions with your landing page). As a general rule, I advise against this practice. There are simply too many real-world issues that already muddy the landing page testing waters, without the need to deliberately introduce additional sources of ambiguity.

Throttling

Throttling is the practice of adjusting the traffic data rate for your test as a whole (or for a portion of it). This is commonly done for three reasons: spreading out the pain, selective focusing on certain parts of your search space, and reaching statistical significance faster.

Spreading out the pain Some online marketers are worried that their conversion performance may actually get worse during their search for a better landing page. Many testers use affiliate traffic as part of their mix and do not want to alienate their affiliates by having them suddenly experience significantly lower conversion rates. It is also possible that few of the alternatives that you test will beat your original, especially in multivariate tests with large interactions.

If you are concerned about worse performance on your alternative recipes during the test, you can devote most of your bandwidth to the current baseline, and reserve a bit for testing the new possibilities. This minimizes the risk of a sudden large drop in conversion rate.

For example, let's assume that the average value for the mix of recipes that you are about to test is 10% worse than your baseline performance. If you were to devote 20% of your traffic to the original, then your conversion rate during the test would drop by 8%:

Conversion rate = 20% × 1.00 + 80% × 0.90 = 0.92

If you devote 70% of the bandwidth to your original, then your conversion rate during the test would drop by only 3%:

Conversion rate = 70% × 1.00 + 30% × 0.90 = 0.97

There is, of course, a trade-off—your test would have to run approximately three times longer to collect the same amount of test data. This can be a problem if your data rate is already low, and you run into seasonal effects during a prolonged test. If you do not see evidence of a significant drop in performance early in your test, you should reallocate more bandwidth to your alternative recipe mix.

Selective focus At SiteTuners.com we normally devote significant data collection bandwidth to the baseline recipe (usually between 15% and 25% of the test traffic), because we want to have a good read on it. Since we are trying to beat the performance of the baseline, we want to accurately measure any fluctuations in it in order to adjust for outside factors in our test. If you simply devote a proportional amount of data collection to the baseline (inversely proportional to the size of your search space), your variance on the baseline data will be high, and you will have to wait longer to make decisions. The exception to this is in A-B split testing, where you will often (and should) devote 50% of available bandwidth to the baseline and alternative version.

You can also use selective focus as a kind of look-ahead—examining recipes that look promising by devoting more bandwidth to them on top of their usual allocation. This lets you get a better sense for whether a particular recipe is really better, or is merely having a short-term run of good luck. However, be aware that uneven bandwidth invalidates many statistical analysis techniques commonly used in multivariate testing.

Reaching significance faster Sometimes you may uncover large improvements over the performance of your baseline. If you are sampling at an equal data rate for all recipes (as measured in the number of visitor impressions), you will end up with more conversions on the best recipe. As you may recall from Chapter 7, "The Math of Tuning," the width of the error bars on the estimated conversion rate depends on the number of samples (conversions) that you have collected. The goal is to have the two bell curves "separate out" from each other. In other words, you want them to "un-overlap" as quickly as possible (until you have reached the desired statistical confidence level in your answer).

In Figure 8.2, you can see two conversion rate bell curves for versions *a* and *b* of a landing page. The observed average values (represented by the vertical lines) are different. The one for *b* is higher (to the right of the one for *a*). But the fact that we can calculate the exact observed average value for our data sample does not imply that we know what the true underlying mean is. One way to represent our uncertainty about the actual underlying mean is to represent it as a bell curve. The higher the bell curve is at a particular conversion rate value, the more likely it is that the actual mean also lies at that value. In other words, the actual mean is most likely to be near the observed mean, and there is a rapidly decreasing chance that it lies further from the observed average value.

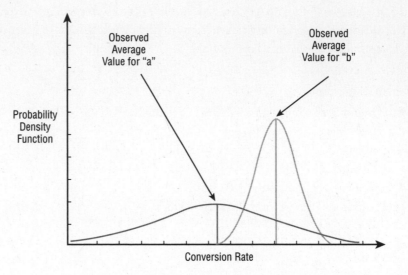

Figure 8.2 Two conversion rate bell curves for an A-B split test

In Figure 8.2, the bell curve for *b* is narrower and taller than the one for *a* because *b* has had a higher number of conversions and we are more certain about the location of its actual mean. But the degree of overlap between the two bell curves is also high because the one for *a* has a wider smudged shape due to the lower number of observed conversions. Your confidence in the superiority of *b* depends on this degree of overlap, which in turn is mostly determined by the width of the wider *a* bell curve.

If *a* had a roughly equal number of conversions to *b*, its bell curve shape would also get taller and skinnier—minimizing the amount of overlap and giving you higher confidence in your answer. The quickest way to separate out the two curves from a statistical perspective is to have an exactly equal number of conversions for each recipe.

If you see a significantly higher percentage of conversions for a particular recipe in your test, you should reallocate your data collection bandwidth to equalize the number of conversions from each recipe. For example, let's assume that you are running a head-to-head test and version *b* is performing twice as well as the original version *a*. In this case, to make a decision as quickly as possible, you should give version *b* half as much traffic bandwidth as version *a*, so that the actual number of conversions is comparable. In other words, you should give *b* one-third of your total bandwidth, and give *a* two-thirds. However, if your conversion rate difference is smaller than the 2-to-1 advantage in this example, you do not need to bother with throttling, since the length of required data collection will not change very much.

Audience Changes

Under ideal circumstances, your landing page is the only thing that changes during your test, so you can attribute causality to any conversion rate changes. You can say that making a certain landing page change *resulted* in the conversion improvement. In the real world, there are often other changes during your test that can influence your results. These fall into two broad categories:

- Internal events
- External events

You should keep your data collection as clean as possible, and try to prevent events that might bias your test. If you cannot, at least have some facilities for detecting significant changes. If you do detect anomalies, you can modify your subsequent analysis to mitigate or compensate for the effects. If that is not possible, you should rerun all or a portion of your data collection.

This section describes some of the things that you can do to avoid, or at least detect, this sort of problem.

Internal Events

Internal events are ones that are directly caused by actions taken within your online marketing program. As I previously mentioned, your overall goal should be to get as wide a cross section as possible of traffic sources, assuming that they are relatively stable, repeatable, and consistent.

Uneven or Flawed Sampling

Some traffic sources may result in uneven sampling. For example, many PPC search engines allow you to specify the exact timing for your campaign. This is okay as long as you subsequently apply your findings during the same time period, but can be a problem if you overgeneralize the results.

For example, you may choose to buy PPC traffic only during the Monday through Friday workweek, and turn off your program on the weekend. The resulting best landing page design from your test should only be used during the same time period. It should not be used during the weekend or evenings without additional testing, because you do not know how that untested audience would react to it.

More subtle sampling problems may occur when you offer a choice of different response mechanisms. For example, let's assume that you want your visitors to either buy online or call your toll-free number and order over the phone. You may test the removal of the toll-free number as one of your tuning elements. It is possible that by doing this you will significantly bias your sample. Visitors who are wary of conducting financial transactions online (e.g., older people or novice Internet users) will now be underrepresented.

If you use a toll-free number, it is usually available at the state or at the national level. This will also preclude most international visitors from responding over the phone. Similar issues exist with chat, Flash, and any customized response mechanisms involving Web browser plug-ins or downloaded software applications. Such response mechanisms will favor more technologically savvy visitors with advanced Internet technology, and undercount the cautious technology late-adopters who do not have advanced capabilities in their Web browser.

Biased Visitors

Bias can be introduced not only from the traffic source or method of sampling, but also from the interactions that a visitor has already had with your company or brand.

If someone has been to your website before, you must consider their whole history. They may have already transacted with you, or received a series of follow-up e-mails after a previous visit. In either case, they must be considered tainted. That is why I don't recommend using e-mail traffic for landing page testing unless you are exclusively tuning for this audience (and using well-respected direct marketing methods).

The basic problem with repeat visitors is that they may be making decisions based simply on familiarity. For example, let's assume that you have a horrible and user-unfriendly website, and are testing an alternative design. First-time visitors may clearly favor the new design. But returning visitors may not. They are already familiar with the old design, and have invested some time and mental effort in becoming familiar with it. Suddenly they are confronted with something different. This may cause them a moment of confusion as they reorient themselves and confirm that they landed in the right place. The anxiety produced by this discontinuity may be enough to wipe out any inherent advantages of the new design. In other words, the return visitor may experience an abrupt change in the page from their previous visit, rather than considering the new page in isolation. In such cases it is often best to test with new visitors only, and to accept the onetime performance drop due to returning visitors seeing different designs. This means you must take the short-term pain (a temporary drop in returning visitor performance) in order to realize the long-term gain (the improved performance of your new design as it applies to all future visitors from the same traffic source).

You will always have a certain proportion of repeat visitors when your landing page is your home page or a permanent part of your website. With controllable traffic sources such as PPC or banner ads, you can aim where the traffic lands. This allows you to minimize the percentage of repeat visitors by using a specialized landing page just for that traffic source. If repeat visitors remain a significant part of your traffic mix, you may want to filter them out during your data collection (assuming that this still leaves you a high enough data rate for your test). Since many people intentionally delete their cookies or access the Web from multiple locations, you will never be able to detect or filter out all returning visitors. Just do the best that you can.

Technically, any prior exposure to your company constitutes a bias. A particular visitor may have seen or heard your offline marketing or advertising, and will act differently than someone who has not, even if it is their first visit to your site. Even direct type-in traffic to your home page should be considered suspect. Why would visitors type in your domain name directly? Obviously they must have heard about your company somewhere. Depending on the context in which your company was presented, they may have already formed some preconceived notions and may not consider your landing page design on its own merits.

Shifts in Traffic Mix

In most cases, you will combine a number of traffic sources for your test. The assumption behind the test is that this combined population of people behaves consistently, and that by testing we can find an alternative landing page design to which they will respond more favorably. So you have to be careful to not to change the composition of your audience during the test. Otherwise, you may tune for one population, and then try to apply the results to a different one.

Examples of changing traffic mix include the following:

- Increasing or decreasing spend significantly on a particular campaign (including turning on new traffic sources or deleting campaigns)
- Using automated bid management tools for PPC campaigns
- Significantly changing the mix of PPC keywords and positions that you are bidding on (even if the overall budget remains the same)
- Adding new high-traffic keywords to your PPC campaign
- Having search engines re-spider your site and increase your search results rankings for a popular keyword
- Negotiating a back link from a popular website

Of course, you cannot put all of your marketing activities on hold for the duration of your test. But try to make as few changes as possible during the data collection. If you introduce new traffic sources, you can usually filter them out and not use them for the test (i.e., continue to show these visitors from new traffic sources your original landing page). If there are significant changes to your traffic mix, you may have to restart your test since your conclusions will be highly suspect, and you will want to properly tune for your new audience mix anyway.

External Events

External events happen as a result of changes outside of your online marketing program. Because of this, you usually do not have very much control over them.

Seasonal external events are different depending on your industry. They may be long duration and build up slowly (such as the fourth-quarter shopping season for many online merchants). Or they may be more abrupt and specific to your industry (such as the exact start date of deer hunting season for a rifle retailer).

If the external events are planned or foreseeable, you can schedule your test around them. If you are tuning for the best year-round behavior of your audience, you may choose to simply discard the data collected during any holidays or seasonal transitions during your test. This is also true during any significant major industry events or gatherings (such as planned conferences or expos). You can gather information about these types of events from industry press sources, and schedule your test accordingly.

Of course, you may want to tune specifically for a short time duration seasonal event because they represent a disproportionate percentage of the value to your business (e.g., a flower site in the weeks leading up to Mother's Day).

Some external events are transient and nonrepeatable. These include:

- Significant announcements from your company
- Major changes in your industry
- Media coverage of your company or industry

You must monitor relevant publications and news sources, during the test period, for events that may impact traffic levels, audience composition, or visitor behavior. If the external events are unforeseen, you may have to discard all of your data for the affected time period.

Technology Changes

Sometimes the mechanisms for proper measurement and recording during your test can themselves impact the results. Some technological anomalies may be hard to detect. But many issues can be seen readily in your Web analytics reports or server logs.

Examples include:

- Page display times (based on Web server load and Internet congestion)
- Broken landing pages (generating Web server errors)
- Crippled landing pages (not displaying as you expect them to on all browsers)
- Upgrades to your Web server, database, content management system, or Web analytics software

Quality control after the implementation stage of your test is especially critical. You may be tempted to simply spot-check a few versions of your landing page in your browser, but this is not rigorous enough. There are often subtle and critical flaws that can only be found by disciplined quality control. For example, let's assume that your new landing page does not display properly for a Web browser that has a 5% installed base among your visitors. During the test, this will show up as a 5% lower conversion rate (because people with that browser version cannot physically complete the transaction), and you may not even notice this drop in your reporting. However, since the page did not load properly, you are actually alienating all visitors with that browser. This has a consequence beyond your test—they may never return.

If possible, you should exhaustively check all possible versions of your landing pages on popular operating systems and Web browsers, and at common screen resolutions. Decide on an acceptable threshold for popularity of a particular technology (e.g., all operating system versions with more than 1% installed base within your audience) and commit to testing with all versions above the threshold. This information is readily available in your Web analytics reports.

Overview of Tuning Methods

There are two key activities in landing page optimization:

- Deciding what to change, and coming up with alternative landing page versions
- Verifying the impact of the changes on your audience

Choosing what elements to test and deciding on alternative versions is very important. If you do not test changes that have a significant impact on conversion, it does not matter how you verify the impact—there won't be any. At the same time, it is critical to understand the benefits and limitations of each tuning method.

Several factors determine the tuning method that you should use:

- The size of your search space
- Your available landing page traffic levels
- The desired level of confidence in the test outcome
- Whether you want to consider variable interactions

Some tuning methods can only handle search spaces with a few total recipes, while others can routinely find the best answer out of millions of possible recipes. Simple tuning methods can work with as few as ten conversions per day (assuming that you are willing to wait months to collect enough data), while others require higher minimum traffic levels. The desired statistical confidence level is completely up to you, and depends on the severity of the consequences from making an incorrect decision. Typically values between 90% and 99% are chosen. As I discussed in Chapter 7, variable interactions play a huge part in online marketing experiments. Some tuning methods do not consider them at all, while others identify them and take them into account in order to produce the best possible results.

The simplest tuning method is A-B split testing. And is a good starting point for getting your feet wet with landing page optimization. Multivariate testing is much more complicated and has several important variations, twists, and considerations that can radically alter the end results.

A-B Split Testing

The most basic tuning method available is *A-B split testing*. The name comes from the fact that two versions of your landing page ("A" and "B" are tested). "Split testing" refers to the random assignment of new visitors to the version of the page that they see. In other words, the traffic is split and all versions are shown in parallel throughout the data collection period (usually in equal proportions). This is an important requirement. As I mentioned earlier, parallel tests should always be conducted (as opposed to sequential ones). This allows you to control for as many outside factors as possible. The random assignment of new visitors to particular landing page designs is also critical, since randomness is the basis for the probability theory that underlies the statistical analysis of the results.

Usually version "A" is defined as your original control page, or baseline (commonly called the *champion* version). The other version is the alternative (commonly called the *challenger*). If the challenger proves to be better than the champion, the challenger replaces the champion after the test and becomes the new champion to beat in any subsequent tests.

In theory, you can have more than two versions in a split test. For example, if you had one original and two alternative versions, you would have an A-B-C split test, and so on. However, split tests rarely have a branching factor higher than ten.

As I discussed in Chapter 6, the variable in your split test can be very granular, or it can be a whole-page redesign of your landing page.

A-B Split Testing Advantages

Split tests have several advantages:

Ease of test design Unlike more complicated multivariate tests, split tests do not have to be carefully designed or balanced. You simply decide how many versions you want to test, and then split the available traffic evenly among them. No follow-up tests are required to verify the results—the best performer in the test is declared the winner.

Ease of implementation Many software packages are available to support simple split tests. If you are testing granular test elements, you can design, set up your test, and be collecting data literally within a matter of minutes. This can be done in most cases without support from your I.T. department or others within the company. You may even be able to collect the data you need with your existing Web analytics tools.

Ease of analysis Only very simple statistical tests (as described in the previous chapter) are needed to determine the winner. Basically, all you have to do is compare the baseline version to each challenger to see if you have reached your desired confidence level.

Ease of explanation No complicated analyses or charts are needed to present your results to others. You can simply declare that you are very confident that a particular version is better than another. You can also give a likely range of percentage improvement (based on the amount of data you have collected and the width of the error bars).

Flexibility in defining the variable values In whole-page split tests, you have complete flexibility in how different the proposed alternatives are. For example, in one alternative, you may simply choose to test a different headline. In another you may completely restructure everything about the page (layout, color scheme, sales copy, offer, and call-to-action). This ability to mix and match allows you to test a range of evolutionary and revolutionary alternatives in one test, without being constrained by the more granular definition of variables in a multivariate test.

Useful in low data rate tests If your landing page only has a few conversions per day, you simply cannot use more advanced tuning methods. But with the proper selection of the test variable and alternative values, you can still achieve significant results in a split test. Improvements in the double or even triple digits are not uncommon.

A-B Split Testing Disadvantages

Split tests also have several drawbacks:

Limited number of recipes As I mentioned, the number of recipes in a typical split test is usually very small. If you did your homework properly, you probably came up with dozens of potential issues with your landing page, and also constructed many alternative variations to test. However, because of the limited scope of split testing, you will be reduced to testing your ideas one at a time. You will also be forced to guess which ideas to test first (based on your intuition about which ones might make the most difference). In other tuning methods, you may be able to test many of your key ideas at once and find all of the changes that improve your conversion rate in one test.

Does not consider variable interactions By definition, split tests consider only one variable at a time, so you cannot detect variable interactions. Furthermore, a series of split tests is not the same as a multivariate test with the same variables. Depending on the variable interactions, you may not be able to find the best-performing recipe at all. Whether you do depends on the order in which you conduct your split tests, and the exact nature of the interactions.

For example, let's assume that you are testing two variables, each of which can take on two values. There are strong interactions between the two variables. The conversion rate for each recipe is as follows:

$aa = 5\%$

$ab = 2\%$

$ba = 3\%$

$bb = 7\%$

If you had conducted a multivariate test and collected data on each of the four recipes, you would have seen the superior performance of recipe *bb* and crowned it the winner.

However, this is not possible if you had simply done two back-to-back split tests (starting with V1 first). You would have tested recipe *aa* versus recipe *ba* (leaving V2 unchanged in its V2a setting). Since *aa* would perform the best, you would conclude that V1 should be locked in as V1a. You would then test V2 in this context by conducting another split test between *aa* and *ab*. After this second test, you would come to the conclusion that V2 should be set to *a*. So the winning recipe would be determined to be *aa*. There is no way to sequentially get to the best answer in this example. This situation is actually quite common. The chances of being led astray from the best solution also increase as you continue to do more split tests over time.

No way to discover the importance of page elements Often, you may choose very coarse variables for your split test. Because of the limited data rate, you are forced to make your best guess at tuning elements that might improve performance. These elements may actually involve many simultaneous changes to your landing page. In the extreme case of a whole-page redesign, you may have changed dozens of details on the page in question and defined them as a single alternative recipe.

However, the same flexibility that allows you to do this *also* limits your ability to interpret the results and attribute credit for the conversion improvement to any particular change that you made. Was it the button color? Or was it the headline change? Or was it the different offer? You will never know. By squashing multiple changes into one variable value, you have confounded their effects and lost the ability to look at them separately.

As I mentioned earlier, this may not be such a huge issue, since many of the so-called "learnings" about the relative importance of variables are based on the spurious assumption that they are all independent. Furthermore, the best effects may be due to the specific variable *values* you have chosen, and not the *variable* itself. For example, a particular headline that you chose to test was very powerful. But this does not allow you to generalize about headlines being more important than the other variables tested.

In any case, you should avoid trying to interpret the results of your split test if the variable values involve changing multiple elements on the page.

Inefficient data collection As you will see in the next section, multivariate tests are often carefully constructed in order to get the most information from a smaller data sample. In effect, they allow you to more efficiently conduct multiple split tests simultaneously, and even to detect certain kinds of variable interactions. Conducting multiple split tests back-to-back is the most wasteful kind of data collection—none of the information from a previous test can be reused to draw conclusions about the other variables that you may want to test in the future.

Multivariate Testing

The purpose of *multivariate testing* is to simultaneously gather information about multiple variables, and then conduct an analysis of the data to determine which recipe results in the best performance.

Multivariate testing approaches differ on two important dimensions:

- How the data is collected
- How the data is analyzed

The data can be collected in a *full factorial* or *fractional factorial* fashion (see the "Data Collection" section below). The subsequent analysis can be either *parametric* or *non-parametric* (see the "Data Analysis" section below). Within parametric analysis there are also significant differences. Some forms of parametric analysis take complex variable interactions into account, while others do not.

I have presented data collection and data analysis as independent dimensions. In fact, they cannot always be separated. If you choose fractional factorial data collection and test design, you automatically lock yourself into a very restricted subset of parametric models (i.e., non-parametric analysis is impossible if you conduct fractional factorial data collection). Figure 8.3 summarizes the possible multivariate testing approaches.

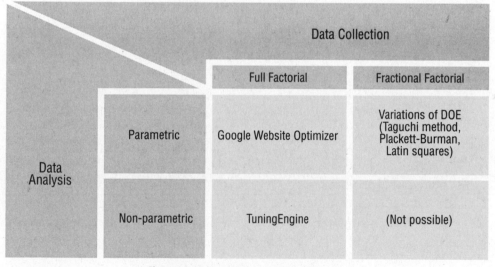

Figure 8.3 Multivariate Testing Approach Overview

Data Collection

Full factorial experimental designs sample data across your whole search space. If this is done properly, the subsequent analysis allows you to consider not only the main effects, but all variable interactions as well (including higher-order ones).

Technically, all *fractional factorial* designs fall under the *design of experiments (DOE)* umbrella. DOE is a systematic approach to getting the maximum amount of useful information about the process that you are studying, while minimizing the amount of effort and data collection required.

By definition, fractional factorial experimental designs make simplifying assumptions about the possible form of the parametric model for subsequent analysis. For example, they may simply assume that there are no higher-order interactions at all (i.e., that the values of the corresponding coefficients in the model are zero). In the extreme case, they can assume that only the main effects matter and that there are no interactions of any kind (even lower-order ones).

One feature of DOE is that it allows you to explicitly define the interactions among the variables that you want to study and examine. This is in contrast to repeated A-B split testing of different variables, which may not find the best solution and depends heavily on the order in which you test the variables.

There is an inherent trade-off among various DOE test constructions. Full factorial parametric designs do not scale very well, but get more complete information about the exact relationship among all main and interaction effects tested. Fractional factorial designs can scale to larger search spaces, but make assumptions about the underlying process that may not be valid and may actually lead you astray.

Data Analysis

Parametric data analysis in landing page optimization builds a model of how the variables tested (the "independent variables") impact the conversion rate (the "dependent variable"). For each recipe in your search space, the model will produce a prediction of the expected conversion rate (or other optimization criterion of interest).

Unless you happened to have sampled data on the exact recipe predicted by the model as being the best, you do not really know if the prediction will hold up. That is why it is critical to run follow-up A-B split tests between the predicted best challenger recipe and the original baseline recipe for all parametric data analysis methods.

By contrast, *non-parametric* data analysis does not try to build a model based on the input variables. Non-parametric methods try to identify the best challenger recipe, but without being able to tell anything about *why* it is the best, or *exactly how much better* it is than your baseline.

The two approaches are unrelated and are answering different questions. They are both a recognition of the fundamental reality that only so much useful information can be extracted from your data collection sample. The only question is what you want to do with the data. You can try to create a general model of the output variable and try to describe it in terms of the input variables, or you can find the best individual recipe and not know why it is the best.

Parametric Analysis

After you collect your data, you can build a model that expresses how your dependent variable (e.g., the conversion rate) varies based on the settings of your independent variables (i.e., your tuning elements and their specific values).

The models are made up of two types of components. *Main effects* describe the impact of an individual variable value on the results. In other words, they look at each variable in isolation, and see how changing its value affects the results. *Interaction effects* consider combinations of variable values, and how they influence each other when presented together. Interaction effects are possible among two or more variable values. For example, if you had five variables in your test, you could have interactions involving any subset of two, three, four, or five variable values. Interactions involving smaller numbers of variables are called lower order, while those involving many variables are called higher order.

As I mentioned earlier, variables are commonly referred to as factors in parametric multivariate testing terminology. Likewise, variable values are often referred to as levels. If a variable has a branching factor of two, the levels are often referred to as "high" and "low" (or are denoted by "+1" and "-1"). Similarly, three levels are often denoted by "+1", "0", and "-1".

Usually parametric multivariate testing uses the general mathematical class of *linear models* based on the analysis of variance (ANOVA). In other words, you are trying to predict the output variable by adding up the contributions of all of the possible main effects and interaction effects of the input variables. You start with the average value of your output variable in the test, and then add in the positive or negative impact of your input variables and their interactions.

Let's consider the simplest possible multivariate example. Assume that you are testing a new call-to-action button and are considering two colors (blue, green) and two font styles (Arial, Times Roman) for the text:

V1a = blue

V1b = green

V2a = Arial

V2b = Times Roman

You can create a model of the conversion rate that "fits" your data as well as possible and uses the average value, main effects, and all interactions. The coefficients (denoted by c's in front of each effect) indicate the magnitude of the contribution of each effect and can be either positive or negative:

$$CR = c_1 + c_2 \times V1a + c_3 \times V1b + c_4 \times V2a + c_5 \times V2b$$
$$+ c_6 \times V1a{:}V2a + c_7 \times V1a{:}V2b + c_8 \times V1b{:}V2a + c_9 \times V1b{:}V2b$$

c_1 represents the average value, c_2–c_5 are the main effects, and c_6–c_9 are the two-variable interaction effects (involving all four possible combinations of the two variables).

Let's assume that your experiment is slightly larger. You now add a third two-way variable to the test (designated by V3a and V3b). The full model with all interactions is shown below (the new terms resulting from the addition of the third variable are bolded).

$$CR = c_1 + c_2 \times V1a + c_3 \times V1b + c_4 \times V2a + c_5 \times V2b$$
$$+ \mathbf{c_6 \times V3a + c_7 \times V3b}$$
$$+ c_8 \times V1a{:}V2a + c_9 \times V1a{:}V2b + c_8 \times V1b{:}V2a + c_9 \times V1b{:}V2b$$
$$+ \mathbf{c_{10} \times V1a{:}V3a + c_{11} \times V1a{:}V3b + c_{12} \times V1b{:}V3a + c_{13} \times V1b{:}V3b}$$
$$+ \mathbf{c_{14} \times V1a{:}V3a + c_{15} \times V1a{:}V3b + c_{16} \times V1b{:}V3a + c_{17} \times V1b{:}V3b}$$
$$+ \mathbf{c_{18} \times V1a{:}V2a{:}V3a + c_{19} \times V1a{:}V2a{:}V3b}$$
$$+ \mathbf{c_{20} \times V1a{:}V2b{:}V3a + c_{21} \times V1a{:}V2b{:}V3b}$$
$$+ \mathbf{c_{22} \times V1b{:}V2a{:}V3a + c_{23} \times V1b{:}V2a{:}V3b}$$
$$+ \mathbf{c_{24} \times V1b{:}V2b{:}V3a + c_{25} \times V1b{:}V2b{:}V3b}$$

As you can see, the number of coefficients that you must now estimate in the model has mushroomed from 9 to 25. For the first time, you see the presence of three-variable interaction effects.

The examples above are among the smallest possible multivariate tests. As you can see, if you have a higher branching factor for each variable, or a larger number of variables, the number of coefficient terms in the model grows very quickly.

> With a large number of coefficient terms in a parametric model, it becomes impossible to accurately estimate each one.

Fractional factorial parametric approaches force you to choose the complexity of your model ahead of time. This means you must somehow decide *in advance* which main effects are important, and also which interactions will be included in the model. The simpler your model is, the fewer recipes will need to be sampled during data collection.

Parametric Analysis Resolution

Based on the complexity of your parametric model, you can determine its *resolution*. The resolution is a scale that describes your ability to separate out the main effects and lower-order interactions with a particular data collection experimental design. The meaning of "confounded" in statistical parlance refers to the failure to distinguish among different things or mixing them up.

Resolution II Main effects are confounded with others.

Resolution III Can estimate main effects, but they may be confounded by two variable interactions.

Resolution IV Can estimate main effects unconfounded by two variable interactions.

Can estimate two variable interactions, but they may be confounded by other two variable interactions.

Resolution V Can estimate main effects unconfounded by three (or lower) variable interactions.

Can estimate two variable interactions unconfounded by other two variable interactions.

Can estimate three variable interactions, but they may be confounded by two variable interactions.

Resolution VI Can estimate main effects unconfounded by four (or lower) variable interactions.

Can estimate two variable interactions unconfounded by other three (or lower) variable interactions.

Can estimate three variable interactions, but they may be confounded by other three variable interactions.

The most common types of designs are resolution III-V. Resolution II designs are not useful because you cannot even estimate the main effects properly. Resolution VI and above are too complex and assume that high-order interactions are common. Higher resolution designs sample across a larger fraction of the whole search space. Simpler resolution III designs are sparse and sample only a small proportion of the search space.

Non-parametric Analysis

It is a practical impossibility to do the following three things simultaneously without a ridiculously large data rate:

1. Find the best-performing recipe (including variable interactions)
2. Search a very large search space
3. Explain why the winning recipe is the best

Non-parametric approaches use a different mathematical foundation and starting assumptions to focus on items #1 and 2. They do not assume anything about the underlying model or even the presence or size of variable interactions.

Parametric approaches focus on items #1 and 3. So in effect, parametric versus non-parametric can be viewed as the inherent tradeoff between being able to model and explain the best recipes, and being able to find it in a much larger search space.

Unfortunately, some companies in our field make ludicrous assertions to the contrary. They claim to be able to test a "virtually unlimited number of variations" of a landing page by using a modified fractional factorial DOE approach, while still taking variable interactions into account, and being able to describe which individual values of the winning recipe contributed to its improved performance. Claims like this make everyone in our industry look bad.

Fractional Factorial Parametric Testing

As I mentioned earlier in this chapter, fractional factorial data collection can not really be divorced from parametric data analysis. So I will refer to the combination of the two simply as "fractional factorial."

In theory, it is possible that every variable that you test has interactions with every specific value of every other variable. In practice, this is usually not the case. During your test, you may discover that many or even most of the elements that you have decided to include do not impact performance at all. They simply do not matter to your audience. It is also common that strong interactions between two variables exist but that higher-order interactions (among three or more variables) are insignificant. In such cases, the behavior of the output variable can be described by looking at the main effects and a few low-order interactions (involving two variables).

This basic idea arises as a consequence of three empirical principles commonly understood in the testing community.

Hierarchical Ordering Principle

Lower-order effects are more likely to be important than higher-order effects.

Effects of the same order are equally likely to be important.

This principle suggests that when resources are scarce (i.e., the data collection rate is low), priority should be given to estimating main effects and lower-order interactions.

Effect Sparsity Principle

The numbers of relatively important effects in a factorial experiment are small.

This is another formulation of the 80/20 rule. Only a few variables combine to produce the biggest effects, and all of the rest will not matter nearly as much.

Effect Heredity Principle

In order for an interaction to be significant, at least one of its parent factors should be significant.

This is another application of common sense. If a variable does not produce any big effects on its own (i.e., it is benign or negligible), it is unlikely to do so when combined with something else. It may be that a big interaction effect is produced by variables that do not show the largest main effects, but at least one of the variables involved in an interaction will usually show some main effect.

The whole idea behind fractional factorial design is that you can collect data on a fraction of the recipes needed for an equivalent full factorial design and still maximize the model's predictive value.

Fractional factorial designs are expressed using the notation l^{k-p} (l is the common branching factor for all variables in the test; k is the number of variables investigated, and p describes the size of the fraction of the full factorial search space used). In mathematical terms, p is the number of generators (elements in your model that are confounded and cannot be estimated independently of each other). In other words, when you increase p, you are really saying that some of your input variables are not independent and can be explained by some combination of the other input variables or their interactions.

A design with p generators will require a $1/(l^p)$ fraction of the full factorial design search space size. For example, let's assume that you have a 2^{6-2} fractional factorial design. A full factorial 2^6 experimental design would require you to sample all 64 possible recipes. But the simpler fractional design will require sampling only 16 recipes (¼ of the total).

Creating a proper fractional factorial design is beyond the scope of this book. The basic steps are as follows:

- Based on the generators (see above) of your design, you can determine the *defining relation*.
- The defining relation specifies the *alias structure*.
- A fractional factorial experiment is created from a full factorial experiment by using the chosen *alias structure*.

One common constraint on fractional factorial tests is that the branching factor is two for all variables. The methods for creating custom test designs outside of this constraint are complex. Many testers simply copy "standard" designs from statistical texts, and restrict themselves to a choice of variables and branching factors that fit the model.

Overview of Common Fractional Factorial Methods

Although there is some difference in common fractional factorial methods, their basic predictive power, required data sample size, and underlying assumptions are pretty similar. The main difference lies in the *shape* of the search spaces that each can be used for.

So if you are going to use any of the methods below, you should base your decision on your familiarity with each and the number and branching factor of the variables in your test.

In the following sections, the sparsest fractional factorial approaches are described in more detail:

- Plackett-Burman
- Latin squares
- Taguchi method

There is no reason to prefer the Taguchi method over Plackett-Burman, or Latin squares. All three fractional factorial methods suffer from the same fundamental issues. These problems are a direct consequence of their origins in manufacturing. Let's take a look at some of the characteristics of this original environment:

Expensive prototypes The underlying assumption is that creating alternative recipes is difficult, time-consuming, or expensive. When applications involve physical processes, human medical trials, or manufacturing technology, this is indeed the case. So the goal is to minimize the required number of recipes (also called "prototypes" or "experimental treatments") in the experiment.

Small test sizes A direct consequence of the expensive prototypes is that you need to keep the number of elements that you test to an absolute minimum, and focus only on the most critical variables.

No interactions As another consequence of the expensive prototypes, you can only measure the main effects created by your variables. The small test size and expensive data collection force you to assume very sparse fractional factorial models that cannot accurately estimate even two variable interactions.

High yields In most cases, the process or outcome that you were measuring had a high probability of success. .

Continuous variables Many of the input variables involved in the tests were continuous (e.g., temperature, concentration of a certain chemical compound). Even though you had to pick specific levels of the variable for the test, you could often interpolate between them to estimate what would happen at nonsampled settings of the variable.

These approaches were transplanted to the online marketing arena (and landing page optimization in particular) because of their relative simplicity and familiarity. Unfortunately, the assumptions that accompanied them came along for the ride, even though they are not applicable to the new environment. Let's take a closer look at the reality of landing page testing:

Free prototypes When you create a test plan, you define exactly which page elements to test, and specify the alternative variable values for each. In most cases, the alternative test elements are easy to implement. They involve changes to the HTML structure of your page, text changes, and graphics.

Once this preliminary work has been done, you have the capability to create any of the recipes in your search space. In other words, the process of creating a different version of your page is completely automated. There is no incremental cost to showing *any* of the possible recipes to your next visitor. So there is no need to restrict yourself to showing only a small percentage of the possible recipes.

Huge test sizes If you critically reviewed your landing page, you were probably able to identify dozens of potential problems (large and small) with it. For each of your original test elements, you can probably come up with several alternatives can reasonably be expected to produce better results and should be included in your test plan. If you did, your search space size would be in the millions (or even billions) of possible recipes. Unfortunately, multivariate testing is specifically designed for very small test sizes. Most real-world tests involve search spaces of a few dozen total recipes.

Significant interactions As discussed earlier, variable interactions play a huge role in landing page optimization. Some interactions are unexpected and are the result of the reduced coherency of the mix-and-match presentation of variables during a test. The effect may be something like Frankenstein's monster—stitched together from functional parts, but not resulting in a very appealing whole.

Other variable interactions are intentional. In fact, as an online marketer you should want to create interactions. You should look for page elements that work together and support each other in getting your visitor to act. These kinds of synergies are at the very heart of good marketing. Yet most fractional factorial designs assume that there are no interactions (or that they are very small).

Low yields Some landing pages have double-digit conversion rates, but most pages have lower rates. Many e-commerce websites have conversion rates that are well below 1%. The limiting factor in the length of the data collection for these pages is the number of conversions (rather than the number of recipes sampled in the test).

Discrete variables Most of the elements that you test on a landing page are discrete. They involve completely distinct choices that are unrelated to each other. For example, if you tested a particular headline for your page, you would not be able to predict the performance of an alternative headline.

By now, you have probably determined my preference for full factorial over fractional factorial data collection for landing page optimization if you are going to use parametric data analysis. There is no efficiency disadvantage to full factorial designs during the data collection stage and significant advantages during the analysis stage.

All three fractional factorial methods I've described below are resolution III designs—and can only estimate the main effects in the model. In other words, they cannot capture all possible two-variable interactions (or any higher-order interactions). Some of them explicitly assume that there are no interactions. They use this radical assumption to dramatically lower the number of sampled recipes and amount of data required to estimate the main effects. An important additional requirement for all of these approaches is that the data collection is balanced across all possible values of a variable (i.e., you cannot use throttling, or it may complicate or throw off your use of standard data analysis).

Let's assume that you want to collect data for each of the variable main effects in the examples that follow. You can construct a series of increasingly larger tests and see how few recipes you can get away with.

The simplest case is an A-B split test containing two recipes, *a* and *b*. You need to split your traffic 50/50 across *a* and *b*. So you need two recipes to measure the two values of variable V1. These two recipes represent your entire search space.

Now imagine that you have two variables, each with a branching factor of two. This results in four possible recipes: *aa*, *ab*, *ba*, and *bb*. You choose to sample only from recipes *aa*, and *bb* (still only two recipes as in the previous example). Note that half of the data that you collect will involve V1a (from recipe *aa*), and half will involve V1b (from recipe *bb*). Similarly, half of your data will cover V2a (from recipe *aa*), and half will involve V2b (from recipe *bb*). As you can see, you have collected equal amounts of data on each main effect, and you did it by sampling only half of your total search space (two out of four recipes).

Let's extend our example to three variables, each with a branching factor of two. This results in eight possible recipes: *aaa*, *aab*, *aba*, *abb*, *baa*, *bab*, *bba*, and *bbb*. You choose to sample only from recipes *aaa* and *bbb* (still only two recipes). Note that half of the data that you collect will involve V1a (from recipe *aaa*), and half will involve V1b (from recipe *bbb*). Similarly, half of your data will cover V2a (from recipe *aaa*), and half will involve V2b (from recipe *bbb*). Half of your data will also cover V3a (from recipe *aaa*), and half will cover V3b (from recipe *bbb*). You have again collected equal amounts of data on each main effect, and have done it by sampling only a quarter of your total search space (two out of eight recipes).

Of course you cannot continue to sample just two recipes and still cover all main effects at larger test sizes. But by clever test construction, you can keep the number of unique recipes surprisingly small (especially when considered as a proportion of the total search space). If you think that the previous examples are a bit contrived and artificial, you are right.

Underlying the use of fractional factorial methods is the assumption that creating a test run is difficult or time-consuming—so you need to keep the number of recipes that you sample as low as possible. This may have been true in the manufacturing setting (e.g., retooling an assembly line to test for a change in production quality), but it is not true or necessary in landing page optimization. Internet technology allows you to easily create any recipe of your landing page test. The page is dynamically created on the fly for each new visitor. For practical data collection purposes, it does not matter how many unique recipes you have in your test.

For the assumption of expensive recipe construction you pay a heavy price during data analysis. By sampling very limited recipes, you destroy your ability to do a comprehensive analysis and find variable interactions later.

Plackett-Burman

R.L. Plackett and J.P. Burman published their paper "The Design of Optimal Multifactorial Experiments" in 1946. In it, they described a very efficient and economical method for constructing test designs.

The requirements for a Plackett-Burman (PB) design are a branching factor of two on all variables, and the number of recipes sampled must be a multiple of four. PB designs exist for 12, 20, 24, 28, and larger sizes. Each PB design can estimate the main effects of one fewer variable than the size of the design (e.g., the PB design with 24 recipes may be used for an experiment containing up to 23 two-value variables).

PB designs are all resolution III and are known as *saturated main effect* designs because all degrees of freedom in the model are used to estimate the main effects. PB designs are also known as nongeometric designs. Because of their construction, they do not have a defining relationship (since interactions are not identically equal to main effects). They are very efficient at detecting large main effects (assuming that all interactions are relatively small).

It was discovered in the 1990s that PB designs have an additional interesting property of being "3-projectible." This means that you can find important interactions involving any subset of three variables in the design.

Latin Squares

Latin squares were first described by Euler in 1782. They are used for a number of applications (including the popular Sudoku puzzles) and have extensive mathematical literature describing them.

Latin squares are square arrangements of numbers and can be different sizes (2×2, 3×3, etc.). Each position in the Latin square contains one of the numbers (from 1 to n) arranged in such a way that no orthogonal (row or column) contains the same number twice.

The two possible Latin squares of size 2×2 are shown here:

$$\begin{bmatrix} 1 & 2 \\ 2 & 1 \end{bmatrix} \begin{bmatrix} 2 & 1 \\ 1 & 2 \end{bmatrix}$$

The 12 possible Latin squares of size 3×3 are shown here:

$$\begin{bmatrix} 1\,2\,3 \\ 2\,3\,1 \\ 3\,1\,2 \end{bmatrix} \begin{bmatrix} 1\,2\,3 \\ 3\,1\,2 \\ 2\,3\,1 \end{bmatrix} \begin{bmatrix} 1\,3\,2 \\ 2\,1\,3 \\ 3\,2\,1 \end{bmatrix} \begin{bmatrix} 1\,3\,2 \\ 3\,2\,1 \\ 2\,1\,3 \end{bmatrix} \begin{bmatrix} 2\,1\,3 \\ 1\,3\,2 \\ 3\,2\,1 \end{bmatrix} \begin{bmatrix} 2\,1\,3 \\ 3\,2\,1 \\ 1\,3\,2 \end{bmatrix}$$

$$\begin{bmatrix} 2\,3\,1 \\ 1\,3\,2 \\ 3\,1\,2 \end{bmatrix} \begin{bmatrix} 2\,3\,1 \\ 3\,1\,2 \\ 1\,2\,3 \end{bmatrix} \begin{bmatrix} 3\,2\,1 \\ 1\,3\,2 \\ 2\,1\,3 \end{bmatrix} \begin{bmatrix} 3\,2\,1 \\ 2\,1\,3 \\ 1\,3\,2 \end{bmatrix} \begin{bmatrix} 3\,1\,2 \\ 1\,2\,3 \\ 2\,3\,1 \end{bmatrix} \begin{bmatrix} 3\,1\,2 \\ 2\,3\,1 \\ 1\,2\,3 \end{bmatrix}$$

The number of possible Latin squares grows very quickly with the size (576 at size 4×4, 161280 at size 5×5, etc.)

Latin squares are used in experimental designs when input variables of interest have a branching factor of greater than two, and there are assumed to be no interactions among the input variables. The combination of the row and columns labels with the cell contents in the Latin square defines a recipe in the experimental design.

For example, let's assume that you want to understand the effect of four different tire rubber compounds on the acceleration of cars. If you have four drivers and four cars available, you could run a full factorial design (for a total of 64 recipes). But you are not really interested in which driver or car is faster, nor any minor interaction effects between tires and drivers and tires and cars. In other words, you are mainly concerned with estimating the main effects (especially the one for the tire compound).

But you also want to make sure that the main effects for cars and drivers do not bias your estimates for the tire compound. So you randomize across all cars and drivers by using the following 4×4 Latin square design, illustrated in Figure 8.4, where each letter represents one of the tire compounds being tested.

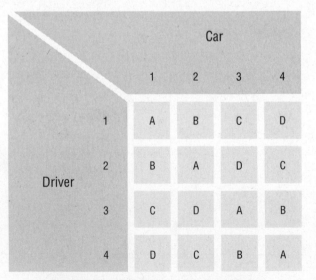

Figure 8.4 Example Latin Squares Experimental Design

As you can see, each driver will try every tire compound, and each car will be driven on each tire compound. The assumption that all variables are independent allows you to complete the study by sampling only 16 recipes (instead of the full 64).

The Taguchi Method

Genichi Taguchi was a Japanese mathematician and proponent of manufacturing quality engineering. He focused on methods to improve the quality of manufactured goods through both statistical process control and specific business management techniques.

Taguchi developed many of his key concepts outside of the DOE framework and only learned of it later. His main focus was on robustness—how to develop a system that performed reliably even in the presence of significant noise or variation. In traditional DOE, the goal is to model the best-performing recipe. In other words, the higher the value of the output variable (e.g., the conversion rate), the better. So the goal is to find the highest *mean*. When taking repeated samples, any variation is considered a problem or a nuisance.

Taguchi had a different perspective. He felt that manufacturing quality should be measured by the amount of deviation from the desired value. In other words, he was concerned not only with the mean, but also with the amount of *variation* or "noise" produced by changing the input variables. So optimization from the Taguchi perspective means finding the best settings for the input variables, defined as the ones producing the highest signal-to-noise ratio (the highest mean with the least amount of variation). An important consideration is how to keep the noise in the output low even in the face of noisy inputs.

The numbers of variables (factors) and alternative values for each variable (levels) is arbitrary in landing page optimization tests. You can easily find additional variables to test, or come up with alternative values for each variable. Unfortunately, basic Taguchi arrays exist only for the following experimental designs:

- L4—Three two-level factors
- L8—Seven two-level factors
- L9—Four three-level factors
- L12—Eleven two-level factors
- L16—Fifteen two-level factors
- L16b—Five four-level factors
- L18—One two-level and seven three-level factors
- L25—Six five-level factors
- L27—Thirteen three-level factors
- L32—Thirty-two two-level factors
- L32b—One two-level factor and nine four-level factors
- L36—Eleven two-level factors and twelve three-level factors
- L36b—Three two-level and twelve three-level factors

- L50—One two-level factor and eleven five-level factors
- L54—One two-level factor and twenty-five three-level factors
- L64—Twenty-one four-level factors
- L81—Forty three-level factors

These test design arrays can be combined in various ways to create additional Taguchi-compliant experimental designs, but you will probably need the help of a statistician to implement them.

The Taguchi method uses orthogonal arrays that obtain a lot of information about the main effects with a relatively small number of recipes. However, many of his experimental designs are *saturated* (allowing no way to estimate interaction effects).

Fractional Factorial Advantages

The following advantages of fractional factorial parametric tests are only from the perspective of A-B split testing. They are *not* advantages when compared to full factorial methods (see the "Full Factorial Parametric" and "Full Factorial Non-parametric" sections later in this chapter).

Data collection efficiency   Instead of performing multiple A-B split tests, you can collect data simultaneously about several variables. As long as your data collection is properly balanced among all variable values, you can take different views (or "slices") of your sample to examine all variables in a single analysis.

Order independence   As discussed earlier, repeated A-B split tests may be unable to find the best solution depending on the order in which the tests are run. Since information about all variables is being gathered simultaneously in a fractional factorial test, the order problem is eliminated, and it becomes possible to find better solutions (although still not necessarily the best ones).

Fractional Factorial Disadvantages

Fractional factorial designs have several disadvantages:

Small test size   Search spaces are very small (it is rare to see landing page tests with more than a few hundred recipes). Most online marketers want to run much larger tests.

Does not consider variable interactions   The most common fractional factorial landing page testing approaches assume a model that is simple, in order to capture important variable interactions. As previously discussed, all of these methods are Resolution III designs and can only estimate the main effects of your input variables. This can significantly skew the results and lead you to costly incorrect conclusions.

Piecewise construction errors   Another common mistake is to take the winning values from each variable and combine them into a single recipe. This piecewise construction does not necessarily constitute the best-performing recipe.

Let's take a closer look at why this is the case. Assume that you have picked a 90% statistical confidence threshold for each variable in your test. In other words, you are 90% sure that the particular value for that variable is the best-performing one. If you had only one variable in your test, you would be wrong 10% of the time, and this might be acceptable to you.

But the likelihood of error grows quickly as you increase the number of variables in your test. For example, in a two-variable test your chances of finding the best recipe depend on you being correct about the best value for each variable independently of the other. This means that you must multiply together the probabilities of being right for each variable.

In our example, this would mean that your chances of finding the correct recipe are 81% (90% × 90%). So your error rate has increased from 10% for a single variable to 19% for two. By the time you get six variables in your test, you are only 53% certain of having found the best recipe. This is only slightly better than flipping a coin.

For this reason, it is critical to run a follow-up head-to-head test between your predicted best answer and your original baseline recipe. But what do you do if the predicted performance of your challenger does not measure up? If this is due to piecewise construction errors, you can raise your confidence threshold, or lower the number of variables in your test. But the unexpectedly poor performance could also be due to huge interaction effects that you have failed to consider. The only way to find these is to rerun the test with a higher resolution design (preferably a full factorial one).

Highly sensitive to streaky data Multivariate test designs are very sensitive to lucky streaks in your data. This is especially a problem if you are collecting very small data samples. For example, let's assume that you are testing a landing page that has a real underlying conversion rate of 1%. Within the first hundred visitors, it is almost equally likely that you would have zero, or two conversions. However, the estimates produced by your models would vary drastically in these two cases. The first model would take the data very literally and conclude that the likelihood of conversion with this landing page is zero (i.e., it will never produce a conversion). The second would conclude that your conversion rate is double its actual value. It is critical to collect a lot of data with multivariate testing models to reduce the problems associated with such possible small-sample distortions.

Requires you to guess at important interactions All fractional factorial models require you to specify exactly what types of main effects and variable interactions are possible in your model. These assumptions must be built in ahead of time in order to simplify the complexity of the model and give you economy in terms of the number of recipes that must be sampled.

In the traditional testing, this might be possible since you know which *physical* processes can have an influence on each other. But in online marketing this is difficult. Unlike physical experiments (e.g., in manufacturing, or pharmaceutical drug trials), landing page optimization is trying to tease out the underlying *psychological* predispositions of people. Since everyone is different, it is impossible to accurately empathize with every member of your audience. You cannot take your own predispositions out of the experiment because you are the one choosing the elements to test. In such a setting, it is impossible to declare which specific interactions matter and which others don't.

Restrictive test design As previously discussed, there must be a certain pattern (in terms of the number of variables and their branching factors) in your test design. So you are forced to either stick with well-known "standard" designs from statistical textbooks or construct your own (with the help of statisticians).

Throttling is very difficult If you throttled your data collection rates and did not devote equal bandwidth to each recipe in your test, your analysis will be invalid for all common fractional factorial designs.

Full Factorial Parametric Testing

A full factorial parametric test collects data on the response of every possible combination of variables (factors) and values (levels). In other words, it collects an equal amount of information about every possible recipe in your search space.

As I discussed earlier, in online marketing we *expect* strong variable interactions. In fact, we are doing everything that we can to create positive synergies among our tuning elements.

> *We at Google are continually surprised by how common and strong variable interactions are in landing page tests.*
> —Mike Myer, statistician, Google

Unlike fractional factorial data collection, full factorial data collection does not lock you into any restrictions during analysis. Full factorial parametric tests do not make assumptions about the underlying model. Analysis of your full factorial data can pinpoint your main effects as well as any interaction effects (lower order or higher order) present in your test.

SiteTuners.com is one of the charter Google Website Optimizer Authorized Consultant companies. The Google Website Optimizer (see the detailed description in Appendix A) is a free A-B split testing and full factorial parametric multivariate testing tool available to all Google AdWords account holders. You do not have to spend any money on AdWords to use the tool. We use it to run all smaller multivariate tests in which the data rate is too low to apply our proprietary non-parametric TuningEngine technology.

I am very glad that Google has chosen the full factorial data collection as their default. Even though the size of the search space is smaller than with comparable fractional factorial testing approaches, you can have a higher confidence in your answer if you run a complete analysis including interactions. However, it is important to note that collecting data in a full factorial design does not mean that you have to subsequently analyze it to look for interactions. You may choose to look at main effects only. In fact, this is what the Google Website Optimizer currently does.

In a full factorial parametric test design, the baseline recipe would receive a fraction of the total traffic that is inversely proportional to the size of your search space (e.g., if your search space is 64 recipes, the baseline would receive 1/64th of the total traffic). Since you are trying to beat the existing baseline, special attention should be accorded to it. You also need to be watching for external and internal changes to your traffic. This means that you want to get accurate conversion information about the baseline recipe even though you may not need to collect a large amount of data for *every* recipe. Because of this, I recommend a modification of the traditional full factorial parametric methodology. As a general rule of thumb, I suggest collecting 15%–25% of your total data on the baseline recipe during a test. This allows you to get tighter error bars on the baseline recipe, and reach statistical significance faster.

Full Factorial Parametric Advantages

There are three main advantages to full factorial parametric tests:

Availability of information on interactions   If you use full factorial data collection coupled with a complete model, you can detect all important variable interactions. This is not the case with fractional factorial Resolution III designs such as the Taguchi method, Plackett-Burman, or Latin squares.

Unrestricted test design   You can choose any number of test variables, and arbitrary branching factors for each one. This is in sharp contrast to the significant restrictions found in fractional factorial designs.

Better estimation of main effects   Even if you discard the interaction data and only build a model of the main effects, you will still be better off with a full factorial design. If there are interactions, your estimate of the main effects will be more accurate than with fractional factorial designs. This is due to the fact that you have collected data evenly across all recipes (all possible contexts and combinations), and are not relying on spot-sampling a small subset of your search space.

For example, imagine estimating the average elevation of the United States. Full factorial sampling could be compared to sampling on a grid with each measurement a mile apart. A fractional factorial design might be much sparser and might sample on a grid that spaces each measurement every hundred miles. The coarse sampling might overlook geographic features that are smaller than one hundred miles wide, and your elevation estimate might be significantly biased based on the exact position of the sampling grid points. This is much less likely to be a problem with the finer grid, since you would capture all significant features greater than a mile wide, and could not go too far astray in your estimate.

Full Factorial Parametric Disadvantages

There are several disadvantages to full factorial parametric tests:

Very small test size Because of the exponential growth of the number of model coefficients as you increase the number of variables (and/or their branching factors), full factorial design quickly hits its limits if you are planning to conduct an analysis of all possible interactions. Because of this, full factorial designs are rarely used in landing page optimization unless your search space is smaller. But remember, the search space size can remain as large as a comparable fractional factorial test if you are planning to only model main effects.

Complicated analysis Although Google Website Optimizer and other full factorial testing tools are available, most of them will only report on the main effects within your test (the significance of the individual variable values). If you collect information about possible variable interactions to ensure that you have a more accurate answer, you will have to have a background in statistics to understand which interactions are meaningful.

May not consider variable interactions If you simply conduct a main effects analysis after collecting the data, you will not find variable interactions. In this situation you will also be subject to the piecewise construction errors that I discussed in the "Fractional Factorial Disadvantages" section.

High uncertainty at the recipe level One other slight drawback of the full factorial parametric approach is that the amount of data that you collect on each individual recipe is small. So you may have poor resolution (a lot of variance) at the recipe level. Because of this, you usually have to run a follow-up test to see if your predicted best answer holds up in the real world. But follow-up tests are also recommended (for different reasons) for all fractional factorial tests.

Full Factorial Non-parametric Testing

Non-parametric data analysis can be used with full factorial data collection. In fact, as I mentioned earlier, it *cannot* be used if you impose any restrictions on the recipes allowed during the data collection. To my knowledge, there is only one deployed and proven non-parametric approach currently being used for landing page optimization, and I will sketch out its unique features below. But I am confident that other non-parametric methods will be developed in the future to address the obvious limitations of parametric analysis in this setting.

Epic Sky (EpicSky.com), SiteTuners.com's parent company, runs large-scale PPC campaigns for clients. A few years ago we also started working for ourselves as a super affiliate. We were driving high-quality PPC traffic to the landing pages provided by each company with whom we had signed up as an affiliate. In many cases, the conversion rate of the landing pages was horrible. This had a direct impact on our affiliate payouts and the scale of programs that we could profitably run.

We figured out quickly that if the conversion rate of the landing pages could be increased, our profits would skyrocket. Out of this self-serving need, we started looking into landing page testing techniques.

Unfortunately, we found that the state of the art at the time was parametric multivariate testing (both full and fractional factorial). Because of the significant limitations of these methods, SiteTuners.com spent over three years developing proprietary math specifically tailored to landing page testing. The result is our proprietary TuningEngine technology.

This approach overcomes the two main limitations common to parametric model building. It takes into account all important variable interactions among your input variables *and* it can scale to very large search space sizes.

What makes this possible is a completely different mathematical framework and approach to the landing page optimization problem. Parametric analysis relies on a model building approach. In other words, it tries to gather enough data to accurately estimate the importance of all variable values to the quantity being measured (i.e., the conversion rate). Once the model is built, it is possible to estimate which variables contributed to the improved performance, and how much they contributed.

By contrast, the TuningEngine asks which combination of variable values (i.e., recipe) is the best-performing one. But it cannot determine which individual variables in the recipe contributed the most to the result.

We have given up the explanatory power in exchange for tangible considerations. Online marketing is a practical discipline grounded in financial and business considerations. Your goal should be to find the landing page that makes you the most money. Explaining why the winning recipe is the best is a secondary academic consideration.

Full Factorial Non-parametric Advantages

The TuningEngine has several advantages over parametric approaches:

Considers variable interactions As I mentioned, the TuningEngine takes variable interactions into account. Although full factorial parametric designs also do this, they are very limited in search space size. Most fractional factorial designs ignore important and prevalent variable interactions altogether.

Handles huge test sizes The TuningEngine can handle very large search spaces. We routinely run tests involving millions or tens of millions of possible recipes. This scale is several orders of magnitude larger than what can be done with multivariate tests (using the same data rate). Unlike other companies in our field, SiteTuners.com does not just collect data on a few dozen recipes at a time. We cover the whole search space.

(i.e., our data collection is not extremely sparse, and we can take variable interactions into account).

No experimental design required Most fractional factorial designs require you to have a very specific construction. This means you may only have a certain number of variables, and their branching factors must also conform to the specifics of the test design matrix being used. This often forces online marketers to limit or change their test plan in order to fit these requirements.

The TuningEngine does not place any constraints on your test design. You simply specify the variables that you want to test along with as many alternative values for each one as you would like. The branching factor for each variable can be different. This is also an advantage for full factorial parametric designs.

Very simple analysis The final phase of a TuningEngine test is a simple A-B split test. The significance of the results is easy to understand (using a single simple statistical test).

Full Factorial Non-parametric Disadvantages

The TuningEngine has three main disadvantages.

Requires higher data rates As a rule of thumb, the TuningEngine requires at least one hundred conversions per day to produce results in a reasonable time frame. This is higher than the minimums recommended for A-B split tests or parametric multivariate tests. Many SiteTuners.com clients actually have multiples or orders of magnitude larger data rates than the minimum, and that is when the technology really begins to shine. However, if you cannot meet the minimum requirement, you may simply have no other option than to use A-B split or parametric multivariate testing.

Cannot tell you why the best landing page works As I discussed earlier, the TuningEngine cannot tell you why the winning recipe is the best. In other words, you cannot decompose the results into the contributions of the individual variables. However, this is not as much of a drawback as it first seems. Since variable interactions are prevalent in landing page optimization, any intuition about individual variables is frequently lost anyway. The value of the winning recipe lies in the *combination* of its variable values. So decomposing it into main effects is often a misleading exercise in fantasy.

Proprietary technology Since the TuningEngine is proprietary, you cannot use it to run your own in-house tests. The only way to access it is to hire SiteTuners for a full-service engagement (or to hire a landing page testing firm that licenses this technology from SiteTuners to run its own engagements).

Congratulations, you have made it through the mathematical part of the book! This chapter also concludes Part II, "What and How to Tune." In the last part of the book, we will focus on practical issues related to getting your tests off the ground. In the final chapters we will cover getting buy-in and pulling together the right resources, developing your action plan, and avoiding common pitfalls.

Getting It Done

In the first part of this book, you learned the background necessary to approach landing page optimization. In Part II, you learned how to uncover and select appropriate page elements for your test, as well as which tuning methods to use. The final part of this book deals with the practical matters of establishing your testing program.

The focus now shifts from the psychology of your audience and landing page design to you and your internal company environment. The skill sets required to get the best results from your landing page testing program are very diverse. You will need to work with a wide range of people whose perspectives may be different from your own. Once you have gathered the right resources, you will have to create the appropriate action plan and watch out for common testing program pitfalls that can derail all of your work.

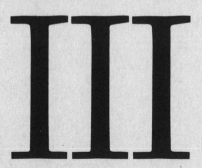

Part III consists of the following chapters:

Assembling the Team and Getting Buy-in

After all is said and done, more is said than done.
—Aesop

As you have seen from the scope of this book, landing page optimization encompasses many disciplines. In this chapter, you will learn about the common roles required to create a successful testing program. Each role brings its own expertise, biases, and needs that must be addressed. You will learn how to bring the necessary people together and move them toward supporting you in your efforts.

Chapter Contents

The Usual Suspects

Your testing program can move forward and still fail. If it does, it will likely happen as a result of a "death by a thousand cuts." Your original test ideas will be reviewed, tweaked, overruled, and co-opted by many others along the way. It is like the children's game of "telephone" in which all participants line up and an original message is repeated and whispered to the next person in line. By the time it reaches the other end, you end up with something completely unrecognizable.

The Blind Men and the Elephant

by John Godfrey Saxe (1816–1887)

It was six men of Indostan, to learning much inclined,
who went to see the elephant (Though all of them were blind),
that each by observation, might satisfy his mind.

The first approached the elephant, and, happening to fall,
against his broad and sturdy side, at once began to bawl:
"God bless me! but the elephant, is nothing but a wall!"

The second feeling of the tusk, cried: "Ho! what have we here,
so very round and smooth and sharp? To me 'tis mighty clear,
this wonder of an elephant, is very like a spear!"

The third approached the animal, and, happening to take,
the squirming trunk within his hands, "I see," quoth he,
"the elephant is very like a snake!"

The fourth reached out his eager hand, and felt about the knee:
"What most this wondrous beast is like, is mighty plain," quoth he;
"'Tis clear enough the elephant is very like a tree."

The fifth, who chanced to touch the ear, Said; "E'en the blindest man
can tell what this resembles most; Deny the fact who can,
This marvel of an elephant, is very like a fan!"

The sixth no sooner had begun, about the beast to grope,
than, seizing on the swinging tail, that fell within his scope,
"I see," quoth he, "the elephant is very like a rope!"

And so these men of Indostan, disputed loud and long,
each in his own opinion, exceeding stiff and strong,
Though each was partly in the right, and all were in the wrong!

So, oft in theologic wars, the disputants, I ween,
tread on in utter ignorance, of what each other mean,
and prate about the elephant, not one of them has seen!

But you have no choice because you need the cooperation of many people. You have to bear the ultimate responsibility for wrangling and herding them roughly in the desired direction. So your skills as a diplomat and persuader will be very important.

A camel is a horse designed by a committee.

—Sir Alec Issigonis (designer of the Mini car)

To help guide you through this process, I have put together a list of the "usual suspects." These are roles that are commonly needed for a successful landing page optimization program. Depending on the scope of your program, not all of them may be applicable to you or your organization. If your company or department is small, several of these roles may be assigned to a single person. In fact, many of them may currently be assigned to you. If that is the case, use extra caution to take yourself and your predispositions into account as much as possible.

Each role in this section has an associated scope of responsibilities or expertise. I have included a section on typical *skills and training* required. Each role also has a *specific overlap* with your landing page optimization program. I will also bring up *common issues* that repeatedly come up in our tests involving each role (with suggestions about how to address them whenever possible).

Remember to pay particular attention when you get to the sections describing your own role or roles. Read them with the additional perspective of understanding how others may view your responsibilities, biases, and working style. Don't become a stumbling block to your own program by ignoring your role in it.

User Experience

User experience (commonly abbreviated as UX) is an interdisciplinary field that examines how users interact with a particular system, object, or device. This includes how they view it, learn about its capabilities, and use it in the real world.

Skills and training In the case of landing page optimization, you are mainly concerned with the Web browser and the content and function of your landing pages, so the UX professionals will likely come from the specific disciplines of human factors, user-centered design, human computer interaction, information architecture, interface design, visual design, or usability testing. Most of these are pretty specialized skills and are not commonly available in most online marketing departments. However, UX people may be working within your software development team. If no one at the company has this background, it is possible to hire consultants on a project basis. With their broad experience, such people can often provide critical insights into which elements to test.

Specific overlap UX specialists are usually given wide scope to improve the overall usability of a system. Because usability is a huge factor in conversion rate improvement, they are usually heavily involved in development of the written test plan (helping to determine the elements to be tested, along with the specific alternatives for each element to be considered). UX experts can also readily construct the roles, tasks, and AIDA decision process steps for your business, and help you identify gaps. They are also experienced at matching important business objectives to the needs of users.

Common issues UX practitioners are generalists. They may have been involved in the design of many websites on a variety of topics. For this reason, it is important to team them with a subject matter expert (SME). Without the support of someone knowledgeable in your industry or business, UX practitioners may miss important aspects of your conversion process or business goals.

UX people are usually good at the *functional* and *architectural* aspects of your design (i.e., common usability issues that are likely to affect all of your visitors). They are usually weaker on the *content* issues, such as text copy, marketing message, and graphical design.

UX practitioners are also believers in the notion that through good design procedures and small-scale usability testing (involving a few representative test subjects) they can come up with a high-performance and coherent design. However, they need to understand that you are not asking them to come up with a perfect design. Their ideas may be used piecemeal as part of your test. It is often tremendously liberating for them to be allowed to come up with ideas without having to be sure they are all good.

The best landing page version will be found statistically (by watching the behavior of thousands of people), not through qualitative or small-scale usability testing. UX practitioners are also often in favor of testing, but they often have problems with statistically based testing such as is described in this book. Because of this, their involvement should usually be confined to helping decide what to test, and not the subsequent data collection or analysis.

Product Manager

Product managers are typically responsible for all aspects of developing and marketing a particular product or service. They may also have profit and loss (P&L) responsibility (i.e., they are held accountable for the profit and loss performance of the product group as a whole). Product managers have operational day-to-day responsibility for the product team, although they may draw on staff members from other departments as needed.

Skills and training Product managers can come from a wide variety of backgrounds, including technical, management, and finance. Their main roles are to manage and facilitate. They are usually effective at putting together cross-disciplinary teams of people. Product managers make sure that the product features are responding to competitive marketplace needs, and that the marketing is effective.

Specific overlap At a minimum, product managers will have to approve any landing page project related to their product. Often they will be the person leading or managing the effort.

They may be needed to secure the help of any project-based people outside of your normal team. Product managers also help push through any approvals required from other departments.

Common issues If your product manager is already behind your landing page optimization project, then you have a valuable ally. If that's not the case, you may have a hard time getting enough of your product manager's sustained attention to make it happen. Product managers typically wear too many hats and are overextended. Since their role is to herd others, they are also commonly interrupt-driven and easily distracted.

Product managers are also often in the "if it ain't broke, don't fix it" mode. If the landing page in question already drives significant revenue or value, you may have a difficult time convincing the product manager that there is a need for landing page testing. He or she may be preoccupied with other problems, and may not understand the financial opportunity presented by improving the conversion rate. This may especially be the case if the landing page testing effort requires the product manager to take on significant extra work to coordinate the project.

You must usually go through the product manager to get budget approval for the project. Often, this individual is not the final financial decision maker, and must in turn get approval from his or her boss. Depending on the scale of your company, you may have to wait until the next budget cycle to get your project authorized.

Webmaster

Your webmasters are responsible for the care and maintenance of your website. They maintain the content, control the site organization, and administer the file-naming conventions (e.g., for page names and graphical images). The webmasters make sure that the site does not have any broken links, missing content, browser compatibility issues, or improper form handling. They also create and review the Web analytics reports for the site.

Skills and training Webmasters commonly come from a programming or technical background (operational focus), or from a creative or copywriting background (content focus).

Specific overlap The webmasters will most likely need to approve (or at least be aware of) the changes that you propose to make to the site. They will need to provide you with the original page elements, and help you upload the new test versions of all pages and graphics.

They will most probably oversee and be involved in the quality assurance and testing of all new page elements. Depending on your tuning technology, webmasters may need to tag all Web pages on the site with additional JavaScript and tracking information. They may also be involved in the cutover from your quality assurance environment to the live data collection. Webmasters may also track and monitor your data collection through Web analytics software.

Common issues Some webmasters are very territorial. They like to control exactly how and when changes happen on their site. This mind-set can often get in the way of testing, because you are perceived as violating their turf and creating extra work for them. In extreme situations, this can result in stonewalling or even outright denial of access to certain parts of the site.

You will need the help of your webmaster to download and upload content to the staging portion of your Web server (i.e., one where you can test changes without affecting the live website). Ideally you should have the ability to transfer files to and from the staging server yourself. But many webmasters will refuse access (ostensibly for security reasons) and insist on doing it themselves. Unfortunately, during quality assurance testing numerous uploads may be required to get rid of all known bugs and problems with your test implementation. If your webmaster is uncooperative or busy, this can drag out your implementation schedule considerably.

Webmasters are also in charge of policing the style guides and naming conventions for the site. They can be very particular about file-naming conventions and HTML coding standards. This can hold up testing if not addressed ahead of time.

Because webmasters are often involved in the testing (and may even be in charge of it), it is always a good idea to get their active cooperation. The best way to do this is to arm yourself with information ahead of time, follow procedures, and communicate clearly throughout. Ask for design guidelines, style sheets, procedures, and Web coding conventions. Address exactly what content changes will be tested in your written test plan. This should include the names and locations of all files and content involved.

System Administrator

Your system administrators keep your server network running and operational. They are responsible for Internet connectivity, the load and demand on your Web servers, keeping software up to date, backing up your data, and computer security.

Skills and training System administrators usually come from very technical backgrounds. They are often detail oriented and keep track of a large number of operational details and procedures related to their job duties.

Specific overlap System administrators will be involved in the following ways in your test:

- Moving from the staging to the live environment
- Rerouting traffic for the test

- Reviewing the proposed testing technology and implementation requirements
- Certifying that personal or private customer data is not disclosed during testing
- Ensuring that network security is not compromised by the testing
- Assuring that server loads and Web page loading times are not significantly affected by the test

Common issues Since choosing a particular tuning technology or testing company partner involves technical elements, system administrators will typically want to get involved. They will vet the underlying technology and project implementation procedures in a lot of detail to understand the impact that it will have on their domain. In some cases, they have veto power over choosing certain kinds of tuning technology approaches.

Part of the system administrator's concern has to do with control over the hosting and presentation of the alternative tuning elements during the test. Some testing technologies rely on outside hosting of site elements on the Web servers of the testing company. This is often strongly resisted by system administrators, because they cannot guarantee the security or response times of another company's Web servers. Other technical approaches allow all new content for the test to reside within the current technical environment of the landing page. In other words, alternative tuning elements are also hosted on the company's Web servers. This is much more likely to put the system administrator's mind at ease.

Additional concerns of system administrators center on security and data integrity. They want to make sure that your testing method does not introduce any new vulnerability. This includes inadvertent disclosure of private customer data (such as e-commerce credit card information or personal contact information). These issues are usually easily addressed if you review the proposed technical approach in detail with system administrators, or arrange for them to talk directly with the technical staff of the proposed testing technology company that you are considering using.

Graphics Designer

The graphics designer is responsible for creating all graphical elements of your landing page.

Skills and training Typically, graphics designers will have an artistic background in the visual arts, including drawing, painting, film, animation, and photography. Some will have had additional training in production graphic design for business. They may also have had additional training specifically in Web design and related graphics, photo editing, animation, video authoring, and Web design software packages.

Specific overlap It is likely that you will need the involvement of a graphics designer for your landing page testing. They can create individual graphical elements such as pictures, buttons, navigation menus, and rollover images. Some of these changes are simple (e.g., changing button text or background colors). Other changes may involve a complete redesign of your landing page and its layout.

Graphics designers may also be needed if your test plan calls for special interactive content (such as comparison shopping guides, product demonstrations, and software wizards).

Common issues Graphics designers usually have an artistic bent. This can mean that they are more concerned with self-expression than with the goals of the business. In their need to keep themselves amused, they often try to work on fun projects or turn routine assignments into artistic outlets.

Unfortunately, this tendency can be at odds with the goals of landing page testing. Internet visitors often respond best to stark landing pages on which visual distractions are kept to a minimum. You must keep tight control over your graphic designers. Use the yardstick of "is it absolutely necessary?" to determine if design elements should be included or emphasized. In fact, it is often a good idea to test the complete removal of existing graphical elements.

The same applies to the use of more subtle color treatments. Bold ones may look more "interesting" to you, but plain ones are often less distracting to the visitor. Anything that draws visual attention on the page (other than your primary call-to-action) should be questioned. Instruct your graphics designers to unclutter the landing page. In other words, emphasis on key elements should be achieved by toning down the surrounding page, rather than by making them even bolder to compete with other graphical elements.

The same applies to the use of animation, sound, video, or fancy interactive demonstrations. To get your approval for inclusion in the test plan, graphics designers must show you that their proposed visual solution is the only acceptable one that accomplishes the business objectives and supports the desired outcome. This is a high hurdle to surmount.

An alternative approach is to allow one "artistic" option for some test plan variables. Who knows, it may even end up being part of the best performing recipe. This, after all, is the whole point of testing.

Copywriter

Copywriters are responsible for the text content of your website.

Skills and training Copywriters come from a variety of backgrounds. Some have a formal education in writing and composition. Others were drafted into the role of technical writer. Still others are experts in their subject matter area and have been asked to write specific content or articles for the website.

Specific overlap Many of the elements that you may want to tune involve copywriting: headlines, body text, sales copy, the call-to-action, the naming of navigation links, button text, figure captions, and text embedded in graphics.

Common issues Copywriters are often generalists. They may need the support of your marketing staff, subject matter experts, or product manager to make sure that your main messaging points and technical features are being presented effectively from the perspective of your intended audience.

Copywriters write for a variety of corporate materials, including informational articles, technical writing, and print collateral. When writing for the Web, they tend to carry over the same editorial style. In fact, effective landing page copy often goes against the very grain of traditional expositional writing and grammar. Copywriters need to be closely monitored to make sure that their Web writing conforms to the guidelines that I covered in the "Language" section of Chapter 5, "Why Your Site Is Not Perfect." This includes use of the inverted pyramid style, factual objective information, and the use of concise sentence fragments or bullet lists.

Marketing Manager

The marketing managers are responsible for the marketing of your product or service. They formulate the marketing plan and oversee its execution.

Skills and training Marketing managers often come from an advertising, communications, finance, or creative background. Depending on the size of your company, they may be generalists who are responsible for everything, or specialists who are only in charge of Web promotion. If your advertising mix includes offline components, they may be responsible for making sure that a consistent view of your product exists across all channels.

Specific overlap As part of your test plan development, marketing managers can often provide a lot of excellent background information. This includes marketing intelligence about competitors and your product's positioning in your industry. They can communicate with the copywriter to ensure that there is compliance with the specific marketing messages that need to be included in your sales copy and headlines.

Marketing managers can also help you understand larger business goals and the potential impact of your landing page test on your business partners, customer service, and offline channels.

Common issues Marketing managers understand the full scope of your promotional and traffic acquisition activities. They have a good handle on the expectations of people landing on the site from different online marketing campaigns and what happens upstream of the landing page. It is important to communicate to them the key requirements for your test traffic. As I discussed in Chapter 3, "Understanding Your Audience," your ideal traffic sources should be recurring, controllable, and stable. The marketing manager can help you to identify the largest subset of your traffic that matches these criteria.

Marketing managers often control the marketing plan and are in contact with public relations and other parts of your company. They can tell you about the timing of external events (such as tradeshows and industry-specific seasonal changes). In addition, marketing managers can tell you in advance about any major public relations or product announcements. You must work closely with them to make sure that your proposed data collection period does not fall during these periods; otherwise, your data may be skewed or irreparably tainted.

Programmer

Programmers are responsible for the functional (as opposed to the strictly visual) aspects of your website.

Skills and training The background of programmers is diverse. There are few acknowledged accreditations in the industry. Many excellent programmers are self-taught. The speed of technology changes requires programmers to become lifelong learners or face the prospect of skill obsolescence. Some programmers are focused on the presentation of information to the end user and are adept at scripting languages that make up the *front end* (i.e., the visual portion of the software application with which the visitor interacts). Others concentrate on the representation, storage, and manipulation of the underlying data that make up the *back end* (i.e., they focus on databases and algorithms).

Specific overlap Any functional changes to your landing page or website may potentially require programming support:

- Mouse rollover behavior
- Reconfiguration of form elements based on visitor actions
- Capturing of additional information (changes to the database)
- Business rules and logic
- Changes in the flow through your pages
- Reorganization of the area where you collect data (and the order in which you collect it)
- Processing any new Web-based forms

Common issues Programmers tend to be poor user interface designers, graphics designers, and copywriters. They think only in functional terms. If a certain capability is technically possible, they will not usually try to optimize or improve the user experience. The result is that landing page changes touched by programmers are often very unappealing to your visitors (with the consequence of lower conversion rates). So you must be specific in your quality control and testing about the details surrounding any changes that the programmers make. This includes background colors, fonts and font sizes, form field order and layout, text labels, and error messages.

The best way to deal with this problem is to have detailed specifications for the required functional changes. Include screenshot mock-ups of the proposed designs. You should also spend some time sensitizing the programmers to the subtleties of good design and emphasizing its importance.

On the other hand, programmers are often very receptive to empirical real-world data. If you can show them that a design option actually performs better than an alternative, they are likely to be very enthusiastic about finding more options like the successful one.

Quality Assurance Tester

The quality assurance (QA) tester ensures that all proposed changes to your website function properly before being released as part of your live site.

Skills and training Most QA positions are not full-time. They are typically project based (e.g., part of a complete website redesign process). Consequently, QA staff have a variety of backgrounds and may spend the majority of their time in other roles, such as webmaster, graphics designer, copywriter, or marketing assistant.

Specific overlap QA should always be involved in the tuning process after the test plan has been implemented (and before the changes are moved to your live site prior to the commencement of data collection). Once problems are uncovered, they are sent back to the implementation team for rework.

Common issues It is important that the person assigned to perform QA is not the same person who oversaw the implementation of the test. Otherwise, there is a clear conflict of interest and a tendency to shortchange the QA testing process.

It goes without saying that your landing page optimization should be based on a formal written test plan document that defines the specific elements and values to be tested. As soon as the test plan is completed, you should independently create a QA plan to go with it. The QA plan should note all important design and technical constraints for the proposed test. The QA tester should use this plan to make sure that all variable values are independently tested and that all key combinations of variables are also considered (see Chapter 10, "Developing Your Action Plan," for additional details).

QA testers are supposed to be detail oriented. In fact, this is a requirement for the role. However, some people take things a bit too far. They refuse to sign off on any deviations from the original test plan that are even a little bit out of compliance. At this point you must often make a judgment call about whether the discrepancies are likely to significantly affect the outcome of the test. You may have to overrule the QA tester and accept the current state of the implementation.

The Company Politics of Tuning

A foolish consistency is the hobgoblin of little minds,
adored by little statesmen and philosophers and divines.
—Ralph Waldo Emerson

In the previous section, I looked at the roles that are typically needed to implement a landing page optimization program. You need the *active cooperation* of the team to pull of the project. Although there are common difficulties with some of the required team roles, there are ways of mitigating these issues.

But there is another class of constituencies within your company that is also critical. Each department in your company described in this section serves a needed function. But eventually they also take on a life of their own, and like any power construct their primary goal seems to become self-perpetuation and reputation building. This is often done by exerting influence in the form of noncooperation. Departmental silos and territorialism are often the biggest obstacles to successful landing page optimization. Unlike the previous group, the power of these people is the ability to *withhold permission*. Remember, it only takes one "no" from any of these people to stop your landing page optimization program in its tracks.

Brand Guardians

The brand guardians within your company can include elements of advertising, marketing communications, product development, and product management. These functions can be augmented by outsourced support from your ad agency, media buyers, or public relations firm. Tangible embodiments of your brand include your logo and acceptable logo presentations, website style guides, public relations messaging points, and color choices.

As I mentioned earlier in the book, a brand can be one of the most powerful assets that a company possesses. It can cut through the clutter in a prospect's mind and serve as a shortcut to decision making. Many companies spend huge sums of money promoting and building their brands for this reason. They also vigilantly guard against distortions or miscommunications of their competitive positioning and messaging points.

There is a danger of a brand becoming fossilized. As the brand becomes increasingly powerful, it takes on a life of its own. The stronger the momentum of the brand, the more difficult it is to make significant changes to it. For better or worse, this is not an issue for many online companies that are contemplating landing page optimization. Chances are your brand is not that well known (at least to the new visitors who arrive on your landing page as a result of your traffic-acquisition efforts).

One of the biggest problems encountered by brand guardians is the lack of consistent messaging about the product. Because of this, brand guardians are often insistent that the key messaging point must be repeated across all media outlets and marketing channels without variation. Although this is generally a worthwhile aspiration, remember that the goal of landing page optimization is to find a landing page design that your audience responds to best.

As a part of this, you are trying to find the right message and the best presentation of it. So brand guardians' insistence on messaging orthodoxy can often shut down the testing of revolutionary new sales copy or headlines that represent outside-the-box thinking. If one of your alternative messages draws a better response, it means that it resonated better with your target audience. The winning element can in fact become part of your new and improved product messaging.

Brand guardians must understand that landing page testing can be an excellent way to conduct market research and understand the changing needs of the target audience. They must not simply insist on the endless (and sometimes mindless) repetition of the current approach. The original messaging and presentation may very well beat out any of the tested alternatives. But at the core of testing philosophy lies the possibility that you may not have the optimal solution, and that you may find better performance through the testing of alternatives.

I.T. Staff

The information technology (I.T.) people in your company may be concentrated in a department of the same name. But they can also encompass anyone with a primarily technical background or role. This potentially includes the webmaster, programmers, system administrator, and your hosting company (if you outsource this function).

I.T. people like to say no, especially to marketing people. The gulf between marketing and I.T. within a company can be wide. The mind-sets of the two groups of people are fundamentally different. I.T. people often see themselves as the high priests of technology and try to keep marketers completely away from their domain.

I.T. staff members are often legitimately busy and overwhelmed. Since their support is often requested (or demanded) by many people in the company, they have developed a multilayered defensive strategy. Even if they do not directly refuse a request for assistance, they can effectively block progress by a series of escalating responses. Common policies and tactics include:

Technical feasibility determinations If I.T. staff does not want to work on a project, they will examine the proposed underlying technology and declare it unfit for some reason. They might insist that it cannot be effectively integrated with existing technologies or systems. In landing page optimization, this approach is commonly used to disqualify the tuning technology. Since the reasons for the objection are often highly technical, few marketers can muster the necessary ammunition to counteract it.

Common reasons for rejecting technologies include incompatibilities, noncompliance with security policies, additional load placed on networks, increased page load times, and dependencies on the testing company's servers for serving some of the landing page content elements.

Luckily, most testing companies, including SiteTuners.com, have come up with noninvasive approaches to testing. The only underlying technologies required are JavaScript (a scripting language available in all popular browsers) and the setting of first-party cookies (allowed by the vast majority of Internet users). With many approaches, the alternative tuning elements can remain in the client's original Web server environment. Uptime levels and response times (collectively referred to as "availability") can also be guaranteed or effectively addressed.

Scheduling and resource allocation I.T. staff may insist that since your project was not scheduled during the last planning cycle it will have to go to the back of the line. In addition, I.T. managers may insist that since no resources were allocated, the project will have to wait until the next budget cycle.

Operational policies Most landing page optimization projects do not require a lot of I.T. support time, but they often involve a number of small interrupt-driven tasks. I.T. has the power to bring the project to a virtual standstill by insisting that detailed, time-consuming, and labor-intensive systems be used to interact with their staff. There are many names for these systems, including "change requests," "trouble tickets," and "issue tracking." Their use is appropriate for larger projects (so component tasks will not be overlooked), but they can be overkill when the required changes can be addressed within a few minutes by the I.T. staffer. In such cases, a small request for help can be tied up for days or weeks in the system without resolution. If this happens repeatedly, it can throw off a landing page project by many weeks.

Common ways to proceed in the face of I.T. delaying tactics include the following:

Work on a landing page outside of I.T. control It is often difficult to get permission to change parts of a company's main website. However, many marketing programs use stand-alone landing pages or microsites that are not connected to the main site. In many cases, such landing pages have significant inbound traffic and are controlled by the marketing department. Since you can control many of the traffic sources for the landing page test, you can redirect their traffic to anywhere you would like.

Get a project-based support commitment You can often get a specific I.T. staff member assigned to you for the duration of your project. As long as you can guarantee that the individual will be used at only a small percentage of the person's total time availability and for a short duration, you can often get I.T. approval. These kinds of arrangements transfer the person nominally to your team (or have that person remain under joint jurisdiction). This allows you to bypass many of the I.T. procedural requirements and have the I.T. staffer complete your tasks with minimal delay.

Prioritize projects based on financial impact If you properly lay out the financial case for your landing page test, you may be able to show the potential for a large profit impact on the company. In many cases, I.T. projects are prioritized based partially on this criterion. By focusing on the financial impact, you may be able to reprioritize your project to the head of the I.T. queue.

Procedural Gatekeepers

There are typically several procedural gatekeepers in a company. They are responsible for avoiding high-impact or publicly embarrassing problems. Common functional areas for gatekeepers are:

Legal Depending on your industry, your legal department may insist on reviewing all publicly accessible documents (including any proposed landing pages). They will make sure that you do not make any wild or exaggerated marketing claims that can expose you to liability. Your proposed headlines and sales copy can be edited into a form that is no longer compelling to your audience. Your legal team may also insist that various disclaimers and policies appear on the page. If you are forced into this situation, try to visually deemphasize this information (by using lower-contrast font colors or smaller font sizes, placing it into a scrollable window, or relegating it to supporting pages via links). Do not allow a long list of fine print to become the dominant visual focus of your page.

Regulatory compliance Some industries are heavily regulated by federal or state laws. If this is true in your case, you may assign an in-house person to make sure that all activities are in compliance with the law. This may require a review of your proposed landing pages. Often, specific language must be used to describe certain features of your product or service. Details of the terms and conditions of your offer must also appear.

Business development Your landing page does not exist in a vacuum. It is possible that your business has significant offline marketing components, multiple distribution channels, alliances, and partnership agreements of various kinds. Some of these may restrict your ability to test various aspects of your landing page. For example, you may be bound by noncompete agreements not to sell certain products or services on the Web, or you may have to enforce minimum pricing standards in order to avoid undercutting your distributors. If you have co-marketing agreements with business partners, you may have to adhere to additional marketing rules that they have in place.

C-whims

"C"-level officers in your company are often driven leaders. In fact, that is how they go to the top. This includes not only the Chief Executive Officer (CEO), Chief Operating Officer (COO), Chief Marketing Officer (CMO), Chief Technical Officer (CTO), Chief

Financial Officer (CFO), but also the top vice presidential levels. They are all different in their roles and responsibilities, but share the authority to fire you (or at least make your life miserable).

Many can effectively delegate responsibilities to subordinates. Others can't. We have seen a surprisingly high level of meddling in landing page testing by managers who should be several levels removed from the operational testing.

Landing page testing is often the target of their attention for the following reasons:

High visibility Landing pages are exposed to the public and seen by huge numbers of your company's potential prospects.

Large potential profit impact In many cases, landing page testing has by far the largest profit impact of any online marketing activity. C-level executives love to follow the money trail, and pay particular attention to projects that can have a large impact on the bottom line.

Testing is fun When you show a high-level executive your proposed test plan, they may want to get involved themselves. The brainstorming process is fun. It lets the creative juices flow. Many C-level execs like to roll up their sleeves and try to guess what your audience will respond to.

Unfortunately, just because C-level executives can get involved in landing page optimization does not mean that they should. Their opinions are based on gut feelings and hunches that are philosophically the polar opposite of large-scale statistical sampling of your audience's actual behavior. And these opinions carry disproportional weight in the decision-making process. So precious slots in the test plan must be relegated to the pet choices of the executives, at the expense of more promising alternatives that your team develops.

Finance

The financial gatekeeper considerations vary based on the size of your business:

Sign-off authority Different levels of managers have different limits on the size of purchases that they can approve independently. Depending on the scope of your testing program, you may need to get several levels of budget approval, including the CFO or even CEO.

Budget cycles The length of your budget cycle and the timing of the next budget planning process can delay your project by many months. You may need to reallocate some funds from the current approved budget in order to start your testing earlier. This is often difficult since it comes out of some other activity that presumably has some internal company support (since it was approved as part of the current budget).

Strategies for Getting Started

A testing program has to be established, and then it becomes an ongoing or periodic activity in the online marketing department. The success of the first project is critical for establishing the long-term momentum for subsequent engagements. There are a number of strategies that you can pursue as you get started.

Start Small

A common way to start your testing program is with a small test. Once you have demonstrated your ability to pull off a complete end-to-end landing page experiment, you should have enough support to continue. The key to this approach is to appear nonthreatening and not ask for a lot of help.

Components of a small test may include:

Unimportant landing page Do not try to fix your home page or highest-traffic landing pages first. Such efforts may be actively resisted before you have proven yourself. Pick a secondary landing page that has a reasonable amount of traffic (perhaps from a single online marketing campaign).

Small diversion of traffic If you have only one landing page, you can still conduct your test by diverting a small percentage of the traffic to testing alternatives. This will guarantee that even if your tested alternatives underperform the current baseline, the overall drop in conversion rate will be small.

Simple page changes If you make simple changes such as headlines, sales copy, and call-to-action buttons, you will not need a lot of outside support to create your alternative tuning elements. You can also make such changes in a short amount of time.

Basic test structure Use A-B split testing (either on a granular or coarse level) for the test. The data analysis is simple—there are no complex variable interactions or complex design matrices to worry about.

Low-cost testing platform Several low-cost tools are available for running basic A-B split and multivariate tests. Many of them are hosted on the Internet and do not even require installation. An excellent choice for this purpose is the free Google Website Optimizer tool available to all AdWords advertisers in their account. The Google Website Optimizer is covered in detail in Appendix A of this book.

But remember, your test must still produce results that are meaningful. This means your data rate must be high enough to complete the test in a reasonable period of time, and the financial impact (or at least the percentage of improvement in the conversion rate) must be significant. Don't run your test if the data rate will be too low, or if the proposed test elements are unlikely to produce conversion improvements on the landing page.

Stay Below the Radar

It's easier to ask forgiveness than it is to get permission.
—Rear Admiral Grace Murray "Amazing Grace" Hopper

Another option for running your first test is to do it out of public view. Sneak it into your normal activities. This can be done by diverting a portion of your existing budget to testing activities. You and your testing team can also run tests "off the clock" in addition to your normal activities.

Many online marketing programs run on a cost-per-acquisition (CPA) basis. If you bring in a reasonable volume of leads or sales at the target cost per acquisition, then people will not care exactly how you do it. In this environment you can spend some of your media dollars on testing and still hit your volume numbers by squeezing more conversions out of the lower ad spend. Once you have a case study pointing to a real success, you can go into the open and get additional budget specifically for testing.

Sneak It Through Your Affiliate Program

You can also consider testing as a part of your affiliate program. Since improved landing pages increase lead volume without changing the affiliate's payout structure, they have a "force multiplier" effect on all of your current and future affiliates. You can legitimately funnel off some of your affiliate program management budget to the landing page optimization effort.

One way to bypass the need for budget approval is to roll your testing into your performance-based affiliate payouts. SiteTuners.com is the only major testing company that will run landing page optimization projects on a strictly performance basis (we also offer fixed-price engagements as an option). In other words, we only get paid if we can demonstrate better performance in a head-to-head test between our best challenger and the company's original baseline landing page. Many companies prefer this approach, because there is no financial risk to them, and SiteTuners.com gets paid only out of the extra value created.

Outsource

We will cover outsourcing in detail in the next chapter. The decision to handle landing page optimization in-house or to outsource can be a complicated one. But if you are considering outsourcing strictly for the initial proof-of-concept test, it has several clear advantages:

Guarantee that resources and skill sets are available Any reputable testing company that you hire will have all of the necessary skill sets in-house. They will often have access to specialists that you cannot afford to hire and do not need on a full-time basis.

No need to ride the learning curve The testing company will also have extensive experience in writing test plans, running tests, and analyzing the results. You do not have to learn based on your own mistakes and are much more likely to have a positive outcome for your first test.

Allows you to shift blame or take credit If the test does not go smoothly, it can be blamed on problems with the testing company. If it goes well, you can take full credit for having had the foresight to hire them.

Make the Financial Case

Most top managers are receptive to financial arguments. They understand that there are two basic ways to improve profits: increase revenues and lower costs. They like and appreciate subordinates who also speak the language of money and understand their contribution to the company's financial success.

As I discussed at length in Chapter 2, "Understanding Your Landing Pages," you should focus on the mission critical parts of your website and understand the value of the intended conversion actions. Take the time to dig up financial information that allows you to estimate the lifetime value of the conversion action. Build your own financial model once you understand the revenue and variable cost percentage for your landing page. Remember to use conservative assumptions and estimates to make your business case stronger and more defensible.

You can use the free SiteTuners.com profit calculator to produce a table of the likely financial impact of your proposed landing page optimization project. Often this can mean large potential profit increases. In fact, your project may be the most financially promising marketing initiative available to the company. Once you get high-level executive buy-in based on the financial case for the project, you should have the political support to move it along and get the active cooperation of other team members.

Build a Coalition

If you are convinced that your landing page optimization program will be ongoing and successful, you can try to build the required commitment and support inside your company from the very beginning. This task will involve significant effort and emotional commitment to rally support for your project and address or neutralize key sources of opposition to it. Coalition building may produce the most durable results, but it is also the hardest and most time-consuming approach that you can choose. For this reason, I recommend starting with one of the other approaches and doing coalition-building activities in parallel on an ongoing basis.

Insource or Outsource?

Should you outsource your testing program or "insource" it by doing everything in-house?

> *Consultants are people who borrow your watch and tell you what time it is, and then walk off with the watch.*
> —Robert Townsend, Author of *Up the Organization*

Do consultants add any real value?

> *Working definition of insanity—doing the same thing over and over again and expecting a different result.*
> —Common quote

Can you make any real progress with your landing page optimization program from your tactical insider perspective?

The decision to insource or outsource your landing page testing project is complicated and depends on many factors:

Core competency focus Some companies consider online marketing in general, and landing page optimization in particular, as functions that are not part of their core competency. They focus instead on product differentiation, manufacturing, distribution, or service fulfillment as the basis for their long-term competitive advantage. They view Internet marketing as a volatile and rapidly changing activity that is best left to specialist companies whose sole mission it is to stay on top of this chaotic environment and deliver the best results.

Other companies view online marketing as their primary revenue-generating activity and the gateway to rapidly growing markets. They are committed to building the required team in-house, and consider a landing page optimization capability to be strategic to their success. Such companies typically spend considerable resources recruiting, training, and motivating key employees. They create systems and processes to monitor and continually improve the way that they carry out testing projects. They view any experience gained during the building of their program and team as a source of lasting competitive advantage, and relish the sense of control that this gives them over their revenue-generating activities.

There is no right answer here. When a business is complicated, it is harder to manage. So this is simply a matter of determining how your organization defines its main focus. If your company feels strongly one way or the other, then the decision to insource or outsource will often be made on the core competency issue alone.

Learning curve and lost opportunity costs As you can appreciate from the scope of this book, landing page optimization is a complex activity that draws on expert skills from a wide range of disciplines. It is unlikely that you already have all of the required skill sets in-house. You can hire people with the necessary skills, or train for your staff members to acquire them (either formally or through on-the-job experience). Either way, there is a significant direct cost to acquiring the necessary skills.

There are also four often-overlooked indirect costs to the insourcing decision. First, as your staff members train, they lose productivity or capacity to do other presumably important work in your company. Second, while the people with the skill sets in this discipline remain in short supply, they may jump to other companies for better pay. This means that you trained them but someone else will get much of the benefit of your investment. Third, their initially low experience level will produce suboptimal results. Since even small conversion rate improvements can be financially significant, this lack of expertise can cost you in terms of lost revenues. Fourth, riding the learning curve takes time, so your improved landing page may become operational some months later than it otherwise might have. The opportunity cost of this delay can be large.

If you consider all of these direct and indirect costs, you may find outsourcing to be a good solution. It allows you to instantly acquire the required skill set and quickly deploy an improved landing page.

Availability of appropriate outsourcing partners Landing page optimization touches mission critical parts of your company. If your landing page test is mishandled or the tuning elements that are chosen actually decrease conversion rates, you can see the results directly in your business performance. So a high level of trust is required if you are going to outsource this function.

Outsourcing also requires a good cultural fit with your prospective partner. This includes an alignment at the business values level. It also requires organizations that operate at the same pace and frequency of communication as your company.

The way that your website is engineered or the specific site elements that you want to test may require you to use specialized technology. As a general rule, free tools or Internet-hosted application service provider (ASP) testing solutions are simpler and have fewer capabilities than some of the advanced testing platforms developed by full-service testing companies. If your tests are relatively simple and your underlying site technology is straightforward, you have many more choices. If you have special needs, you may have to outsource to one of the few firms that can accommodate your technical requirements.

Testing companies may have their own requirements to consider you as a potential client (besides your ability to afford their services). If you have a bureaucratic company that requires reviews by several gatekeepers, testing companies may not want to work with you. Most testing companies also have minimum requirements for data rates on the landing pages that you are tuning.

If you cannot find a partner that is in alignment with you on these issues, you may have no choice but to go it alone.

Perspective   Thinking outside the box is difficult if you work in it. Your experience in your industry, company, and department conspire to straightjacket you with invisible assumptions. It is hard to throw away all of your biases and beliefs and come up with truly original approaches to testing. Your current landing page may loom like a huge case of writer's block and prevent you from seeking any radical change. It probably already represents your best thinking.

When you outsource, you will bring fresh minds to your testing program. The people at the testing company are experts in testing. But they are not knowledgeable about your specific industry and business. This allows them to bring a "beginner's mind" to the problem at hand. They may ask silly and naïve questions, or question assumptions that you hold as sacrosanct. They may also break your fixation with sales copy and messaging and focus on more fundamental usability issues that you did not even know your landing page had.

Capacity and schedule   Can you dedicate full-time staff to move your project along or will they be distracted and pulled in too many directions? If you do not have someone on your team whose primary responsibility is the success of your testing program (as opposed to being in charge of testing along with several other higher priorities), you probably will not achieve the best possible results.

Outsourcing has several advantages from this perspective: a larger dedicated team, significant prior experience, better systems and processes to deploy tests faster, experience with complex implementations, working knowledge of powerful testing tools, and an awareness of common mistakes in analyzing test data.

Affordability and payment methods   As I discussed earlier, by means of bizarre accounting and thinking, your own staff do not count toward the cost of a project, while a comparably small expense for an outside service is an "extra" cost. Of course this is nonsense, and your employees are expensive (double their salary as a rough guide to burdened costs with overhead included). They should be working on highest-impact activities that contribute the most to your company's success. Given their skill set and other company responsibilities, this may not be landing page optimization.

Even if you consider the burdened staff time and other carrying costs, outsourcing may be more expensive over the length of the actual test. But you also have to keep in mind the cost of keeping your in-house capability around and idling between tests. This can be even more expensive in the long term—especially considering the stop/start momentum required to reactivate the team for each test.

Another consideration is which budget "bucket" the testing funds come out of, and the payment options available from outsourcing partners. For example, many testing companies offer extended payment terms or allow you to pay a flat-fee monthly subscription for a certain ongoing level of testing work. Some offer guarantees of various kinds. As I mentioned earlier, SiteTuners.com offers a no-money-upfront pure performance-based payment option. The payments begin after the test (out of the future improved cash flow once the new better-performing landing page has gone live).

Once you have assembled your team and built internal company support, it is time to get to work. In the next chapter we will cover the specific steps required to execute your landing page optimization program.

Developing Your Action Plan

He who fails to plan, plans to fail.
—Proverb

All of the preceding chapters in this book have in a sense been a preparation for this one. Hopefully, you now have a comprehensive understanding of the key issues surrounding landing page optimization. But all of this knowledge will do you no good if you do not apply it. This chapter will give you a step-by-step framework for developing your landing page optimization action plan.

Chapter Contents
Before You Begin
Understand Your Business Objectives
Build Support and Assemble Your Team
Determine Your Landing Pages and Traffic Sources
Decide What Constitutes Success
Uncover Problems and Decide What to Test
Select an Appropriate Tuning Method
Implement and Conduct QA
Collect the Data
Analyze the Results and Verify Improvement

Before You Begin

Much of the material condensed here relies on previously presented material. I strongly suggest that you go back and revisit all appropriate prior book sections as you prepare your plan.

When we start an engagement at SiteTuners.com, the first thing we do is gather some background information about the client's business and online marketing programs. This framework guides our action plan development and identifies constraints or potential issues early in the process. The simplified sample questionnaire in the sidebar "Resource: Preliminary Questionnaire" can help you understand the big picture before you start your test. If you do not know the answers to some of these questions, you may want to gather them from the appropriate sources in your company.

Resource: Preliminary Questionnaire

Marketing and External Factors

- Are there any seasonal traffic spikes or bumps in your industry?
- Are you planning to launch any significant marketing or PR campaigns?
- Are you planning to introduce any new products?
- Are you planning to significantly change the functionality or pricing of existing products?
- Who are your three biggest online direct competitors?
- What are your main differentiators and positioning points against your competitors?

Site Performance and Traffic Levels

- What traffic source(s) will be used for the test?
- How many conversion actions per day do they represent?
- What site elements have you tested in the past? What were the results?
- What site elements would you be interested in testing? Why?
- Do you have any service-level or response time guidelines for your Web servers?

Site Appearance and Functionality

- Do you have a formal creative brief for your logo and/or site?
- Are there any technical requirements for your site (screen resolution, plug-ins)?
- Are any portions of your site design or organization "off-limits" for our test and may not be changed?

Use the contents of the simplified questionnaire as a starting point. You may want to create a more detailed or modified set of questions to suit your particular needs and environment.

Understand Your Business Objectives

As I discussed in Chapter 2, "Understanding Your Landing Pages," you must begin with a solid understanding of your business objectives, and know how your landing page or website supports them.

What drives your business? Is it sales, subscriptions, leads, downloads, e-mail sign-ups, or advertising and page views? What portion of your business marketing intersects with the Web? Is all of it conducted online? Are key parts influenced by offline marketing, or do they require subsequent phone or in-person follow-up? You may not have control over the whole process and may be a single step in the value chain. Your goal should be to make your piece as powerful and efficient as possible.

You may be tactically focused on hitting your cost-per-action (CPA) numbers or growing your volume by a certain percentage. But you may not have a good sense of your contribution to the company as a whole. Dig for financial information. Go as high up the financial management ladder as necessary to get the numbers that you need. Your managers will likely appreciate your newfound interest in the company's bottom line. In fact, you may be speaking their language for the first time.

Building the Financial Model

You must build a model of the lifetime value (LTV) of your conversion action. If you base your program simply on the revenue from the initial transaction, you may severely underestimate the true worth of your marketing activities in general and the value of landing page conversion improvement in particular. After you have calculated the LTV, take seasonal factors into account and calculate the annualized revenue run rate of your conversion activities.

It is also critical to properly understand your variable cost percentage. As I previously discussed, this is different from the standard accounting definition, and is not directly related to your current profit margin. For purposes of landing page optimization, all of your in-house media buying (including banner ads and PPC traffic) are a fixed cost and should not be included in this number. Reread "The Financial Impact of Conversion Rate Improvement" section of Chapter 2 to learn how to calculate the revenue and variable cost percentage for your specific business type.

The data that you ask for may not be readily available. You may be the first person to request it in the format that I have described. It is okay to use estimates or averages when appropriate financial reports are not available. You should also be conservative when dealing with ranges, and always err on the side of caution. Once you have the raw numbers, you may still have to make additional assumptions. Again, try to be conservative. In most cases you will find that even your most cautious scenarios still represent significant potential improvement to your company's bottom line. Use the Conversion Improvement Profit Calculator (mentioned in Chapter 2) to determine the range of likely financial outcomes from your test. See the sidebar "Resource: Building the Business Case" for additional background.

Resource: Building the Business Case

- What is the primary desired conversion action (click-through, form-fill, download, purchase, time-on-page)?
- Are there any additional conversion actions?
- What is the number of annualized conversion actions expected from the traffic sources to be used for this test (repeat for each conversion action)?
- What is the lifetime value (LTV) of the conversion action (repeat for each conversion action)?
- What is the annualized run rate of LTV for all conversion actions from your test traffic sources (sum over all possible conversion actions)?
- What is your variable cost percentage (VCP) on an incremental conversion action (use a weighted average across all possible conversion actions)?

Build Support and Assemble Your Team

As I discussed in Chapter 9, "Assembling the Team and Getting Buy-in," you need to diplomatically rally all important contributors and gatekeepers around your cause. Always understand every stakeholder's concerns, limitations, and biases. Show them why it is in their best interests to help you, and how the project will make them look good.

If this is your first landing page test, then review the "Strategies for Getting Started" section of Chapter 9 as well, and pick the one that is most appropriate for your company and political environment. Since you have prepared the financial model to describe the impact of your proposed test, you should try to get the buy-in of the highest management levels that you can. If they have blessed it, it should be much easier to secure the cooperation of the needed team.

Of course, not everyone is likely to fall into line. In some cases the best that you can hope for is to neutralize active opposition. Another strategy would be to bypass potential sources of conflict or trouble altogether.

Assembling the Team

Assembling your team is not really a one-shot activity—the cast of characters will change throughout your project. It is an ongoing process. The composition of your team will vary dramatically depending on the scope of your proposed test. In some cases, you may test a very granular text change (such as an alternative headline). These kinds of tests you may be able to handle yourself with self-service landing page testing software tools. At the other extreme, you may be considering redesigning your whole site and re-architecting your conversion process in fundamental ways. This might involve changes to your branding, information architecture, content management system, or back-end databases. You may need the active participation of usability experts, graphics designers, copywriters, programmers, product managers, and your advertising agency.

In addition, you may have to deal with a complicated I.T. environment involving network administrators, webmasters, and QA testers. This may require intricate and formal code or file upload, separate staging areas, and elaborate quality control procedures before your test changes are approved.

As I discussed earlier, it may be appropriate for you to outsource your entire project to a full-service landing page testing company. This is largely dependent on the skill sets you already have in-house, as well as people's availability during the proposed testing period. Sometimes you may need specialized technology that is not available from landing page testing software packages. In such cases, you may have no choice but to work with a full-service testing company that has developed the specific technical capability that you need. See the sidebar "Resource: Assembling the Team" for additional details.

Resource: Assembling the Team

In-house Resources and Procedures

- Which roles can you and your immediate team fill?

  - User experience and interface design

  - Product manager

  - Webmaster

  - System administrator

  - Graphics designer

  - Copywriter

  - Marketing manager

  - Programmer

  - QA tester (should not be you unless this is your only role)

- Which of the above roles can other members of your company fill?

- Identify specific people and the approximate level-of-effort (in total hours) that may be required for all the roles in the preceding two questions.

- Who will have the *primary* responsibility for each of the following steps in the process?

  - Overall test

  - Identification of landing page problems

Resource: Assembling the Team *(continued)*

- Brainstorming testing features

- Drafting test plan

- Reviewing and approving the test plan

- Approving budget and allocating staff resources

- Implementation

- Quality assurance

- Move from "staging" to "live" environment

- Data collection

- Analysis

- Presentation of results

- Are there any reviews of your test required by the following entities?

  - Brand/style (logos, style sheets, colors, messaging)

  - I.T. (testing technology, uploading of files, policies)

  - Legal/compliance (legal requirements, disclaimers)

  - Product manager (copywriting, offer, call-to-action)

Determine Your Landing Pages and Traffic Sources

After you have determined your business goals, you should be able to identify the mission critical parts of your website that lead to the desired conversion action or actions. Review the appropriate sections of Chapter 2. Remember, unless a page or website section directly supports the completion of the conversion action, it is not likely to be mission critical for the purposes of landing page optimization.

Determine the type of landing page that you have: main site, microsite, or stand-alone. Each type has different implications for what can and cannot be tested. For example, if you are modifying the header and navigation structure of a page that is part of your main site, you will have to carry the changes over to the rest of the site. By contrast, you can often make arbitrary and radical changes to a stand-alone landing page that is used to convert visitors from a specific online traffic acquisition campaign.

Selecting Traffic Sources

Before the test begins, determine what subset of your audience you will be tuning for. Sometimes this may be traffic from all available sources. By choosing the widest possible cross section of your audience, you have the opportunity to improve average conversion performance for everyone significantly. At other times you may want to segment for specific online campaigns. This is especially important when the traffic sources represent different kinds of people, with significant differences in their propensity to convert.

You may also want to "geo-target" and segment your audience by their location or preferred language. Time-of-day or day-of-week filtering is also common. For example, you may want to test which landing page design is preferred by your weekend versus weekday visitors, or your workday versus evening visitors.

Regardless of the filtering or segmentation that you have chosen, it is important to make sure that you have enough traffic from each source. Do not run separate landing page tests for traffic sources that do not meet the minimum data rate requirements of the tuning method that you have chosen. Review the appropriate sections of Chapter 8, "Tuning Methods," for additional details.

As I discussed in Chapter 3, "Understanding Your Audience," you should carefully consider the traffic sources that you use and make sure that they are from recurring sources, are controllable, and are stable. You should generally try to avoid spiky sources such e-mail drops to in-house lists. Unless you are tuning specifically for repeat visitors, try to get your test traffic from fresh sources of visitors who are uncontaminated by prior exposure to your company brand, website, or offers.

Once you have picked your traffic sources, do not make the mistake of overgeneralizing the results of your test. Remember, even if you have no significant problems with data collection, audience bias, or analysis of the data, the advantage of your winning page is only predicted to hold up for your *original traffic source mix*. Do not start showing the new version of your landing page to audiences that were not part of your test. If you must use the same page for everyone, at least run a head-to-head test on the held-out traffic sources (i.e., the ones not in your original test) to make sure that the new page does not result in lower conversion rates for this new audience. See the sidebar "Resource: Landing Pages and Traffic Sources" for more information.

Resource: Landing Pages and Traffic Sources

Landing Pages

If multiple landing pages are included in the proposed test, answer the questions in this section for each one.

- What is the landing page?

- Is the landing page a stand-alone page, part of a microsite, or part of your company's main site?

- What is the conversion page (on which the conversion action happens)?

Resource: Landing Pages and Traffic Sources *(continued)*

- What is the confirmation page (page displayed immediately after the conversion page)?

- What intermediate sequence of pages must be traversed between the landing page and the conversion page?

- Are the pages static, or are portions created dynamically on the fly?

- What other components are needed for the proper construction and display of the pages (include files, database, cookies)?

- Do you have access to all components of the page (including original graphics files from which the page images were created)?

Traffic Sources

- Do you have a Web analytics package installed?

- What are the traffic sources that you will use for the test?

- How many conversion actions per day do they represent?

- What tuning methods will be possible at this data rate?

- Are the traffic sources steady or sporadic?

- Can you filter out any undesirable sources (e.g., e-mail drops to in-house lists)?

- Can you filter out any visits from your own company or agents (e.g., call centers or customer service staff)?

Decide What Constitutes Success

At this point, you should already understand your business goals and the lifetime value of your desired conversion actions. From this, you can determine what you will measure in your test. The simplest measure is conversion rate. For many environments this will work well. However, if you have multiple conversion goals or multiple items for sales in an e-commerce setting, you may have to calculate and measure either conversion revenue or gross margin contribution. The math required to analyze this kind of data is much more complicated than the simple counting involved in conversion rate optimization. Please review the "Measuring and Counting" section of Chapter 8 to determine the correct success measure for your test.

As you will see in Chapter 11, "Avoiding the Pitfalls," delayed conversions need to be taken into account. Depending on your specific audience and conversion action characteristics, a significant portion of your visitors may convert after a long period of delay. If this is the case, you may have to take this into account and "age" your data appropriately before making decisions.

Selecting the Right Confidence Level

Another key decision you will have to make is how confident you need to be in your answer. Remember, statistical confidence only tells you the *likelihood* that the new version of your landing page is better than the original. It does not tell you exactly *by how much* it might be better. If your landing page represents the lifeblood of your business and significant economic value runs through it, be conservative and accept only a tiny chance of being wrong.

However, if you are aggressively testing and time is of the essence, you should accept lower confidence levels. As I discussed in Chapter 7, "The Math of Tuning," three major factors determine the length of your test: your data rate, the size of the effects that you find, and the confidence level that you choose. You have no direct control over the first two factors once the test starts, but by setting your confidence level lower, you can often significantly decrease the length of the data collection period.

Another way to look at this trade-off is that you may have to collect data for a much longer time to reliably find improvement effects of a certain size. Please review the "How Long Should My Test Run?" section of Chapter 7 for additional discussion of this topic. This implies that if you have a fixed amount of time to collect data, perhaps due to seasonal factors or business deadlines, you will have to accept the fact that you will be unable to find effects of a certain size, and may have to hope that some big improvement will be found during the test. If the threshold for detectable improvements is very high, you will have to resign yourself to the very real possibility that you may have inconclusive test results. See the sidebar "Resource: Defining Success" to guide you through the success definition process.

Resource: Defining Success

Conversion Action

- Do you have a single conversion action or multiple ones?

- If you have a single conversion action, does it always have the same value?

- If its value differs, can an average value be estimated?

- Decide on your conversion criterion (what will you be optimizing):

  - Conversion rate—For single conversion actions with identical values or a steady average value

  - Revenue per visitor—For e-commerce catalogs with similar profit margins on all products, or multiple conversion goals with different values

  - Profit per visitor—For e-commerce catalogs with substantially different profit margins on products or product categories, or for price tuning

Resource: Landing Pages and Traffic Sources *(continued)*

Confidence Level

- Does a significant percentage of your company's value pass through the landing page(s) to be tested?

- Are you planning a single test or an ongoing campaign of testing?

- Is a significant part of your test traffic from affiliates or performance-based business partnerships?

- Is your conversion action immediate or delayed? If delayed, what is the delay required for 90–95% of visitors to eventually convert?

- Is your data rate high or low?

- Decide on your confidence level:

  - Low (90–95%)—If you plan to conduct multiple tests, have lower data rates, or have little performance-based traffic.

  - High (95–99%+)—If you have high data rates, significant business value flowing through the landing page, or have a lot of performance-based test traffic.

- Decide on how much bandwidth to devote to the baseline recipe:

  - Low (15–25% devoted to baseline recipe)—If you have a high data rate, a multivariate test, and little performance-based test traffic.

  - Medium (50–60% devoted to baseline recipe)—If you are running an A-B split test. Use the higher end of the medium range if you have significant performance-based test traffic.

  - High (75–90% devoted to baseline recipe)—If you have a very conservative company management culture, a high percentage of performance-based test traffic, or are planning to test radical alternatives to your landing page design or content.

Uncover Problems and Decide What to Test

Remember your "ugly baby" from Chapter 5, "Why Your Site Is Not Perfect"? It's still there, crying out for your attention. The unflinching courage and clinical detachment with which you examine the existing problems of your website or landing page will in large part determine the success of your landing page optimization program.

Use all of the applicable tactics in the "Uncovering Problems" section of Chapter 5 to dissect your site. Try not to sensor yourself or your information sources. This is brainstorming with no right or wrong answers. Simply record any issues dispassionately, regardless of how trivial or fundamental they may appear to be.

Once you have collected all of the raw data from this process, classify the issues into broad groups of themes. Group your findings under the broad categories covered in the "Usability Basics" section of Chapter 5. Does anything jump out at you? Typically you will see that your problems cluster in areas such as page structure and emphasis, too much disorganization or clutter, unclear calls-to-action, verbose writing, or improper editorial style.

Deciding on the Tuning Elements

Now that you have listed and categorized all of the problems with your landing page, it is time to prioritize them. As I discussed in Chapter 6, "Selecting Elements to Tune," think about the severity of the negative impact of your landing page problems, and the corresponding amount of improvement if the issue is fixed. Consider the breadth of your problems. Prioritize those that are standing in the way of completing the conversion action, affect the largest segments of your audience, and are prominently featured on your page.

The combination of your data rate and the length of time that you have allotted for your data collection will be another important factor in deciding how you define your tuning elements. If your data rate is low, and you want the test to complete in a reasonable amount of time, you will have to combine or "chunk" multiple design changes into coarser test elements. In the extreme case you may decide to completely redesign your whole landing page and include all of your desired design changes at once. If you have a high data rate and are using an advanced tuning method, you may be able to get very granular in the definition of your tuning elements.

Try to test elements that will have a long-term and consistent impact on your business. Unless your business peaks around a specific season or holiday period, avoid testing seasonal content or promotions. Once the appropriate season has passed, they will lose their relevance and impact completely.

Consider the "Timeless Testing Themes" in Chapter 6. These themes consistently produce solid gains in a wide variety of landing page tests that we have conducted at SiteTuners.com.

As I discussed in Chapter 9, there are many political dimensions to your landing page testing. Some of the design elements that you may wish to test come with significant baggage. This may be in the form of control and turf, skillsets needed, availability and cost of resources, or a long and difficult approval process. Regardless of the specific issues surrounding the design element, you will have to decide whether it is worth your time, reputation, and effort to fight for its inclusion in the test.

After you have decided exactly what to test, document your specifications in a written test plan. The formality and level of detail of your test plan depends on the scope of your test and the involvement of other people in the project. If you have a small team, the test plan can be informal. If you are doing a simple A-B split test on very granular text elements (such as a page headline), you may not even need a written plan. However, if you have many people involved in the project, I strongly suggest that you make your test plan as detailed as possible.

However, many tests are much more complicated. They involve multiple variables, which often depend on one another. The test implementation may require changes to website navigation, page flow, form contents, or back-end data storage and processing. In such cases the test plan needs to be very formal and detailed because it will serve as the implementation blueprint for your user interface specialists, graphics designers, programmers, and network administrators. See the sidebar "Resource: Test Plan Overview" for the important sections of a typical plan.

Resource: Test Plan Overview

A typical test plan will contain the following sections. The test plan should have enough detail to clearly communicate the desired tuning elements to the implementation and QA teams.

Overview

The overview is an executive summary that allows someone to understand the purpose of your test without reading the rest of it. Typical information includes:

- Description of the big picture—how the landing page supports the goals of the business, what constitutes a conversion action, and how its value is defined

- Landing page(s) chosen—include URLs and screenshots of the "before" pages

- Traffic sources—a description of the traffic sources chosen, approximate aggregate number of conversions per day, and notes about seasonality and stability of the traffic

Constraints

Describe any marketing, branding, technical, implementation, and schedule constraints. Discuss any page or site elements or pages that must not be modified during the test.

Variables and Values

This section should be the centerpiece of your plan. To facilitate communication among the test team members, it is helpful to visually block out the tuning element locations on the page and overlay them with descriptive names that will be used later in the test plan. Note the number of variables in the test, the number of possible values (branching factor) for each variable, and the total number of unique recipes (search space size). Please review Chapter 8 for additional details and definitions.

You should clearly define what specific page elements you are going to test, along with all possible variable values (including the original and any alternative versions).

Continues

Resource: Test Plan Overview *(continued)*

Actions and Value

Define the set of conversion actions that are possible in your test. For each action, define the value. For equal-value conversions, the value does not matter. But if you sell a variety of products, or have multiple conversion actions, you must use revenue or profit margin as the metric.

Implementation and QA Notes

As you will see later in this chapter, you will also need to prepare an implementation plan and a QA plan. In this section of the test plan you identify and flag any potential issues that will impact these areas.

The sidebar "Sample Test Plan Excerpt: RealAge.com" shows some key portions of the test plan conducted by SiteTuners.com on behalf of RealAge.

Sample Test Plan Excerpt: RealAge.com

Overview

The goal of this test is to improve the conversion rate of the landing page shown in Figure 10.1. The page has previously been extensively tested and previously optimized to improve conversions. The traffic sources for this test originate solely from PPC campaigns.

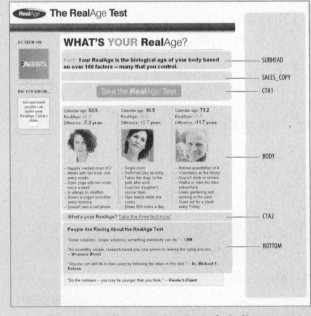

Figure 10.1 Test Plan Landing Page Overlay for RealAge.com

Sample Test Plan Excerpt: RealAge.com *(continued)*

Constraints

The top header graphic, left page column, and page headline may not be modified.

Variables and Values

This test consists of 10 variables that can take on 49 different values. The resulting search space contains 3,265,920 unique combinations of variable values ("recipes").

Note: The following is an excerpt of only certain variables, and values, and is not complete.

Variable 1: SUBHEAD The subheader is under the page headline as shown in the SUBHEAD section of the landing page overlay.

Note: Existing font size, color, family, and emphasis will be maintained for all versions.

A: OrigSUBHEAD "Fact: Your RealAge is the biological age of your body based on over 100 factors—many that you control."

B: TheTruth "Find out the truth."

C: YourLifestyle "Is your lifestyle making you younger?"

D: Change "Change you life today!"

E: Get "Get your RealAge today!"

F: Shocked "Prepare to Be Shocked"

G: None Completely remove the SUBHEAD text.

. . .

Variable 3: CTA1_TEXT The first call-to-action appears in the CTA1 section of the landing page overlay. It currently consists of the text on the button.

A: OrigText "Take the RealAge Test"

B: Start "Start the RealAge Test"

C: StartNow "Start the free test now!"

D: TakeTest "Take the test"

E: FindOut "Find out my RealAge"

F: GetMy "Get my RealAge"

. . .

Continues

Sample Test Plan Excerpt: RealAge.com *(continued)*

Variable 4: CTA1_FORMAT The current format of the first call-to-action section is indicated in the CTA1 portion of the landing page overlay.

A: OrigFormat Orange round edged button with white text.

B: OrangePlus Orange button with identical text link below it.

C: Green Dark green button with drop shadow and white text.

D: GreenPlus Green button with identical text link below it.

E: BlueOrange RealAge blue color button with orange text.

F: LargeText Large bold text link: no graphical button.

...

Variable 8: PIC_SLATES Each landing page contains a set of three featured profiles within the BODY section of the landing page overlay. The set of three images is collectively referred to as a "slate."

Note: All picture backgrounds on the final implemented slates will be white.

A: OrigSlate

B: Slate2

Sample Test Plan Excerpt: RealAge.com *(continued)*

C: Slate3

Actions and Value

The conversion action is the completion of the RealAge test after a visit to this landing page. Each test will have a fixed value of $X. The conversion optimization criterion is the percentage of conversions.

Select an Appropriate Tuning Method

The tuning method that you choose will depend on several factors. Depending on your technical requirements, the choice of tuning method will influence your choice of available tools. This, in turn, can influence whether you choose to run the test in-house or outsource it. Factors you'll want to consider include:

Size of your test As I discussed in Chapter 8, use the right tool for the right job. If your test plan involves only one variable, you can do an A-B split test. If it involves a small number of variables (with a search space of a few dozen total recipes), you can use some variation of parametric fractional factorial or full factorial multivariate testing. If your search space consists of millions of possible recipes, you will have to use proprietary advanced non-parametric full factorial methods such as the SiteTuners.com TuningEngine.

Cost Software for conducting and tracking landing page optimization tests comes in three general varieties: free tools, paid tools, and packaged paid tools and services. Free tools include the Google Website Optimizer (described in detail in Appendix A). Basic free tools are built into a growing number of Web analytics software packages. Paid tools are available from stand-alone testing tool software companies or can be unbundled from landing page testing companies. In some cases, you must buy full testing engagement services from landing page testing companies to get access to their tools and technology.

Technical capabilities The sophistication of landing page optimization tools varies widely. The most advanced tools are available from dedicated landing page optimization testing companies. Basic tools can handle A-B split tests involving a single landing page. More advanced capabilities will be required for multivariate testing, segmentation of visitors by traffic source, segmentation by physical location, segmentation by time-of-day or day-of-week, nested variables (one contained physically inside another), and the need to implement business rules (changes to your website functionality or appearance based on the visitor's history of interactions with your site). If you have a high-traffic website, you will also have to take into account the consequences of testing on your server response times and load balance across your network of servers. You may require a service-level agreement (SLA) with your testing company to ensure proper performance of your website during the test. An SLA guarantees certain minimum levels of uptime or specific maximum response times.

In-house vs. outsource decision As I discussed in Chapter 9, you will have to make a decision about conducting your test in-house or outsourcing all or a portion of it. If you outsource, you are locked into the tools and tuning methods available from the testing company that you have chosen. You may choose to outsource only the construction of the test plan and the subsequent analysis of the data, and handle the implementation and data collection yourself with the help of testing software. This is appropriate if you have the usability expertise, graphics, and programming support to handle the implementation. The statistics behind the test construction and interpretation of results can be handled by outside experts.

The sidebar "Resource: Selecting a Tuning Method and Outsourcing" guides you through the decision process.

Resource: Selecting a Tuning Method and Outsourcing

Appropriate Tuning Method

- What is your data rate (measured in conversion actions per day)?
- Are you planning to test complete landing page redesigns or granular elements?
- What is the number of variables in your test?
- What is the search space size of your test?
- Do you expect significant variable interactions among the tuning elements that you have chosen?
- Do you want to run one test or multiple tests on the same page?

Resource: Selecting a Tuning Method and Outsourcing *(continued)*

- Consider A-B split testing if:

    - The data rate is greater than 10 conversions per day.

    - The search space is less than 10 recipes.

    - You are testing a whole page redesign.

    - You are testing a single granular variable (e.g., headline).

    - You are planning only a single test.

- Consider fractional factorial multivariate testing if:

    - The data rate is greater than 50 conversions per day.

    - The search space is 10–100 recipes.

    - You are planning to test multiple page variables.

    - You are willing to ignore variable interactions and find only main effects.

    - You are planning to conduct multiple tests.

    - You want to explain and estimate main effects.

- Consider full factorial parametric multivariate testing if:

    - The data rate is greater than 50 conversions per day.

    - The search space is 10–100 recipes.

    - You are planning to test multiple page variables.

    - You want to consider variable interactions (if you conduct a full analysis of your data and don't build a main effects model only).

    - You are planning to conduct multiple tests.

- Consider non-parametric full factorial methods if:

    - The data rate is greater than 100 conversions per day.

    - The search space is 1,000,000+ recipes.

    - You are planning to test over a dozen page variables.

    - You want to consider variable interactions.

    - You want to run one large-scale test (not a series of smaller ones) and get your answer.

    - You do not need to understand why the winning recipe performs better.

Continues

Resource: Selecting a Tuning Method and Outsourcing *(continued)*

Outsourcing Considerations

- Is landing page optimization going to be a core competency of your company?

- Do you have anyone in the company whose primary responsibility is the successful completion of the test (in other words, who will "own it")?

- Do you have all necessary staff in place to execute your program? If not, which roles are missing?

- How long will it take you to find, hire, and train the required staff? What is the estimated cost of these activities?

- Do you have enough ongoing work to keep the new staff productively occupied? If not, what is their ongoing burdened salary "carrying cost"?

- How long will it take to assemble the complete team?

- Based on your business case, what is the range of lost-opportunity costs involved in waiting this long to start your testing program?

- Can your planned testing tool or technology implement all of the tuning elements that you may want to test?

- Do you have special technical requirements or constraints (such as software, content management systems, or dynamic content generation) that are incompatible with the use of certain landing page testing tools?

Implement and Conduct QA

As soon as your test plan is completed, start developing two additional documents: the *implementation plan* and the *QA plan*. As I mentioned earlier, the teams responsible for implementation and QA should not be the same, but it is okay for the same person (or group of people) to write the two plans.

Implementation

The implementation of your test can be a complicated undertaking and require significant coordination. Over the course of many engagements at SiteTuners.com, we have created a template for an implementation plan that allows us to efficiently develop all required content. The sidebar "Resource: Implementation Plan Overview" gives you the perspective needed to tailor it to your specific situation.

Resource: Implementation Plan Overview

Team and Shared Resources

List the names, contact information, and scope of responsibility for every member of the implementation team. List the access procedures and login information for any databases, staging areas, or file uploading directories that will be used for the implementation. If security and compartmentalization are an issue, you may chose to disseminate the appropriate information directly to specific team members.

Content List

Describe the list of content and files that are affected by the test. This should include the landing pages, any downstream pages that will be changed, graphics, supporting multimedia, and programming code, as well as the postconversion confirmation page that will be displayed (your conversion tracking code will typically be inserted into this confirmation page). If you are proposing changes to the page structure or shell, contain them within include files or Cascading Style Sheets (CSS). Otherwise, you have to manually change each page in the site in order to maintain a consistent look and feel. If portions of your site are dynamically generated, you will need to include any necessary programming code, database changes, and business rules. If portions of your landing pages are stored in a content management system or database, clearly identify exactly which pieces will be touched by the test.

For each file, graphic, or code element, include the filename (or location) and a description. Use a specific naming convention for all required content. Often this is related to the variable number and value in question. For example, assume you had two variables in your test: two call-to-action button colors, and two different text treatments for the button text. This would result in four distinct buttons defined by the specific values of the two variables: V1aV2a, V1aV2b, V1bV2a, and V1bV2b. If you use this kind of naming convention, it is easy to tell at a glance to which variable and value (or combination of variables and values) the content is related.

Task List

Based on the content list, develop a detailed task list of the specific content and functional changes that you will need to implement. Broadly speaking, these changes fall into the following categories:

- Text content: headlines, sales copy, or new site content
- Page structure and layout: HTML, CSS, JavaScript, or other scripting code
- Graphics and multimedia: images, animations, video
- Functional or page-flow changes: programming, form processing, changes to data gathering or storage
- Operational: changes outside of the website itself, procedures, staff training

Continues

Resource: Implementation Plan Overview *(continued)*

For each task, assign a team member and schedule. Try to take into account any dependencies among people working on the implementation. Sometimes relatively small tasks can hold up important parts of the implementation if they are not attended to. Track the progress of the implementation via the task list. Add new items as follow-on tasks or "problem tickets" until all known issues with the implementation have been resolved. Also include some aspect of version control in your content naming convention. This will allow you to track changes and be able to quickly identify previous versions or iterations of your content.

Quality Assurance

Once the implementation is completed, the QA process can start. At SiteTuners.com we use a *launch page* to conduct our testing. A launch page is the gateway to examining any version of the landing page that we want to see. By selecting the exact settings for the value of any variable in the test, you can create any recipe in your test. Figure 10.2 shows the launch page for RealAge.com (a subsidiary of Hearst Corporation) for the engagement referenced earlier in the chapter. Similar preview functionality is available in most landing page testing tools.

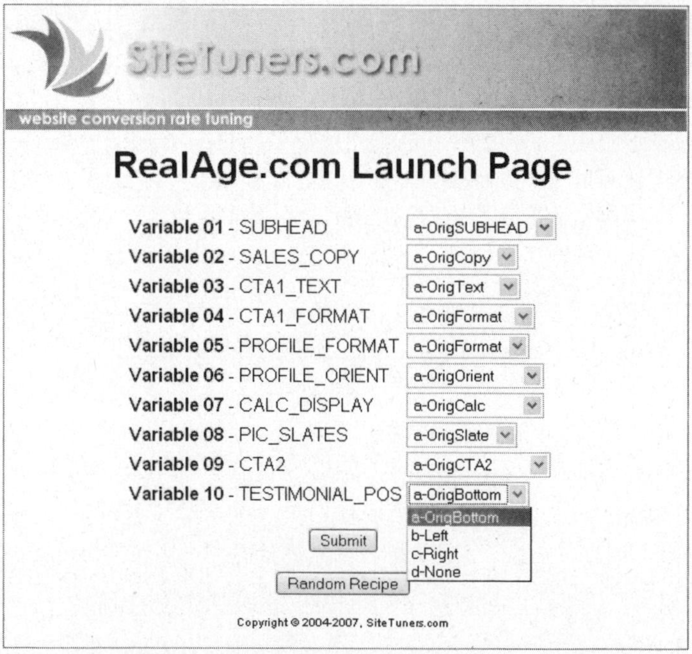

Figure 10.2 Example recipe preview "launch page" for the RealAge.com

If your test is small-scale (fewer than a couple dozen total recipes), you may be able to exhaustively check all recipes and make sure that they were implemented properly. As the number of recipes grows, this quickly becomes impractical. At SiteTuners.com, we specialize in large engagement size and routinely run tests with millions or tens of millions of recipes. In such an environment, we can no longer check everything by brute force. A properly constructed QA plan can help to overcome this problem and make testing manageable. See the sidebar "Resource: QA Plan Overview" to understand how to approach QA plans.

Resource: QA Plan Overview

Piecewise Review

The simplest kind of testing to conduct is element by element. You cycle through every variable value in your test plan to make sure that it looks and functions as expected. Even in large tests (with search space sizes in the millions of recipes), the total number of variable values is still manageable (typically no more than a couple of dozen).

Interaction Review

Piecewise review only looks at each variable value *in isolation*. However, you need to consider some of your variable values *in the context of* other variable values. Explicitly call out the important dependencies among your chosen tuning elements.

For example, imagine if one variable defines the button color and has five distinct values, and another one defines the button text and also has five distinct values—that means you have ten total piecewise elements to consider. But in reality, there are 25 separate buttons that needed to be created, and each one must be reviewed individually.

Note that the "interactions" that I am referring to here are not the variable interactions discussed in Chapter 7. They are visual or functional interactions among your variable values. As a result, you can identify them ahead of time and include them in your QA plan.

Constraints and Dependencies

As I discussed in the "Test Construction" section of Chapter 8, you may have variable values that are dependent or contingent on the existence of another variable value. Depending on how you have chosen to define your variables and values, make sure that these constraints have been properly enforced. For example, if you add or delete steps in your conversion process, you must make sure that there are no disconnected parts or features of your site (that can't be reached through available links and navigation), nor any "orphaned" content or functionality that still exists when it should have been removed.

Continues

> **Resource: QA Plan Overview** *(continued)*
>
> **Coherency Review**
>
> Even if you have conducted all of these QA steps, you may still have problems with coherency (see the "Coherency" section of Chapter 6). Don't miss the forest for the trees. Even if everything was properly implemented, the end result may look odd because of unexpected juxtapositions. For example, if you remove a page element completely, you should examine the effect on the surrounding elements that now butt up against each other. Subtler coherency issues involve changes in emphasis and visual balance. For example, if you replace a short test description with a longer block of text, the main visual focus of the page can change because more of the screen real estate is now devoted to the text. If the coherency issues are severe enough, consider changing the test plan to address them.

Maintain a "problem ticket" or known issues list. This is similar to the bug-fix process that is used in software development prior to a new release. Classify or rank your unresolved issues by severity and work down your list in order. Once your issues get small enough, you may just decide that they will not materially change the outcome of your test and you can proceed without addressing them. In such cases, you always have the option of correcting them after the test if they are part of the winning recipe.

Collect the Data

Collecting data during the test is a two-part activity. First you must properly prepare for data collection. Then, you must closely monitor the data collection process.

Preparing for Data Collection

Preparing for data collection is a critical activity and involves the following steps:

Tracking Test to make sure that your Web analytics tool still works and that all campaign tracking is coming across and has not been messed up by your test code and content changes. Such problems are especially common if you are changing flow through the site or renaming pages. Look for sudden drops in traffic from particular campaigns or referring websites. Uncover any breakdown in tracking by troubleshooting the issue.

If you have alternative contact methods such as toll-free numbers, you may have to temporarily set up multiple numbers (one per unique recipe in your test) in order to properly track and attribute activity.

Traffic filtering Implement any required traffic filters. If certain traffic sources are not meant to be a part of your test, the affected visitors should still see the original version of your site. Filters can be implemented by routing traffic to the original or alternative page, or by displaying different content within the same page depending on passed-in parameters on the inbound URL.

Procedural changes Some tests may require changes to company procedures or training, or the addition of extra staff. If your company is currently running at full capacity, identify the critical bottlenecks ahead of time and put in contingency plans to quickly respond if the conversion rate during the test increases substantially. This may require keeping extra inventory on hand or training contract workers as extra surge capacity. If you are changing the method, amount, or sequence of the data that you collect online, brief all affected staff and departments ahead of time. For example, if you remove some fields from an online form (to make it shorter and less imposing), instruct your call center staff to collect the missing information on their subsequent follow-up calls.

Scheduling You must determine your approximate data collection period ahead of time. Ideally you would like a long window that is not affected by seasonal issues, significant business plan changes, or outside events. If it is impossible to avoid short-term disturbances in your data collection (e.g., due to industry tradeshows or holidays), plan for them, and decide what you will do with the data from those time periods. You can choose to leave the data in your sample unaltered, try to compensate for the bias introduced, or discard it altogether.

You may decide to leave your data collection period somewhat open-ended. This is appropriate since you do not know the size of the effects that you will find ahead of time, and may choose to simply wait you have reached a high statistical confidence in your answer. Conversely, if your data collection period is fixed, you should be able to calculate the size of effects that you will be able to identify (see the "Size of Improvements Found" section of Chapter 7). If the size of effects that you can resolve is large, the test elements you have chosen are more likely to produce inconclusive results.

Cutover to "live" Your implementation and QA should be done on a separate copy of your landing page in a *staging environment*. Before you start data collection, move all appropriate files, code, and data structures to the live environment. The live environment may be different from the staging environment, so this move can introduce additional instabilities and problems. It is best to make your cutover outside of your peak business hours, and you should have your network administrator, webmaster, and programmers standing by during this process.

It may be impossible to test some elements of your new landing page without being live. For example, you may not be able to test your e-commerce checkout process because it is only hooked up to your live site and is difficult to duplicate in your staging environment. Make sure that you run end-to-end tests (and back out any resulting data or transactions).

Your QA process is unlikely to have caught all issues during staging. Your cutover problems can range from severe (e.g., your conversion process is broken and the conversion action cannot be completed) to mild (e.g., some small percentage of visitors may experience a nonstandard presentation of your landing pages under unlikely circumstances). You must have contingency plans in place to quickly back out and reverse your changes, and restore the live site to its original state.

Monitoring Data Collection

Once your actual data collection has started, make sure that everything is going according to plan. Typical monitoring activities include the following:

Check data recording Make sure that impressions and conversions are being recorded across all recipes in your test. Make sure that no corrupted or incomplete data is ending up in your tracking.

Check data rates Verify that the expected number of visitors is being recorded based on the traffic sources that you are using for the test. Very low traffic numbers may indicate that your filters are too restrictive or are not working properly. Very high traffic numbers may indicate that you have not filtered out all undesirable traffic sources. Cross-check your data rates against other Web analytics tools you may have in place, or examine their recording at the origin (e.g., in the PPC account, affiliate tracking software, or ad network where the traffic originates).

Watch for any anomalies in the data rate. These may indicate unexpected external events. They may also alert you to the presence of sporadic or spiky traffic sources that you neglected to filter out.

Check conversion rates Make sure that the conversion rate being recorded for your baseline recipe is comparable to historic figures. Very low or very high conversion rates may be a sign of improper counting or recording. However, you should not worry if the conversion rate is on the low side initially, since delayed conversions are often a significant part of the total and will not happen until the data has been "aged" by the passage of time. Check the conversion rates of other recipes in your test.

Correct for sampling bias Even if your data rate is high and you quickly reach statistical confidence in your answer, continue to collect data across all appropriate time periods. As a general rule, correct for time-of-day and day-of-week effects by collecting data in one-week increments.

The sidebar "Resource: Data Collection" gives you a checklist to conduct proper monitoring.

Analyze the Results and Verify Improvement

How you analyze your data depends on the exact elements in the test plan and their constraints, the conversion actions and their respective values, the tuning method, and the specific landing page testing software chosen. In the simplest case, an A-B split test can be stopped when statistical confidence has been reached via a simple spreadsheet calculation. If you have a complicated multivariate test and are examining variable interactions, you may need the assistance of an outside statistician to properly interpret the results.

If your test proves inconclusive, you have three options:

- Abandon your test if the reasonable data collection window has passed.

- Start another test with different test elements.

- Continue to collect more data until the desired confidence level has been reached. Remember that this may happen rather slowly since your ability to resolve an effect does not depend directly on the number of conversions, but rather on the *square root* of it.

Even if your test finds significant improvements, you may still have work ahead of you. One of the assumptions behind the landing page statistics is that the behavior of the audience does not change over time. In reality this is not the case. Nothing remains the same forever. You may launch additional customer acquisition programs and change your audience mix. Seasonal issues may encroach after the completion of the test. Your audience's sophistication and familiarity with your company or industry can also change, affecting the perceived value of your offer. New competitors may enter the fray, or functional substitutes may appear that begin to supersede your product or service.

You can't assume that performance improvement observed in your test will hold up over time. This is especially true if the tuning elements that you have chosen are short-lived or transient (such as changing the offer or running a seasonal promotion). Basic usability improvements should have a much longer shelf life. The best way to protect yourself against such changes is to continue to run your original version at a low level (e.g., 5% to 10% of the total traffic) even after your test completes. It is likely that your baseline will continue to underperform the winning challenger recipe. However, you may want to hedge and give up a bit of the possible improvement as an insurance policy against downside risk. The sidebar "Resource: Data Analysis" makes sure that you do not overlook anything in your analysis.

Resource: Data Analysis

- Have you reached your desired statistical confidence level?

- If not, should you continue the test?

- Have you eliminated any questionable data collection periods or spikes from your data?

- Have you considered variable interactions of just main effects?

- Have you run a follow-up A-B split test involving your winner and the original baseline recipe?

- Is your program relatively stable in terms of traffic volumes and conversion rates? If not, what percentage of your ongoing traffic should you dedicate to the losing recipe?

By now you should be able to develop an effective action plan. In the next chapter, you'll learn how to avoid some common pitfalls that can undermine your work.

Avoiding the Pitfalls

*No battle plan survives contact with
the enemy.*
—Helmuth von Moltke (1800–1891),
   Prussian Army Chief of Staff

*How do you reconcile the need for planning
required to develop your action plan in the previous chapter with this quote? They seem contradictory, yet both are true. This chapter is about
the real world. After all the planning is over, you
still have to sidestep many pitfalls in order to
complete a successful landing page test. This
chapter can help you learn from other people's
common mistakes.*

Chapter Contents

A Final Warning

Before we begin, here's a warning: if you have diligently read this book, many of the pitfalls described in this chapter should be a review. But chances are you have ignored some of my previous cautions and injunctions along the way. So I'll repeat them here for additional emphasis.

Many of these issues consistently trip up even experienced testers. All the planning in the world will not save you. Neither will being really smart. Most of the topics described here can only be learned through painful and costly experience. My hope is that this experience may come from me, and that you will take full advantage of it.

Ignoring Your Baseline

At SiteTuners.com we once ran a client engagement and saw performance improve on our challenger recipe from a 4.63% conversion rate in week one to 5.03% during week two. Normally you would be happy to see this kind of increase in conversion during your data collection period. But was it really a good thing?

We had to look more closely at the data. It turned out that our original baseline recipe had a conversion rate of 3.59% during week one and 6.18% in week two. In other words, during week one, our challenger recipe had a *29% advantage* over the baseline. During week two it was actually *19% worse*!

What had changed? Week two was a holiday week. Presumably the composition of the audience had changed. So while the new audience preferred the challenger a bit more than the old audience, they also preferred the baseline by an even higher margin over the old audience. We would have never found this out if we had not looked at the baseline performance.

Do not get distracted by changes in your conversion rate during your test. Your conversion rate may fluctuate for a number of reasons (including not collecting enough data and seasonal factors discussed in a moment). The purpose of your test is not to get the *absolute highest* conversion rate on your challenger recipe during your data collection period. What is important is whether you are beating your baseline.

To do this you must collect enough data to have a very good read on the performance of your baseline recipe. If you simply assign a proportional amount of data to it (as is commonly done in full factorial multivariate testing data collection), you will require a lot more time to zero in on its true performance. As I mentioned, we typically devote 15–25% of the available traffic to the baseline recipe during multivariate tests. However, you should note that for certain parametric multivariate testing approaches, disproportionate data collection on the baseline recipe may invalidate the subsequent analysis (which assumes that the data collection design is balanced). Please review the "Throttling" section in Chapter 8, "Tuning Methods," for additional information.

Collecting Enough Data

One of the advantages of online marketing in general (and landing page optimization in particular) is the ability to measure everything. All online marketing campaigns and programs should be run "by the numbers." The difficult part is in knowing *which* numbers to use and *when*.

Many online marketers like to watch the pot boil. They come to resemble stock market day traders who get hooked on the action and make frequent changes to their programs. Some even use automated tools (e.g., for PPC bid management) to make decisions more frequently than is humanly possible. There is nothing inherently wrong with automated tools or frequent changes per se, but each change must be made after collecting an appropriate amount of data. Unfortunately, this is often not the case in practice.

Let's consider the dangers of small sample sizes. Let's assume that you have had four visitors to your e-commerce website. One of the visitors has bought something. So what is your conversion rate of visitors to sales? If you answered 25% (one sale out of four visitors), you are probably way off. Most e-commerce sites we have seen range from 1% to 5%. Unless your product is unique, indispensable, and available for sale only from your site, the 25% conversion rate is highly unlikely. Similarly, if you had no sales after the first four visits, you would probably be wrong to conclude that your conversion rate was really zero, and that you would *never* get a sale. This example may seem a bit extreme, but too many landing page tests are decided with inappropriately small data samples. As I mentioned earlier, your sample size is expressed in the number of conversion actions, and not in the number of unique visitors.

Once you start the data collection in your test, resist the temptation to monitor the results frequently, especially early in the test. Otherwise, you run the risk of getting on an emotional roller-coaster caused by the early streaks in the data. One moment you may be euphoric about excellent results, and the next you may be despondent as the indicated improvement vanishes like a mirage. So pick a statistical confidence level in your answer and wait until you have collected enough data to reach it. You need to have the self-discipline not to even look at the early results.

Remember, the law of large numbers tells us that our measured conversion rate average will eventually stabilize at the actual value. But it does not tell us exactly how long this will take. It is possible to have large deviations from the actual mean early in the data collection. Even if you are confident in the fact that your new landing page converts better than the original, you still do not have a clear indication of exactly how much better it is if you haven't collected enough data. Do not simply use the observed difference in lift as your reported answer. Always present it with the correct error bars (also called "confidence intervals"). I strongly urge you to review the appropriate sections of Chapter 7, "The Math of Tuning," to solidify your understanding.

Collect Enough Data

- Don't watch the pot boil, especially early.
- Collect enough data to reach your desired confidence level.
- Always present data with error bars.

Variable Interactions

With the growing popularity of landing page optimization, certain approaches have been canonized and have taken on an almost mythical reverence among the ranks of online marketers. It is almost as if the buzzwords themselves confer some special power on the practitioner (e.g., "DOE", "multivariate testing," and the "Taguchi method").

As you may have already surmised from my discussion in the "Multivariate Testing" section of Chapter 8, "Tuning Methods," there is a huge mismatch between the original environment in which fractional factorial testing was developed and how it is usually applied to landing page optimization. It was basically transplanted to online marketing because it is relatively easy for a nonmathematical audience to understand, and not because of its appropriateness or fitness for the task.

The Drunk Who Lost His Car Keys

A policeman on patrol noticed a man on all fours crawling around under a streetlamp in the middle of the night. After stopping to take a closer look, the policeman quickly determined that the man was very drunk.

"What are you doing, mister?" he asked.

The drunk looked up at him bleary eyed and replied, "Looking for my car keys—I can't seem to find them."

"Where did you lose them?" the policeman asked.

The drunk scratched his head for a few moments, and then said, "Over there" as he pointed to the end of a dark alley several hundred yards away.

"So why are you looking under this streetlamp?" asked the confused officer.

"Because the light is better here," replied the drunk.

You need to step back and take a critical look at the tuning method you are about to use and its implications for your test. Are parametric multivariate testing methods better than A-B split testing, assuming that you have a high enough data rate? Sure. But don't let that blind you to one of their glaring defects—most common multivariate techniques do not take variable interactions into account. Like the drunk looking for his car keys, they are usually looking only at the main effects of your individual test variables because that is where "the light is better," and not because it is where the best solution lies.

Variable interactions are very common and strong in landing page optimization testing. This should not be a surprise to anyone, since online marketers are intentionally trying to create landing pages that are greater than the sum of their parts. You should be looking for synergies among all of your page elements and trying to eliminate combinations of variable values that undermine your desired outcome. Please review the "Variable Interactions" section of Chapter 7 for additional background.

As I have already discussed in the "Full Factorial Parametric Testing" section of Chapter 8, full factorial data collection does allow you to later examine variable interactions. However, you need to be clear about full factorial *data collection* versus subsequent full factorial *data analysis*. They are independent of each other. Currently the Google Website Optimizer is the only widely used parametric multivariate testing tool that allows you to collect data for a full factorial design, but the reporting and analysis still only looks at the main effects (please see Appendix A for a detailed look at the Google Website Optimizer). In theory, you can export the complete data and conduct a more complicated analysis, but this is not supported in the tool.

So the dirty little secret is out. If you still choose to ignore variable interactions, you have no one but yourself to blame for suboptimal results. The bottom line is this: if you do not have the minimum data rate to use non-parametric tuning methods like the TuningEngine (which can handle very large test sizes *and* considers variable interactions), then you should at least use full factorial data collection coupled with a proper subsequent analysis that estimates variable interactions. Identifying interactions can be a complicated and unpleasant business. You may have to learn some additional statistics or bring in outside experts to help you to design the test and analyze your results, but this is the only way to consistently get the biggest possible benefits.

In Appendix A, "A Closer Look at the Google Website Optimizer," I walk through the experimental setup and results for SiteTuners.com client SF Video. Two landing page headlines were tested with two layouts of client logo trust symbols (a total of four possible recipes). If you had only looked at the main effects, you would have concluded that the new headline was the best (96.6% confidence) and that the original client logo layout was superior (93.5% confidence).

But this does not tell the whole story. A closer look reveals that changing the headline and leaving the client logos unchanged had a significant and large impact on the conversion rate. However, there were no big changes in conversion rate with *either* headline in the presence of the new client logo layout.

The SF Video experiment was very simple—in fact you can't have a simpler multivariate test construction. Why did the headline have a very large impact in the presence of the original client logo layout, while it had none in the presence of the new one? Who knows? The point is that surprisingly large interactions can exist even in such small test designs.

Don't Ignore Variable Interactions

- Interactions exist and can be very strong.
- If you ignore them, you will not get the best results.
- A-B splits and fractional factorial parametric testing generally assume that variable interactions do not exist.

Seasonality

As I mentioned in the "Biased Samples" section in Chapter 7, it is a big mistake to conduct sequential testing. In other words, you should never run one version of your landing page design *followed by* another one. Too many outside influences can cloud or invalidate your results. The reason that you should collect data in parallel (by randomly splitting your traffic among the alternative recipes in your test) is to account for as many of these outside factors as possible.

However, even if you properly conduct data collection in parallel, you may still run into obvious or subtle seasonality issues. As I previously discussed, underlying all landing page testing is the statistical framework that calls for an *unchanging visitor population* that *behaves consistently* over time. Unfortunately, neither of these prerequisites is likely to be strictly true in practice. Your audience mix changes as you change your marketing activities, or even as your competitors change theirs. Even the same population of visitors may start to change their behavior over time as they gain more familiarity with your product, company, or industry.

In the "Traffic Sources and Their Variability" section of Chapter 3, "Understanding Your Audience," I discussed very spiky seasonality in some industries and how this may significantly complicate a test. Sometimes your goal is to specifically tune for such a short-term seasonal period. Conversely, you may actually attempt to filter out any short-term holiday periods and treat them as anomalies as you try to tune for "normal" visitor behavior during the rest of the year. Please review the "Audience Changes" section in Chapter 8. You should also note the discussion of scheduling in the "Collect the Data" section of Chapter 10, "Developing Your Action Plan," for additional information.

As a general rule, you should adhere to the following guidelines in order to get the best results:

Make Peace with Seasonality Issues

- Choose recurring, controllable, and stable traffic sources.

- Don't change your marketing mix during the data collection.

- Plan data collection around any major product or company announcements.

- Average across obvious sampling biases (day-of-week, time-of-day).

- Schedule around any known seasonal trends or important industry events.

- Remove or mitigate data from unexpected external events.

- Continue ongoing low-level data collection on the original recipe even after the test is completed.

Assuming That Testing Has No Costs

I have heard many people opine that landing page testing is a silver bullet. You pick some page elements to test, collect your data, and all of a sudden you have a better-performing landing page. In fact, not all of your test plan ideas are going to make a positive impact on your conversion rate. Unfortunately, you don't know ahead of time which of your variable values will be successful. If you did, you would not need testing in the first place.

A certain kind of mental reframing is required as part of the proper perspective for landing page optimization:

Each landing page test has a cost. You will have to expend time and effort to set up the test, monitor data collection, and analyze the results. Even if your test is successful, you still have to consider alternative marketing activities that you could have been engaged in instead of testing, and the lost opportunity cost of not doing them. In other words, if you have bigger opportunities for making an impact on your program's profitability, attend to those first.

A test may not yield any positive results. It is possible that the tuning elements you have selected will not create any noticeable conversion improvement. A few may actually make things worse and lower your conversion rate. At the end of the test, your original baseline recipe for the landing page may still remain the champion and will have bested all challengers. This is not a problem. You cannot base your testing program on the outcome of a single test. You will guess wrong a significant percentage of the time when selecting alternative variable values to test. But this should not deter you from trying. Testing is an ongoing activity, and until you have completely exhausted all of your meaningful ideas, you should keep trying.

However, it is likely that you will see a law of diminishing returns if you continue to tune the same page over and over. Chances are you will get your biggest gains during your early tests, because at that point your landing page is in its worst shape and your ideas are most numerous and original. During subsequent tests, you will probably be tinkering with smaller refinements that are not as likely to produce dramatic conversion improvements. So you have to soberly evaluate whether another test on the same page is warranted.

Performance may drop during a test but still lead to positive results. It is possible that the mix of alternative recipes you are testing will perform worse than the baseline recipe. Often some of your variable values are worse than their baseline counterparts while others are better, creating a sampled blend of recipes that has lower overall conversion. As a result, you will see an often significant drop in revenues early in your test. Don't panic or abort your test. Have the self-discipline to collect data with high statistical confidence.

If some variable values or recipes continue to underperform, you can eliminate them from the mix that you are testing. Eventually after several experiments (or follow-up test runs), you should be able to cut out all of the poor performers and focus on what is working the best. This may get you into positive territory (where your final challenger recipes perform better than the original baseline).

In one particular series of landing page tests run by SiteTuners.com, we started out with all of the possible recipes that we were considering. The resulting mix initially performed *19% poorer* than the baseline (see Figure 11.1). Had we ended the program at this point, we would have thought that we did not find anything better than the baseline. However, over several additional test runs we zeroed in on successively better-performing recipes, and were eventually able to identify a challenger recipe that performed *27% better* than the baseline in the final head-to-head test.

However, all is not rosy simply because of the positive outcome. The shaded portion of the graph below the "0%" line is proportional to the lost revenues during the data collection period, and the shaded portion above that line constitutes extra revenues collected during the test as a result of improved performance. As you can see, the lost revenues are greater than the extra revenue, indicating that there was a net loss of revenue during the test. But this is okay because the new and improved landing page will presumably continue to outperform the original for a very long time, so by using it the company will recoup the difference and then accrue additional extra revenues going forward.

Average Conversion Rate Improvement Versus Baseline

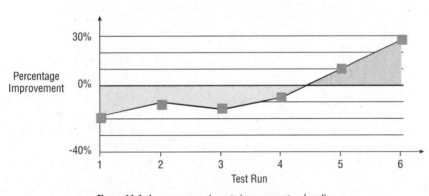

Figure 11.1 Average conversion rate improvement vs. baseline

There's No Free Lunch:

You must be willing to suffer short-term pain during landing page testing in order to attain the long-term gain of improved performance and higher conversions.

Delayed Conversions

Carefully consider delayed conversions in your data collection and subsequent analysis. A delayed conversion happens when a visitor acts only after a noticeable delay or on a subsequent return visit to your landing page. Such delays can range from hours to many months.

Depending on your audience and landing page, you may have a low percentage of delayed conversions. This is usually the case when the landing page is stand-alone and single purpose. The required conversion action is usually nonthreatening and does not involve payment or the disclosure of a lot of personal information.

For example, imagine that you run a lead-generation company in the financial services industry. You sell the contact information from people who download your free retirement planning guide to local financial planners around the country. The visitors are generated from PPC campaigns on major search engines. The traffic lands on a stand-alone page that offers the guide in exchange for the visitor's name, e-mail, and contact phone number. In such a situation you would expect the number of delayed conversions to be low. There is not a lot of information on the landing page—nothing to ponder or digest. It is basically an impulse decision to get the guide. If visitors decide not to get it, they are unlikely to type in the same keyword and click on your ad again. Since there is no other way to find your landing page, this is a one-shot attempt to get the conversion.

Figure 11.2 shows the conversion delay graph for a typical lead-generation SiteTuners.com client. The graph is on a logarithmic scale (i.e., the horizontal axis displays the conversion delay time in orders of magnitude and not linearly). As you can see from the graph, most conversions have happened by the two-hour mark indicated by the "elbow." After that, you get a small stream of stragglers. But these do not change the end result significantly. Even after a thousand hours of delay (about six weeks), the stragglers constitute only 5% of total conversions. Even on a logarithmic graph, the conversion rate after the elbow stays pretty flat.

By contrast, there are situations where stragglers constitute a significant percentage of the total conversions. This is most likely to happen when the conversion action is significant or requires an online purchase. There is growing evidence that online consumers are getting more comfortable looking for information on the Internet. One of the implications for e-commerce is that the conversion delay (from first landing page visit to the sale) continues to grow. Internet users are comfortable comparison shopping and gathering additional information before committing to the transaction.

Figure 11.3 shows the conversion delay graph for a typical e-commerce catalog SiteTuners.com client. The traffic sources are from a mix of PPC, SEO, and type-in traffic. There is a possibility that someone will bookmark the page where they landed in the catalog. Repeat customers are also a significant part of the traffic mix. Notice that the elbow is not quite as pronounced as in the lead-generation example. The percentage of stragglers is also greater (as indicated by the higher slope of the graph past the elbow point). In fact, stragglers in this example constitute a full 15% of total conversions. So if you would have measured the conversion rate after one hour, you could expect it to drift up by almost 20% over the following few weeks.

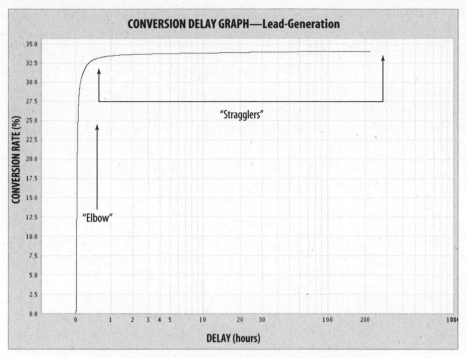

Figure 11.2 Conversion delay graph for a lead-generation landing page

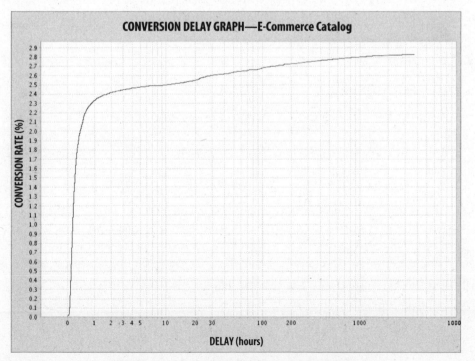

Figure 11.3 Conversion delay graph for an e-commerce catalog

The important implication for landing page testing is that you have to understand the behavior of your stragglers and compare apples to apples. This can be done in one of two ways:

Ignore the stragglers If your percentage of stragglers is very low, you could simply measure at the elbow point on the graph. In other words, you can disregard all of the conversions that happen after a certain maximum delay time (which corresponds to the elbow for your particular landing page). Since the percentage of stragglers is small, this does not change your results significantly and allows you to nearly instantly compare the newest results to those from previous data collection periods.

"Age" your data Age your data from the most recent data collection period to make sure that you are comparing properly against past periods. As you can see on the graphs in Figure 11.3 (as displayed on the logarithmic delay time-scale), the conversion rate increase will usually begin to flatten out at some point. So you should wait the appropriate amount of time before looking at the conversion rate. Exactly where to make this cutoff is a judgment call. As a rough guideline, I recommend the point at which you reach 95% of the final conversion rate. Usually this time period is between a few days and a few weeks.

Consider Delayed Conversions

- Understand the behavior of your "stragglers."
- Compare properly aged results only.

Case Study: Power Options

One of SiteTuners.com clients, Power Options (www.poweropt.com) sells access to their advanced stock option research database on a subscription basis. Clients can research the full universe of 250,000+ tradable options and use the patented software to find the best possible trades.

The company offers an unrestricted 14-day trial without requiring any credit card information. After the trial is completed, some people continue with the service on a paid basis. SiteTuners.com's goal was to increase the percentage of visitors who signed up for the free trial.

The original free trial sign-up process involved landing on a very information-rich page (shown in Figure 11.4). The page had a lot of information about stock option trading, Power Options, and related subjects.

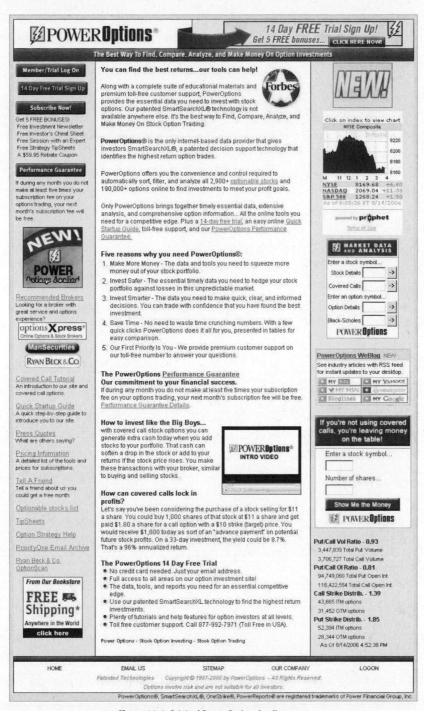

Figure 11.4 Original Power Options landing page

A couple of the graphics on the landing page were links to the follow-on page, which allowed you to register for the free trial (see Figure 11.5). The registration page also had a lot of text as well as thumbnail screenshots of some sample software reports.

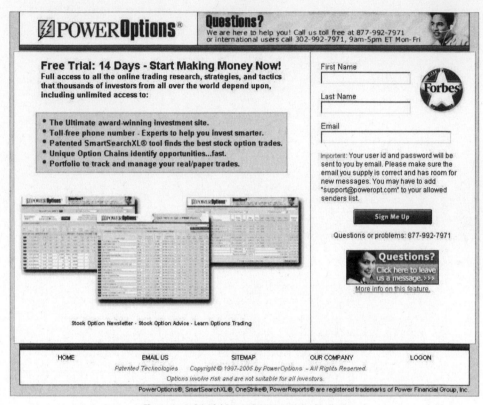

Figure 11.5 Original Power Options registration page

Power Options had a low data rate on the landing page in question, so we elected to use an A-B split test. As I mentioned in the "Granularity" section of Chapter 6, "Selecting Elements to Tune," SiteTuners.com decided on a "coarse" approach. In other words, instead of tinkering with a specific landing page element, we combined all of our ideas into a single best-practices redesign of the free trial process.

In our proposed redesign (see Figure 11.6), we reduced the two-page process to a single page. Among the most striking changes was our radical simplification of the page. The focus shifted to a simple description of the free trial offer. We eliminated all supporting information that described stock option trading and the details of the Power Options software.

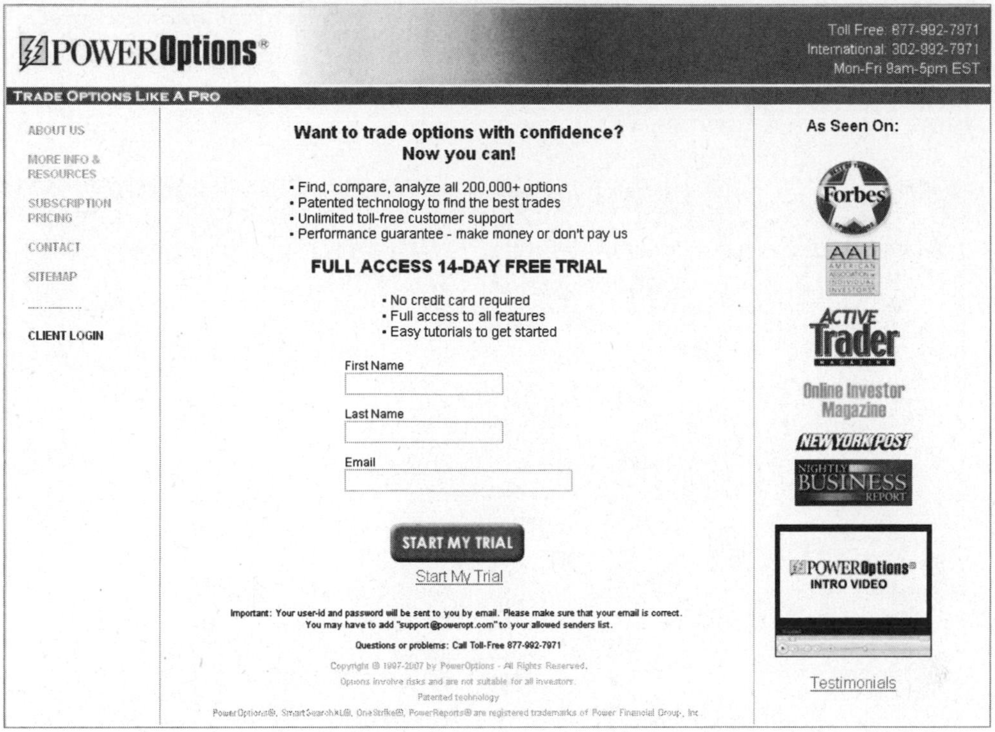

Figure 11.6 Redesigned Power Options registration process

When we showed the proposed alternative landing page to the client, we got a lot of pushback. We were told that this kind of radical simplification would not work with their target audience. The stock option trading community is very sophisticated and mathematically inclined, and needs a lot of supporting information. Power Options insisted that our simplified version did not do enough to educate the visitor. We insisted that, on the contrary, the original page was turning away a lot of people who might otherwise take the low-risk step of activating a free trial.

Did the information-rich original page instill loyalty and provide valuable information to visitors? Or did it serve to scare away prospects with its voluminous text, complicated page layout, and unclear call-to-action?

As it turns out, both sides were right—to a degree. Although our redesigned challenger version of the page ended up having much higher conversion rate to free trials, the baseline registration process instilled more loyalty and resulted in significantly higher delayed conversions among the stragglers. In order to understand this better, look at the conversion delay graph in Figure 11.7.

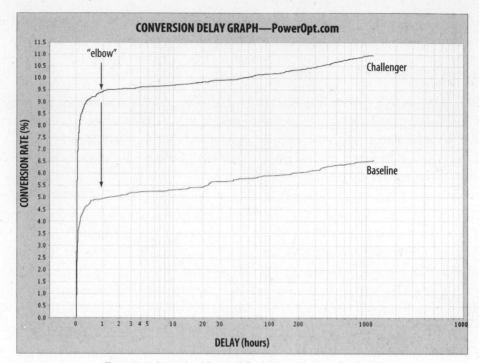

Figure 11.7 Conversion delay graph for the Power Options A-B split test

Usually we see a clear elbow and then delayed conversions trickling in. Sometimes the slope of the delayed conversion "tail" is proportional to the height of the elbow (when displayed on a logarithmic scale like the image below). In other words, the percentage of delayed conversions is the same for all tested versions of the landing page. But this is not always the case.

In the graph in Figure 11.7, our challenger version had an elbow at 9.5% and an 11% final CR (an increase of 16%). The original baseline version of the site had an elbow at 5% and eventually peaked at 6.5% (an increase of 30%). So the original baseline had a higher percentage of delayed conversions but a lower overall conversion rate at the end of the day.

Tracking the actions of the stragglers was critical to predicting the percentage improvement accurately. If we had measured at the elbow point (one-hour delay), we would have predicted a 90% improvement (9.5% divided by 5.0%). Once we aged the data, we saw the more accurate 70% figure (11.0% divided by 6.5%). This was very close to the actual 75% observed revenue-per-visitor increase after the free trial was completed. Our subsequent analysis showed that the original version influenced a higher percentage of committed visitors to return later, and closed some of the performance gap against our simplified challenger over time.

If you observe different straggler behavior among the landing page versions that you are testing, you must age your data before analyzing the results.

Search Engine Considerations

The topic of search engines and search engine marketing is vast and beyond the scope of this book. Often a significant portion of the traffic to a landing page comes from SEO. Because of this, I will touch on some important considerations about search engines as they pertain to landing page testing. I will focus on Google in recognition of its dominant position in these areas.

SEO is a very tricky business. There is an ongoing race between the search engines and people who are trying to understand them and optimize their content to appear near the top of the results. The stakes are pretty high. If you can dial in the right set of features and practices, you may be able to get significant traffic to your landing pages without a direct per-visitor cost. Of course, long-term SEO success requires a significant ongoing commitment of resources and time, so it should not be viewed as the source of "free" traffic.

The following client concerns often come up in our testing: fear, technical issues, and cloaking.

Fear

If you are lucky enough to receive significant SEO traffic to parts of your site, you may be scared of testing changes to your current design. Many online marketers have this "If it ain't broke, don't fix it" mentality. They are afraid of changing even the smallest details for fear of losing their top ranking.

This fear is largely unfounded or inappropriate for two reasons. First, the search engines regularly change their ranking algorithms. So keeping your site the same is not a guarantee of ranking stability. You may lose your position even without testing. Second, the main contributors to your high ranking are all off-page factors that have nothing to do with the text, design, or appearance of your page. Such off-page factors include the authority of your domain name (including how long it has been active), the number and quality of inbound links to your page from other respected websites in your industry, and the presence of the keywords in your page title (even though this is actually an on-page factor, it is easy to preserve and maintain during your test). If you have properly addressed these factors, you will have gotten 80–90% of the potential SEO benefit.

On-page factors are insignificant compared to the off-page factors and should not deter you from testing. You should not make radical changes such as creating your landing page completely in Flash technology, removing all of the text from the page by putting it into include files, or changing all text to corresponding graphics (which cannot be properly read or indexed by the search engines).

Technical Issues

Some online marketers are concerned that simply adding the required testing code and scripts to their landing pages will create technical problems that will get them disqualified from the search engine results. This concern is baseless. *Search engine spiders* ignore most programming code and basically look at the text of the page (along with hyperlinks). Most testing software uses JavaScript code to alter the contents of the page based on the contents of a first-party cookie on the Web visitor's browser. This happens *client-side*. In other words, the changes happen after the Web server has created the page and handed it off to the Web browser software. Since the spider does not know how to interpret the JavaScript code and does not accept cookies (which are used to control the behavior of the test page), it cannot possibly know what page a human visitor would see. As a result, the spider always sees the same page as it was before the data collection for the landing page test was started.

Cloaking

Over the years, I have had many people indicate to me that one of the reasons that they have not done conversion tuning on their site is that they are afraid they will be accused of *cloaking* by Google and lose their high position in the search results.

Cloaking is the practice of showing different content to the search engine spiders and to actual human visitors to your page with the intention of deceiving the spiders and changing the page's ranking in the search results. In extreme cases this can be used as a bait-and-switch tactic to draw an audience to your page and then show them completely unrelated content. Obviously if a lot of websites did this, the trust level in search results would go down, and search engines would have a lot of heat directed at them.

At the same time, search engines also want people to find relevant information, and the whole point of landing page optimization is to find out what appeals to your visitors.

Google has recently clarified their policy on cloaking as it applies to landing page testing (this policy may be changed in the future, so please check directly with Google on their latest pronouncements). Ethical landing page testing is not considered cloaking. Follow these general guidelines:

- Keep your alternative versions on the same theme and topic as the original page.
- Remove testing code and install your new champion version of the landing page(s) as soon as the test is completed.
- Always show your original version as part of your recipe mix during data collection.

However, there is also a more subtle and fundamental issue underlying the cloaking discussion: what the spiders need to rank your page well is not what your audience wants to experience when they visit your page. There will always be this inherent tension.

Studies have shown repeatedly that Internet visitors don't "read" when they look at Web pages. For many landing pages that we have tested at SiteTuners.com, a stripped-down, stark version of the page works best. All of the clutter and detailed information is often removed so that visitors can focus on their task with minimal distractions.

But Google prefers content-rich, static-text pages that fall within a particular word count range. Anyone who does not write pages to this editorial style will suffer. So the mantra of "do what's best for the visitor" that Google trots out frequently to justify its policies just does not fly. The minimum word length and clear page structure are necessary only for Google's algorithm so that it can extract meaningful statistics about word frequency and the theme of the page.

At SiteTuners.com we have developed a number of specific techniques to change the overall appearance and improve the openness of the design while preserving most of the existing text. These techniques still leave the overall "theme" of the page for the spiders while changing its visual emphasis for the end user.

> **Don't Use Good Organic Ranking as an Excuse Not to Test:**
> All major SEO-related issues can be addressed if handled properly.

PPC

Since you are paying for PPC traffic, you have the right to land it anywhere you want (that is relevant and within the editorial guidelines of the search engine). PPC is basically an auction model that tries to maximize the revenue per visitor for the search engine by considering the maximum bid amount that you are willing to pay and the click-through rate (CTR) when deciding where to place your ad in the search results.

Because of these characteristics you might think that PPC would be immune from search engine issues. However, Google has introduced the notion of a landing page quality score (QS) as part of its ranking algorithm. A poor QS can cause your keyword to have a prohibitively high bid in order to appear at all in the search results. Since landing pages are often specifically designed for short-term PPC campaigns, they cannot be measured by the same standards as stable long-term pages on your website. In other words, there are no off-page factors such as inbound links or domain quality to consider. Only on-page factors can be used.

In theory, this can mean that your conversion rate improves through testing, but the resulting page causes your QS to get much worse. The net result would be that you would have greatly diminished (or no) PPC traffic to your new and improved page. In practice, this should not be a concern. Remember that from the standpoint of search engines, the whole point of landing page testing (and the announcement of the tools like the Google Website Optimizer) is to increase the conversion rate. This improved landing page performance should translate into higher PPC prices paid by the most efficient advertisers. I do not think that Google will cripple their main cash flow machine. In fact, they are proactively working to encourage landing page testing.

Inaction

I hope that I have not paralyzed you with fear about all of the things that can possibly go wrong with your test. It all comes down to this: as you are reading the last few words of this book, you have a choice to make. Hopefully you have learned something useful about landing page optimization. But your knowledge may remain in the realm of intellectual concepts only. I guarantee that if you do nothing, you will not improve your conversion rate.

You must *act* to produce any results. This does not have to be some giant undertaking. Start small. Take baby steps. Test something very simple. Even if you do not have a good outcome, you will learn something. And you will build the excitement and psychological momentum needed for your landing page optimization program to succeed in the longer term.

> **Start Testing Immediately:**
>
> A little bit of something is better a whole lot of nothing.

Now close this book and go do some testing. If you need a practical place to start, please visit the companion website for this book at LandingPageOptimizationBook.com. Best of luck!

A Closer Look at the Google Website Optimizer

The recent introduction of the Google Website Optimizer software is undoubtedly the biggest visibility boost and endorsement to the growing field of landing page optimization. Its backing by Google, its wide availability, and the unprecedented free price point combine to instantly make it a force to be reckoned with. But what are its true capabilities, strengths, and limitations? I will help you answer these questions and walk you through a hands-on demonstration of key Google Website Optimizer features.

Background

The release of the Google Website Optimizer (GWO) software as a beta test in the fall of 2006 was a low-key event. Even when the final version was announced in spring 2007 it did not get much notice. This was despite the fact that powerful landing page testing capabilities were suddenly available for free to anyone with a Google AdWords PPC account.

I continue to be amazed and somewhat befuddled by this. I personally know many PPC advertisers who fine-tune almost every aspect of their campaigns. They dig deep to find the best search term portfolios, test their ad copy, and actively manage the bids at a keyword level to maximize ROI. Yet there is a limit to the efficiencies and revenue gains that can be captured by these activities. But for some inexplicable reason the same companies have ignored testing the landing pages on which all of their traffic lands, despite the fact that the potential performance improvements can be staggering.

What is GWO? Simply put, it is a free, self-service tool that allows you to run A-B split or full factorial parametric multivariate tests on your landing pages. The data is collected in a full factorial fashion (with every possible recipe in the test receiving an equal percentage of the available traffic). Once you have identified the projected winner in a multivariate test, you can also immediately start a head-to-head follow-up test against the original landing page with the click of a button.

Despite common misconceptions, GWO landing page tests do not have to be run exclusively on Google AdWords traffic. The traffic sources are not restricted in any way. Moreover, you do not have to spend any money on AdWords in order to use GWO. You simply have to have an AdWords account.

Why did Google create GWO? It was a mix of altruism and self-serving business considerations. Testing makes landing pages more effective and Web search more relevant for the intended audience. It also provides better bang-for-the-buck for Google advertisers, allowing them to temporarily lower their cost per acquisition by raising conversion rates.

The longer-term implication is that Google is trying to increase the revenue that it generates from advertisers. It is difficult to squeeze out efficiencies simply from tuning a PPC campaign. As more and more sophisticated competitors start using PPC in each industry, the cost of the top few positions in the paid search results will continue to climb. This is inevitable since being in the top positions results in the lion's share of the traffic. If you do not improve your conversion rate, you will eventually be pushed from the top positions by more efficient competitors who want the extra exposure and have the business economics to support it.

So for the advertisers, it is largely a zero-sum game—if one wins, the others lose. But for Google and other popular PPC search engines, higher conversion rates allow their advertisers to pay more for the same click.

An important characteristic of GWO is that it is a tool that is intended for self-service use. This creates some challenges and opportunities around its adoption by different groups of potential users. On one hand, its wide availability makes it possible for just about any online advertiser (big and small) to test their landing pages. On the other hand, the free price-point and self-service designation lower its perceived value in the marketplace.

Among very small companies, there may be few alternatives for landing page testing tools. However, these companies are also the least sophisticated technically and mathematically. Many of them may try GWO and fail to produce any positive results either because of implementation challenges (no matter how simple Google makes their tools and supporting information), or because of their poor choice of testing elements (which may not result in significant conversion improvements). The very low data rates of some smaller businesses may also result in unacceptably long data collection times for a test, or may cause the results to remain statistically inconclusive.

At the other extreme, larger companies may need a robust technology platform that includes advanced features and is scalable to larger test sizes. They may also want the testing expertise and analytical support that a landing page optimization partner provides. Such companies may not have the time, experience, resources, or inclination to grow an in-house testing program from scratch and may have to outsource.

Google recognized the need for additional support and created the Website Optimizer Authorized Consultant (WOAC) program. Each prospective company must meet stringent criteria to qualify for the program. WOACs provide support in all aspects of GWO: consultation, implementation support, training, and full-service engagements.

The companies are drawn from different backgrounds. Many are Internet marketing generalists who may only provide landing page optimization services as a small part of their offerings. Some are also Google Analytics Authorized Consultant companies (GWO is built on the same technology platform as Google Analytics), and have deep technical implementation skills but lack significant testing and usability experience. Others are Google AdWords qualified and are migrating into landing page testing as a way to increase the efficiency of the PPC spending.

SiteTuners.com was one of only five charter WOACs, and is one of a small number of companies whose focus is exclusively on landing page optimization. We use GWO for most engagements involving A-B split testing or multivariate testing. As mentioned in Chapter 8, "Tuning Methods," we have also developed our own proprietary TuningEngine technology and use it for large tests that exceed the capabilities of GWO and meet higher minimum data rate requirements.

Requirements and Capabilities

In this section, I will outline some important technological and implementation considerations of GWO.

Technical Requirements

GWO requires two basic technical capabilities: the availability of JavaScript, and first-party cookies. JavaScript is a Web programming language that allows changes to be made to the landing page on the fly as it is being displayed in the visitor's Web browser. Because of this, it does not matter whether the landing page is static HTML or whether it has been created dynamically via a database or some content management system. The changes are made *after* the landing page has been requested from the Web server and properly constructed (i.e., JavaScript technology is *client-side*).

A first-party cookie is a small information file that is left on your computer by a website that you visit. It is normally used to identify you during return visits, and to customize your experience in some way. Because of this convenience, the vast majority of Internet users leave the first-party cookie setting "on" in their browser software. However, because of concerns about computer privacy, many people regularly delete their cookies. As I discussed earlier, this may lead to undercounting of repeat visitors (since they will look like first-time visitors after their cookies have been erased).

The JavaScript and first-party cookie requirements are common among landing page testing tools, and allow approximately 95% of all Web visitors to be tracked during a landing page test.

Alternative Content Variations Stored by Google

There are two basic approaches to storing the alternative tuning elements during your test. Each has its pros and cons.

Google has chosen to host all alternative HTML content on its own servers. When a piece of content is required to construct the landing page, Google returns it to the visitor's Web browser, and it is incorporated into the page. An advantage of this approach is that the alternative content for the test can usually be created by the author of the landing page without the support of the webmaster or I.T.

The disadvantage is that a delay is created as the content is retrieved from a remote server. This is minimized by the fast response times of Google's servers. But the latency of retrieving *any* data over the Internet still remains. Google mitigates this problem by using several dozen server farms that are spread throughout the world. Since the data is retrieved from the closest available server, the latency is typically kept to very low levels.

Another limitation of the current implementation is that the total for the HTML test elements stored by Google cannot exceed 64KB when compressed. In practice, this means that large pieces of content (such as large text blocks) cannot be stored by Google. Instead, they must be included *by reference*. In other words, they must be stored on the same server as the landing page (or some other non-Google server).

Some companies have a philosophical or operational aversion to having part of their landing page stored on a remote server. They want the feeling of control that comes with storing content locally. It also allows them to guarantee shorter server response times. You can try to reference as much local content as possible during a GWO test. However, even if you simply reference local content, you will still experience the latency, as the reference itself is retrieved from Google's servers. As I mentioned earlier, this should not be a significant issue in practice, but it should be understood as a concept.

Some landing page optimization tools (such as the SiteTuners.com's TuningEngine) have chosen to leave all content on the client's local servers. The only dependency on the testing platform is to determine which recipe to show a new visitor, and the reporting of any completed conversion action. However, this approach typically requires the cooperation of the webmaster and I.T. staff to upload files during test implementation and QA.

Page Rendering and Scripting

The GWO implementation requires three main programming scripts (written in JavaScript) to create each test page.

The *control script* is placed near the top of the page file. It determines if the current visitor is already a test participant by looking for the presence of an existing first-party cookie. If the visitor is new, it assigns them a recipe and saves the information in the cookie. If they are a returning visitor, the control script determines which recipe they previously saw and makes sure that they will see it again.

Each block of content on the page that contains a test element is surrounded by a set of *page section* "begin" and "end" tags. As each block is reached, JavaScript is used to replace the original content with the appropriate alternative variable value (by overwriting the original content on the page).

At the bottom of each page is a *tracking script*. This is used to record the fact that the page was displayed correctly. If the page is a confirmation page that follows a conversion action, the tracking script records the conversion.

There are two advantages to this implementation approach. First, the page is drawn sequentially (similar to how normal pages are rendered by the browser).

Alternative implementation methods may display nothing until the page load is complete. In addition, they may cause a momentary flicker or blink as the original page content is replaced and rewritten with the alternative content. Second, if the alternative content is unavailable on Google's servers, there are no Web browser errors and the original page is simply displayed to the visitor (without counting that visitor as part of the data collection).

Possible Types of Tests

Several types of tests are possible with the current implementation. Although more flexible and freeform tests can be implemented, they require specific technical knowledge of workarounds and are beyond the capabilities of most intended self-service users.

The most basic type of test possible is an *A-B split test* on a single landing page (followed by a confirmation page that records the completed conversion action). *Split-path* A-B split tests are also possible. A split-path test is an alternative linear flow of pages. For example, you may be testing a three-page registration process, or a two-page flow containing the same information.

A *multivariate test* involving elements of a single landing page is possible. You may also choose to implement a *multiple-page multivariate test*. In such cases your test elements may be different on each page, or may repeat (as long as they are identical) on multiple pages.

If you do not have a confirmation page following your landing page, you may also choose to implement a *time-based* test. The conversion action will be recorded based on a minimum time that you specify being spent by the visitor on the landing page.

It is also possible to record multiple conversion actions in your GWO test. These may be on the same page or spread across multiple pages. Each conversion will simply be counted and added to the total. All conversion actions are assumed to have the same value.

Example Test Setup: SF Video

This section will walk you through the setup and results of an actual GWO experiment. The specific screenshots and capabilities shown here may soon become obsolete as the GWO continues to evolve. The purpose of this example is to show you the general flavor and architecture of the tool and how it is used in a real-life example. Detailed documentation and implementation guides are available from Google; this section is not meant as a technical specification or a replacement for Google's documentation.

The GWO is accessed from the Campaign Management > Website Optimizer submenu in your Google AdWords account (see Figure A.1). When you start, you will be asked to choose an A-B split or multivariate test.

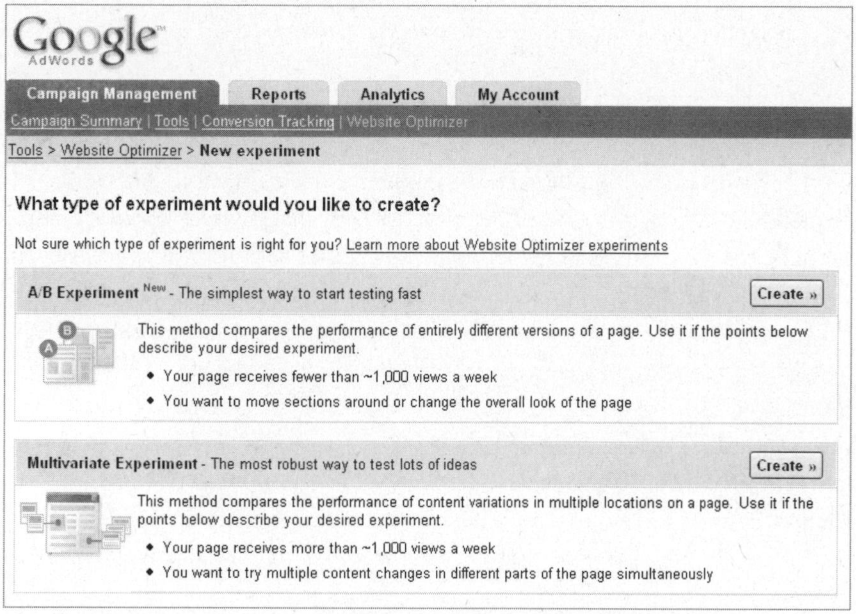

Figure A.1 GWO test setup screen

The example that I will use is from SiteTuners.com client SF Video (mentioned earlier in the "Variable Interactions" section of Chapter 7, "The Math of Tuning," and in the "Variable Interactions" section of Chapter 11, "Avoiding the Pitfalls"). We chose to conduct a simple multivariate test on the PPC lead-capture form of the company.

Step 1: Identify Experiment Pages

In the first step of your test setup, do the following (as shown in Figure A.2):

- Select a unique experiment name.
- Select your landing page.
- Select a conversion confirmation (or "goal") page.

GWO will check to make sure that both the landing page and confirmation page are accessible from the Internet before continuing.

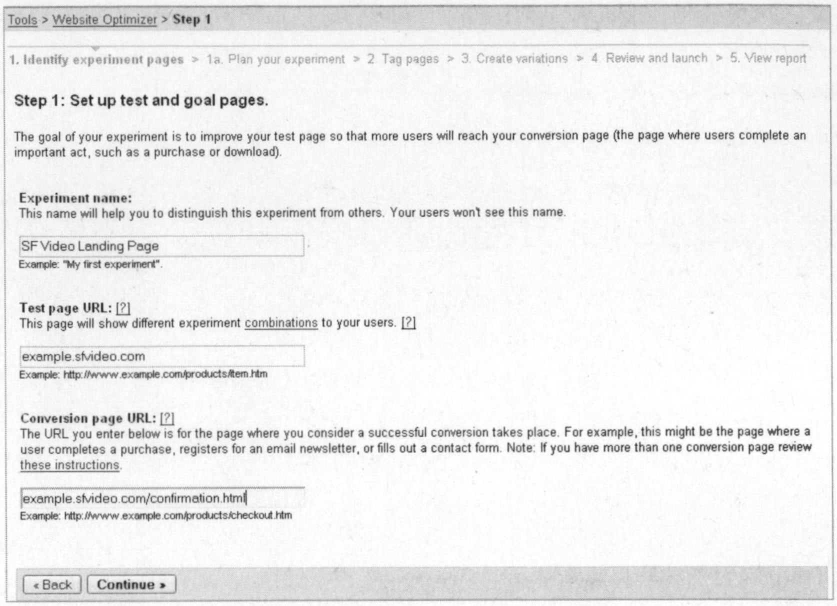

Tools > Website Optimizer > Step 1
1. Identify experiment pages > 1a. Plan your experiment > 2. Tag pages > 3. Create variations > 4. Review and launch > 5. View report
Step 1: Set up test and goal pages.
The goal of your experiment is to improve your test page so that more users will reach your conversion page (the page where users complete an important act, such as a purchase or download).
Experiment name:
This name will help you to distinguish this experiment from others. Your users won't see this name.
SF Video Landing Page
Example: "My first experiment".
Test page URL: [?]
This page will show different experiment combinations to your users. [?]
example.sfvideo.com
Example: http://www.example.com/products/item.htm
Conversion page URL: [?]
The URL you enter below is for the page where you consider a successful conversion takes place. For example, this might be the page where a user completes a purchase, registers for an email newsletter, or fills out a contact form. Note: If you have more than one conversion page review these instructions.
example.sfvideo.com/confirmation.html
Example: http://www.example.com/products/checkout.htm
« Back
Continue »

Figure A.2 GWO Step 1: Set up test and goal pages

Step 1b: Test Page Section Planning

The next step is to identify the sections of your page that you will be testing. This is simply a planning placeholder step before you proceed, and is indicated by the screenshot in Figure A.3. It instructs you in more detail to:

- Choose your page sections
- Discuss them with your technical team

Tools > Website Optimizer > SF Video Landing Page > Step 1a
1. Identify experiment pages > 1a. Plan your experiment > 2. Tag pages > 3. Create variations > 4. Review and launch > 5. View report
Step 1a: Plan your experiment
Before you can begin the technical set-up of the experiment, you'll need to decide which specific content you'd like to test on your test page.
Heading
Image
Description
Examples of page sections to test.
Choose your page sections
Your marketing team should decide which sections of your test page you would like Website Optimizer to vary. Some examples of potential test page sections could be headlines, images, testimonials, buttons, and promotional copy.
Review desired page sections with your technical team
Before you can begin implementing the experiment on your site, your marketing and technical teams will need to agree on which sections to test. Once you have chosen your page sections, proceed to Step 2 so that you or your webmaster can copy the Website Optimizer JavaScript tags and add them to your test page's source code.
For a full overview of the experiment set-up or to review upcoming steps, visit the Quick Start Guide.
After you've selected your page sections and reviewed them with your technical team, click 'Continue »' to begin adding the JavaScript tags to your page.
« Back
Continue »

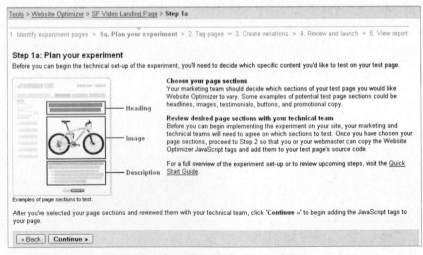

Figure A.3 GWO Step 1b: Plan your experiment

For the SF Video landing page (shown in Figure A.4) we chose to test the following two elements:

- Headline of the form input section
- Number of SF Video client logos

Figure A.4 "Original" SF Video landing page (original headline and 36 client logos)

For the form headline variable we included two alternatives:

- "Free Quote Request" (the original)
- "Instant Quote"

For the number of logos variable, we also included two alternatives:

- 36 (the original)
- 7

The resulting test had a total of four possible recipes ("combinations" in the terminology of GWO). The remaining three combinations are shown in Figure A.5, Figure A.6, and Figure A.7.

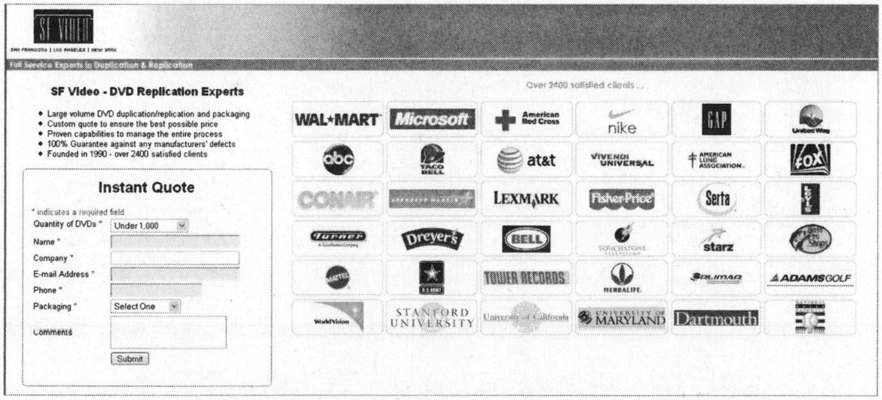

Figure A.5 "Combination 1" SF Video landing page (new headline and 36 client logos)

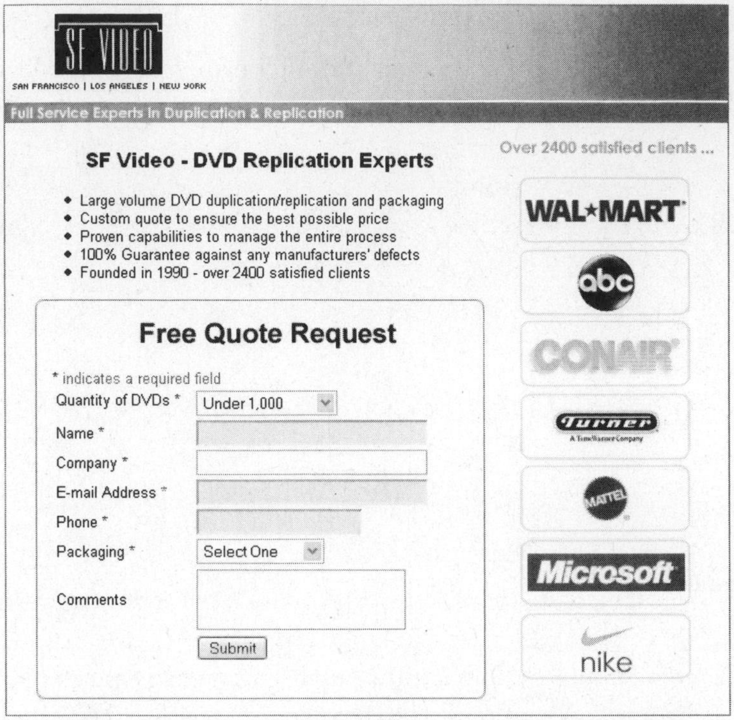

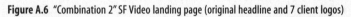

Figure A.6 "Combination 2" SF Video landing page (original headline and 7 client logos)

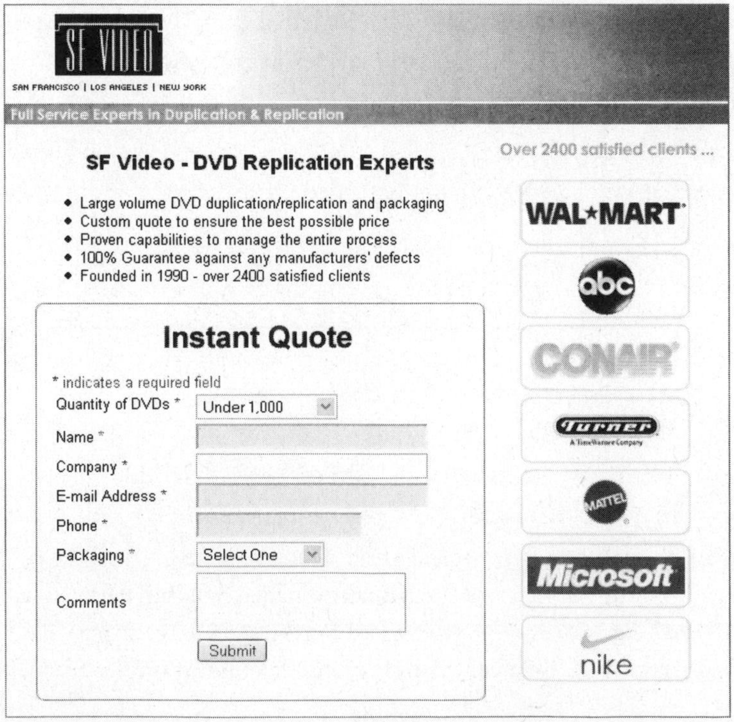

Figure A.7 "Combination 3" SF Video landing page (new headline and 7 client logos)

Step 2: Add Tags to the Experiment Pages

Adding the JavaScript to your landing page and confirmation page actually involves multiple substeps:

Step 1: Cut and paste the control script into the top of the page Simply cut and paste the JavaScript code snippet supplied into the top of your landing page.

Step 2: Identify and add page section script for page sections The exact code that you will need to do this depends on exactly what content you will be alternating as part of your test elements. Google provides simple examples for swapping out text or a graphic (see Figure A.8).

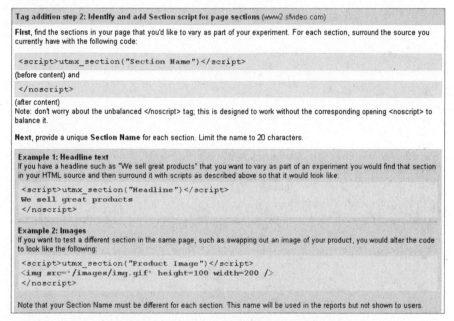

Figure A.8 Example *page section script* for text and graphics

Step 3: Install Tracking script on test page Cut and paste the JavaScript code snippet supplied into the top of your landing page. This code will record an impression (unique visit) during the data collection.

Step 4: Install Tracking script on the conversion page Cut and paste the JavaScript code snippet supplied into the top of your landing page. This code will record a conversion during the data collection.

Step 5: Validate the JavaScript tag installation Once you have added all of the necessary JavaScript to your landing and confirmation pages, you have to run a validator to ensure that everything was done properly (see Figure A.9). If your new pages have not been uploaded to the Web, you can first check the JavaScript on the files without uploading them. However, in order to proceed to the next step, you will need to eventually run the validator on the files in their live location.

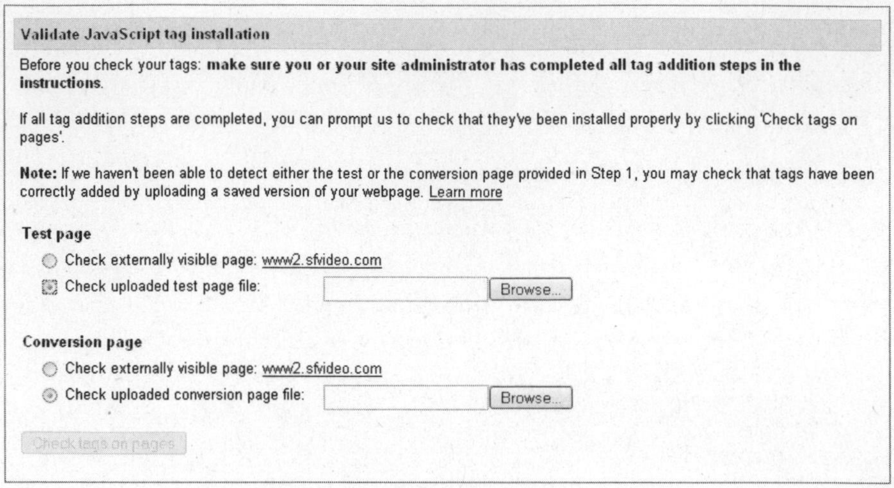

Figure A.9 JavaScript validator

If the validator finds problems with your JavaScript tagging, it will produce a detailed list of problems (see Figure A.10) to help you troubleshoot.

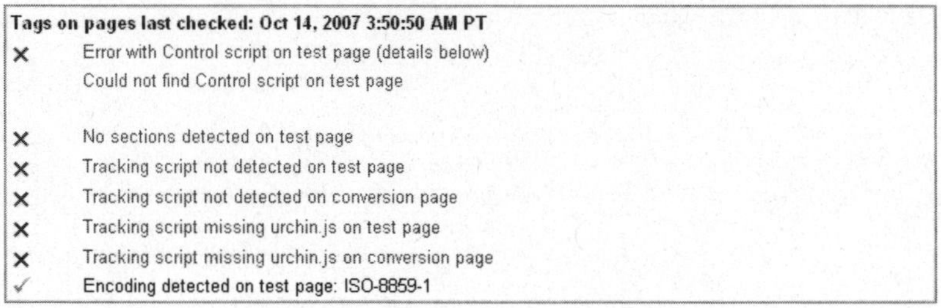

Figure A.10 JavaScript validator error report

Step 3: Create Variations

At this point GWO will contain noneditable original versions of each page section that you have tagged with a *page section script*. You will be able to add additional variations (variable values) one at a time for each variable. Once you are done adding all of the alternative variable values, you can preview any possible version of your page by clicking on the preview link. You will see the preview control pane at the top of your screen and the current page version at the bottom. You can select the combination number or the individual settings for each variable to display the desired page.

Step 4: Review Experiment Settings and Launch

After you have completed your tagging and created alternative variable values, you can review the experiment settings before launching. In addition to double-checking all of your information, you can specify what percentage of the traffic to the page you want to use for your test (see Figure A.11). Note that whatever percentage of traffic you select will be divided equally among all of the combinations in your test. In this example, Site-Tuners.com used all of the available traffic to the page. Each of the four combinations received 25% the available traffic.

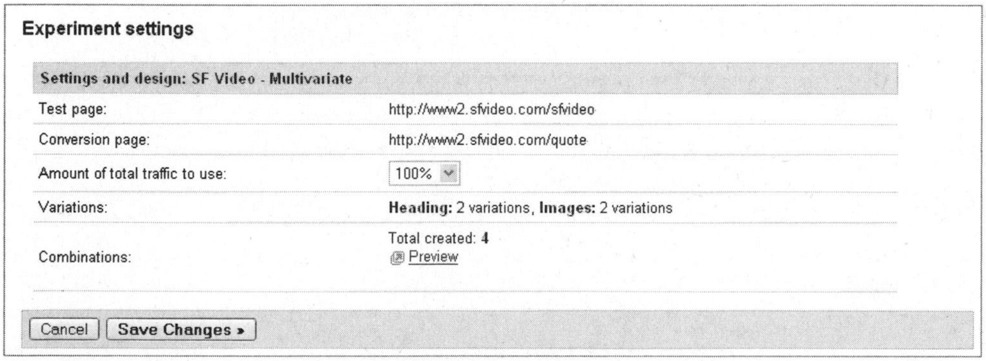

Figure A.11 GWO experiment settings

Step 5: View Reports

Once you start collecting data, you will have access to two reports. The reports are not real-time. They are a bit delayed—just like in your Google AdWords account. You can pause and resume your data collection at will once your experiment starts running. After enough data has been collected, GWO will estimate the time required for your test to reach a 95% statistical confidence in your answer. However, if you test variable values that have no effect on your conversion rate, it is possible for the test to run a very long time without reaching any conclusive results. In such cases, you will have to determine when you have invested enough time in data collection and cut the test short.

Combinations Report

The first tab on the reports screen displays the *Combinations* report (see the final SF Video report in Figure A.12). This report shows you the performance of your baseline recipe (labeled "Original") versus the best- or worst-performing recipes (called "combinations" in GWO). The report will show only a few of the best or worst combinations. If your test is very large, you can also export the data into a Microsoft Excel spreadsheet for further analysis.

Combinations	Page Sections					
Analysis for: Mar 29, 2007 1:04:35 PM PT - Oct 9, 2007 1:50:23 PM PT						
View: ⊙ Best 3 Combinations ○ Worst 3 Combinations				Download: T		🖶 Print ⊡ Preview
Combination	Estimated Conversion Rate Range [?]		Chance to Beat Orig. [?]	Chance to Beat All [?]	Observed Improvement [?]	Conversions / Visitors [?]
Original	2.73% ± 0.6%	⊢▭—⊣	—	0.96%	—	38 / 1393
Combination 1	4.33% ± 0.7%	⊢——▭—⊣	98.7%	96.3%	58.7%	57 / 1317
Combination 3	2.86% ± 0.6%	⊢▭——⊣	58.4%	1.85%	4.97%	39 / 1362
Combination 2	2.70% ± 0.6%	⊢▭—⊣	48.5%	0.91%	-0.85%	36 / 1331

Figure A.12 GWO Combinations report

If your search space size is large, the amount of data that you collect on each particular recipe may be small. A common mistake is to select a winner just because it has "separated out" to a 95% confidence level. Remember, the confidence calculation is only valid if you are considering two items in a head-to-head test. Let's consider a hypothetical example to illustrate the dangers of misusing this. If you have 100 combinations in your test, you would expect on average to find five of them that significantly outperform the original just *based on random chance alone*. In other words, those five are simply on a short-term lucky streak. So it is critical to run a follow-up head-to-head experiment and collect a lot more data to see if your expected improvement really does hold up. It is appropriate to look at the "Chance to beat all" column and wait until it reaches your desired confidence level. If you do this, it does not matter how many combinations you are looking at.

The following columns are displayed in the report:

Estimated Conversion Rate Range The conversion rate is expressed as a numeric range and graphically as a set of error bars. The numeric range includes the measured conversion and a "plus or minus" range that takes the sample size into account. For example, the original recipe shows a range of 2.73%±0.6%. So we can be 95% confident that the actual conversion rate of the baseline lies between 2.13% and 3.33%. Similarly, combination #1 shows a conversion rate range of 4.33%±0.7%. So we can be 95% confident that the actual conversion rate of the combination #1 lies between 3.63% and 5.03%.

The graphical error bars are shown in three colors. The portion that overlaps vertically with the original is shown in gray. Values numerically above the range of the original (to the right on the scale) are shown in green. Those below numerically (to the left on the scale) are shown in red. As soon as a combination goes to all-green, you are 95% sure that the combination has a higher conversion rate than the original. The more horizontal space there is between the top of the original's error bars and the bottom of the combination's error bars, the more they have "separated out." That means your confidence level actually increases beyond 95%.

Chance to Beat Original This is a calculation of the combination's chance to beat the performance of the original recipe. Be careful not to act too quickly. You will typically need at least 95% confidence to make a decision.

Chance to Beat All This is a calculation of the combination's chance to beat the original recipe *and* all other combinations in the test as well. Since there are other potential competitors for the top-performer spot, this number will typically be somewhat lower than the *chance to beat the original* (unless all other combinations are performing significantly worse than the original).

Observed Improvement This is the improvement percentage based on the observed conversion rates of the combination and the original. Note that this is based on the sampled data only. For small sample sizes, the error bars will be very wide.

This is probably the most misunderstood part of the report. Remember, just because you are very confident that combination #1's conversion rate *is better* than the original's, that does not mean that you know *exactly how much higher* it is.

In the previous example, the observed improvement for combination #1 over the original is 58.7%, but based on the error bars for both conversion rates the range of possible improvements is between 9% and 136% (with a 95% confidence). Please review the "How Much Better Is It?" section of Chapter 7 for additional background.

Conversions / Visitors This column provides the raw data on which all the other calculations are based. The number of conversions is a count of the conversion actions f or a particular combination based on the visitors who converted within a half hour of seeing the landing page. The GWO cookie length is currently set to a fixed amount of time (check the Google documentation for the latest cookie length). After that, the cookie is erased and the visitor is treated like a new test participant upon a return visit (and is shown a new randomly assigned combination).

Unique visitor sessions are counted based on the same cookie. So a visitor who takes longer than a half hour to return to the page without converting will be "recycled" and treated as a first-time participant in the test.

Page Sections Report

The second tab on the reports screen displays the *Page Sections* report (see the final SF Video report in Figure A.13). This report shows you the performance of each of the variable values ("variations") in your test grouped by variable ("page section"). The names of the columns and explanation of calculations is the same as in the *Combinations* report. The following issues need to be understood when using the page sections report.

Combinations	Page Sections					
Analysis for: Mar 29, 2007 1:04:35 PM PT - Oct 9, 2007 1:50:23 PM PT						
Sort By: Relevance Rating Order Created				Download: T ⊡ ⊠ | 🖶 Print | 🖾 Preview		
Relevance Rating [?]	**Variation**	**Estimated Conversion Rate Range [?]**	**Chance to Beat Orig. [?]**	**Chance to Beat All [?]**	**Observed Improvement [?]**	**Conversions / Visitors [?]**
Heading 2 / 5	Original	2.72% ± 0.4%	—	3.39%	—	74 / 2724
	Instant Quote	3.58% ± 0.5%	96.5%	96.6%	31.9%	96 / 2679
Images 1 / 5	Original	3.51% ± 0.5%	—	93.5%	—	95 / 2710
	6 Images	2.78% ± 0.4%	6.55%	6.45%	-20.6%	75 / 2693

Figure A.13 GWO Page Sections report

Amount of data on each variation The amount of data collected for each variable value will depend on the branching factor of the variable. For example, in the SF Video example earlier, each form heading received approximately half of the total traffic because only two variable values were possible for the form headline (the original, and the "Instant Quote" alternative). If there had been four possible values for this variable, each would have received one quarter of the available traffic. If your search space size is large, the amount of data collected on each variable value will be much greater than that collected on individual recipes.

Relevance Rating The report can be sorted by an additional Relevance Rating column. This five-point scale indicates how much conversion rate difference there is among all of the values of a particular variable (page section). In other words, it is possible that there is wide variation and clear separation among the values of one variable, while other variables do not impact the conversion rate at all. If a particular variable has a low relevance rating after collecting a lot of data, you may decide to cut the test short. Under these circumstances, you can lock in the winning values for the highly relevant variables, and leave the original values for the ones that have low relevance.

Dangers of piecewise construction One of the temptations of looking at this report is to simply pick the best value for each of your variables and declare the resulting combination as the winning recipe. If you take this approach, there is a significant chance that you will be led astray from the best solution. This is especially true if you have a larger number of variables in the test, have low statistical confidence in some of your individual variable values, and experience strong variable interactions (as is often the case in landing page optimization). Please review the notes about piecewise construction errors in the "Fractional Factorial Disadvantages" section of Chapter 8, "Tuning Methods." As I mention there, I strongly urge you to run a follow-up head-to-head test of your predicted best challenger in order to verify the results.

Advantages

GWO has several strengths, which we'll examine in this section.

Full Factorial Data Collection

GWO is the only multivariate testing tool that uses full factorial data collection. In other words, it samples data equally from all recipes in the search space. Despite common misconceptions to the contrary, full factorial data collection for landing page optimization is *not* any less efficient than fractional factorial approaches (such as the Taguchi method) if you are only planning to conduct a main effects analysis. Please review Chapter 8 for additional background.

It is true that full factorial data collection results in smaller sample sizes on each recipe (because every possible recipe in the test receives an equal and proportional percentage of the available test traffic). So you will not reach the desired confidence level as quickly for a particular recipe (unlike fractional factorial, which concentrates data collection on a small subset of carefully selected recipes). But this is not really a weakness.

The point of collecting the data is not to wait long enough for a single recipe to pull ahead as the winner. Rather, it is to *build a model* that *predicts* which recipe is likely to be the best. This is true of both fractional and full factorial approaches. Since you only sample a small number of recipes in a fractional factorial test, it is likely that you will have collected *absolutely no data* on the best recipe as predicted by the model. That is why follow-up head-to-head tests are required for parametric multivariate testing.

Full factorial also has the advantage of ease of test setup. Instead of carefully constructing balanced arrays and matrices, you simply pick the variables that you want to test along with the desired variable values. Unlike with fractional factorial approaches, the variables can have arbitrary branching factors, and you can have as many variables as you need (constrained only by your available data rate). Once your variables have been defined, you simply start data collection in a random and balanced fashion across all your recipes.

Full factorial data collection also allows you to later uncover all important variable interactions. As I have discussed in Chapter 7, variable interactions are a critical part of landing pages. As marketers, we often want to create synergies among the different elements on the page. Yet commonly used fractional factorial approaches (along with repeated A-B split testing) assume that *variable interactions do not exist*. This is a dangerous and inappropriate assumption that will lead to suboptimal results. With full factorial data collection, you at least have the option of conducting a more sophisticated analysis to uncover important interactions. Common fractional factorial methods force you to build models consisting only of the *main effects* of each variable.

Even if you choose to ignore the presence of strong variable interactions and build only a main effects model, full factorial data collection still has an advantage over fractional factorial. Since full factorial sampling evenly covers your whole search space, you will more accurately model the main effects. You will not be at the mercy of the specific recipes that are sampled in the sparse fractional factorial test designs.

Robust Technology

GWO was built on top of the Google Analytics technology (originally developed by San Diego–based Urchin Software and purchased by Google). Google Analytics is a proven Web analytics platform that has been widely deployed in its free hosted application form and also features a stand-alone server version. A large number of Google Analytics Authorized Consultant (GAAC) companies worldwide support deployments on the platform.

Like all Google operational product deployments, GWO was designed from the start to be scalable and have very high availability. Since the system is distributed across a number of data centers worldwide, the latency time to retrieve content should be low regardless of the Web visitor's location.

Ease of Implementation

Simple A-B split or multivariate tests can be set up in minutes, while largely bypassing I.T. assistance. The example in the previous section should have familiarized you with the basic process. As GWO develops, setup wizards and documentation will improve even more. After you have successfully deployed your first test, it becomes simple to create additional ones. Your focus can shift to the creation of the best test variables and values, and away from the mechanics of implementation.

Price Point and Staying Power

By offering GWO as a free tool, and putting their clout behind it, Google guarantees widespread adoption and their long-term dominance in the landing page optimization tools field. It's hard to beat "free" as a price point. Many companies (or at least enterprising online marketers within them) will rally around GWO as a quick and easy way to jumpstart their landing page testing programs.

I am convinced that GWO is absolutely strategic to Google. It allows the most value to be extracted from their biggest business line (AdWords). I expect that once the tool reaches adoption critical mass, many of Google's larger advertisers will jump on the bandwagon of landing page optimization. Their needs and requirements will be more demanding than those of the early adopters. For this reason I expect the GWO team to continue investing significant financial resources and rapidly evolving the capabilities of the tool.

Drawbacks

There are several drawbacks to the GWO. Some have to do with its self-service nature. Others have to do with its relatively recent creation and launch. I suspect that many of these limitations will be addressed in upcoming product upgrades.

No Variable Interaction Analysis

As I discussed earlier, the full factorial data collection of GWO gives it an edge over fractional factorial methods. But one of its biggest advantages currently lies untapped. The Page Sections report is a *main effects* report only. In other words, the analysis after the data collection has been completed is rudimentary and not that different from what can be found with other multivariate tools. The power to uncover and consider variable interactions is critical to achieving the best results. Currently GWO does not support this, although the raw data can be exported for additional analysis outside of the tool.

Does Not Support Recipe Bandwidth Changes

GWO does not support throttling or recipe bandwidth changes. The current implementation of GWO distributes available traffic *evenly* across all recipes in a test. The follow-up test capability lets you test only *one* challenger recipe against your original champion. So you are faced with an all-or-nothing proposition. There is no way to run a follow-up test on a larger subset of your search space. There is also no way to modify the bandwidth assigned to a particular recipe or recipes, even if they might be of particular interest. This is especially a problem when considering the original baseline recipe. Since you are trying to beat the performance of the original, you need to have a good estimate of its behavior. As I mentioned earlier, at SiteTuners.com we normally devote 15–25% of available bandwidth to the original recipe.

GWO does allow you to select what percentage of your traffic to use for the test (see the "Throttling" section of Chapter 8). Unfortunately, this is done in a wasteful way. Because all of the traffic not included in the test will see the original landing page, there is an opportunity to find out more about its behavior. Unfortunately, under the current implementation this data is simply not tracked, and discarded. It would be much more elegant to specify what percentage of the available traffic should be dedicated to the original recipe, and allocate the remaining traffic evenly among the remaining recipes in the search space.

Big Brother Sees All

I have heard many people comment about their unwillingness to use any tool provided by Google that exposes details of their online business operations. They are concerned that Google will analyze the resulting data (even if anonymously and in aggregate) to find more efficient ways to extract additional revenues from them. They fear that Google will become more vertically integrated, opaque, and more monopolistic in its practices. They would prefer to use third-party landing page testing tools and services simply to keep their activities as much as possible out of Google's sight (the same thinking has slowed adoption of Google Analytics at some companies). Regardless of whether these concerns are warranted, they are shared by a significant number of people and need to be understood.

No Easy Support for Nested or Conditional Testing Elements

GWO does not easily support nested or conditional testing elements.

The cleanest implementations of the GWO involve test variables that do not physically overlap with one another (or interact in their underlying HTML coding). Under its standard implementation, GWO cannot handle physically nested variables (such as changes to high-level page structure), or embedding one variable conditionally inside of another. It is possible to implement these kinds of test designs, but it requires an intimate knowledge of the tool and some specific programming work-arounds.

Only Works for Counting Conversion Events

GWO can only count conversions, so it can only be used to improve conversion rates of equal-valued events (such as click-throughs, downloads, form-fills, or purchase of a single product). Technically, GWO can record different types of conversions (spread across multiple pages), but it does so by assigning them an equal value. In other words, it just lumps them together regardless of type and counts them.

This leaves out a significant class of landing page tests including, most notably, e-commerce catalogs that sell multiple products. Google Analytics already supports tracking multiple conversion goals (including ones that have an associated revenue value). ROIRevolution.com (another WOAC company) has recently developed and publicly described techniques for more tightly tying together GWO and Google Analytics. This allows you to conduct sophisticated analyses on your data and segment your traffic and results along standard Web analytics lines. This is a welcome step, and I suspect that GWO and Google Analytics may become more closely linked in the future.

However, this does not change the basic problem: GWO does not allow you to *optimize* for criteria other than conversion rate. If you had multiple products or conversion actions with different values or profit margins, you would be unable to use the tool. See the "Measuring and Counting" section of Chapter 8 for additional discussion.

Rough Edges

GWO has a number of rough edges. These minor limitations and design choices make the tool more cumbersome than it should be:

Arbitrary combination naming convention Combinations are numbered sequentially instead of being expressed as the settings of variables.

Fixed naming for Original elements There is no way to override the default "Original" with more descriptive variable value ("variation") names.

Fixed confidence limits All of the reporting is based on 95% confidence limits. Users should be allowed to set this parameter depending on their specific needs.

No notification features There are no provisions for e-mail alerts when a combination or variable value goes to statistical significance.

Requires Engagement Support

GWO can be somewhat tricky to implement when you expand its use beyond a single landing page. Although it is possible to handle the implementation if you have technical skills, this normally takes the test out of the domain of true self-service for most online marketers.

Many self-service would-be landing page testers do not really know what to test, or how to analyze the results. They choose landing page elements that are unlikely to produce conversion rate changes and then get frustrated when the test does not produce definitive results in a reasonable timeframe. Even if the tool itself is easy to use, there is no substitute for competent and experienced support in designing the test plan and deciding which alternative page elements to create.

The deceptively simple GWO reporting interface can also lead to improper conclusions as the data is being collected. Many of the intended users do not have any background in statistics, or even a rudimentary understanding of confidence intervals or error bars. Because of this they often cut the data collection inappropriately short, or report the results in an inappropriate way.

As I mentioned in the first section, recognition of these limitations led Google to create the WOAC program. Over time, their plan is to develop an ecosystem of companies that can provide appropriate support to anyone who needs it.

Lacking Enterprise-Level Features

GWO currently lacks many of the features that would make it an enterprise-level testing platform for large and complex websites.

Test size Current tests are limited to a maximum of eight variables (with a branching factor of 128 each). The search space size is limited to 10,000 total recipes. Users who want to test more than that are forced to conduct multiple smaller back-to-back tests.

Reporting lag The reporting in the GWO interface is slightly delayed.

Segmentation GWO cannot handle segmentation of incoming visitors (e.g., by traffic source, physical location, or time) and show each class of visitors different content.

No business rules or triggers No provision for business rules or event triggers are incorporated into the GWO. Thus, it is impossible to change the landing page or personalize it in significant ways based on the past history of behavior with a visitor.

Content size The content alternatives that reside on Google's servers are restricted to a 64KB compressed total for a single test.

Cookie length Currently the cookie length is fixed. Any preset value is bound to be inappropriate for many applications. The cookie length should be a user-settable parameter. Please see the "Delayed Conversions" section of Chapter 11, "Avoiding the Pitfalls," for additional discussion.

GWO was announced as a free self-service tool, and it may not be fair to compare it to specialized platforms available from landing page optimization companies. Yet many companies and pundits in the field did just that shortly after its announcement in an attempt to marginalize or position it.

I believe that we are seeing the very early days in the evolution of the product. Basic capabilities were included in the first release (which was produced under tight deadlines), but right from the start everything was built on top of Google's top-notch infrastructure. It will be relatively easy to add features in the future that would significantly broaden its capabilities and appeal. This seems almost inevitable given that Google wants to provide extra value to its biggest advertisers. Although the exact product evolution of GWO is somewhat unclear, it would be imprudent to count Google out of the enterprise landing page tool market.

Glossary

A

A-B split testing The simplest form of landing page testing. A new visitor to the page is randomly shown either the original version ("A") or an alternative version ("B").

above the fold The portion of a Web page that is seen without vertical or horizontal scrolling in a Web browser window.

affiliate In online marketing, a company or individual that voluntarily chooses to promote the products or services of another company. Affiliates are paid based only on measurable and trackable tangible actions that result from their promotional activities.

affiliate program A performance-based marketing program set up by a company. Affiliates join the program and are compensated based solely on their performance. Typical payment methods include a percentage of sales revenue generated, or a fixed amount per specified action on the company's website (see *affiliate*).

B

B2B Acronym for "business-to-business." Refers to vertical industries or businesses whose clients are also businesses (rather than retail consumers).

B2C Acronym for "business-to-consumer." Refers to vertical industries or businesses whose clients are consumers or the retail buying public (rather than other businesses).

back end The portion of a website or Web application (including the underlying database) that does not directly interact with the end user.

back links A hypertext link from another website to a page on your site. A sufficient number of properly constructed back links from reputable websites can increase your position on search engine results pages (see *SERPs*).

banner ads Rectangular graphical ads of various dimensions that appear on a website. Banner ads may contain animation or other interactive features. Normally the website owner does not have control over the content or color scheme used in a particular banner ad shown on their site.

banner blindness The tendency of website visitors to ignore and tune out banner ads.

baseline The original version of your landing page that is used as the benchmark against which other design variations are measured. Also called the "champion" or "control."

blacklist A list of "junk" e-mail addresses from which an e-mail program will not accept messages. Blacklisting is one form of spam filtering.

breadcrumbs A type of Web page navigation that shows the trail of pages that a visitor passed through to arrive at the current page.

bounce rate The percentage of visitors who land on a Web page and immediately exit without visiting any other pages linked from it.

brochure ware Websites that are static in nature and provide high-level descriptive information only, lacking any interactive features.

business-to-business See *B2B*.

business-to-consumer See *B2C*.

C

Central Limit Theorem An axiom of probability theory that states that regardless of the original distribution of a random variable (such as conversion rate), its average will conform to a normal "bell curve" distribution (see *random variable*).

challenger A new version of your landing page that you are testing against your current "champion" version (contrast with *baseline*).

champion See *baseline*.

clickstream analysis A capability of Web analytics software to display and represent popular sequences of pages that visitors navigate on a website.

click-through rate The percentage of Web page viewers who click on a particular link (also abbreviated CTR). CTR is often applied to the percentage of Internet users who click on a PPC advertisement and land on the advertiser's landing page.

client-side Programming functionality that takes place in the visitor's Web browser software after the page has been loaded. Many landing page testing changes are implemented via client-side technologies.

cloaking The practice of showing different content to search engine spiders and human visitors to a Web page for the purposes of manipulating the ranking of the page in search engine results (see *SERPs*).

continuous variables Variables, such as temperature or pressure, that can take on a range of numerical values (contrast with *discrete variables*).

control See *baseline*.

conversion action A desired measurable action on a landing page performed by an Internet visitor. Examples include click-throughs to another page, form-fills, downloads, or product purchases.

conversion rate The percentage of landing page visitors who take the desired conversion action.

cookies A small informational file stored by the Web browser software on an Internet user's PC that records information about current or past visits to a particular website.

cost per thousand impressions The dollar cost to be paid by an advertiser for each thousand appearances of an advertisement on a particular Web page or set of websites (also abbreviated as "CPM").

CPM See *cost per thousand impressions*.

CRM An abbreviation for "customer relationship management." This type of software is used to track the whole history of a company's interactions with a particular person across multiple channels, including the Internet, telephone, mail, and in-store visits.

CTR See *click-through rate*.

customer relationship management See *CRM*.

D

deep link A hyperlink to a Web page with very specific information. Such a page may reside deep within a website, several links removed from the home page (see *deep linking*).

deep linking In PPC campaigns, the practice of landing traffic on the most relevant landing page possible within a website (see *deep link*).

descriptive statistics A branch of applied statistics that is used to describe and summarize attributes of the data collected in an experiment. Typical descriptions include the mean (or average), median, variance, and standard deviation of the data.

design of experiments A discipline for multivariate testing and optimization that includes fractional factorial data collection and parametric data analysis. Examples include Taguchi method, Plackett-Burman, and Latin squares. Abbreviated as "DOE" or "DoE" (see also *fractional factorial*).

discrete variables Variables that can take on a set of distinct, enumerated values (contrast with *continuous variables*).

DOE See *design of experiments*.

E

error bars An indication of the uncertainly regarding the true value of a sampled quantity. Error bars can be represented graphically, or expressed as a numeric plus-or-minus range around the average or mean observed value.

event In probability theory, an event is the set of all possible outcomes to which a probability is assigned. In landing page testing, the event is commonly defined as the possibility of converting or not converting.

experimental studies A statistical method in which you observe a control condition and then modify the environment in a preplanned way to see if the modification resulted in an observable change in the desired outcome.

F

first-party cookies Cookies set by the particular Internet domain or website that an Internet user is visiting (see *cookies*).

fractional factorial A subset of DOE multivariate testing that seeks to cut down on the proportion of recipes sampled from the total search space in order to extract the most useful information from the smallest number of recipes. Fractional factorial methods (such as the Taguchi method) make simplifying assumptions about the underlying model and often ignore variable interactions (see *DOE, full factorial, main effects*, and *variable interactions*).

frames A method of designing Web pages in HTML by which information is pulled from a number of distinct sources and constructed in a collage-like fashion into the final page.

front end The portion of a website or Web application that interacts directly with and is seen by the visitor. Often used interchangeably with the term *user interface*.

full factorial A subset of multivariate testing data collection that samples data evenly across all recipes in the search space. Allows for the most complicated and accurate models during subsequent data analysis by taking variable interactions into account (contrast with *fractional factorial*).

G

Gaussian distribution A data distribution also known as a bell curve.

gross margin contribution In accounting, the dollar amount that a purchase adds to the gross margin after subtracting all variable costs. Gross margin for websites is often used instead of profit for optimization (and is often referred to as profit) since the design of the website rarely has any impact on the difference between gross margin and profit. This book follows this convention and makes little distinction between profit and gross margin.

I

inferential statistics The branch of applied statistics used to predict or model the behavior of an underlying system based on an observed test sample.

information foraging theory A branch of applied computer science that describes the behavior of people when faced with a lot of available information in their search for a specific solution to a current need.

information scent The extent to which a person's attention can be kept on a particular task or desired outcome based on the visual cues such as text or links placed on Web pages (see also *information foraging theory*).

input variables The variables in a landing page test that are assumed to have an impact on the conversion rate or other optimization criterion. Also called *independent variables*.

interruption marketing Marketing in which visitors must be interrupted in the course of their normal activities. Examples include billboards, television commercials, and Web banner ads (contrast with *permission marketing*).

inverted pyramid A website copy-writing style in which important information is put at the beginning of the page and summarized, and detailed information is provided lower on the page or accessed via related links.

K

keywords A word or phrase typed in by Internet searchers. A portfolio of keywords related to a particular topic or industry is commonly used as the basis for constructing PPC campaigns (see also *PPC*).

L

landing page The first page that a visitor lands on as a result of a traffic acquisition activity. The landing page can be a stand-alone page, a part of a special-purpose microsite, or a page on the company's main website.

Latin squares A fractional factorial multivariate testing method (see *fractional factorial*, *design of experiments*).

lifetime value The full economic value resulting from a particular conversion action as measured over the whole lifetime of that visitor's relationship with a company. Abbreviated as "LTV."

launch page A Web page used in landing page testing quality assurance to display any possible recipe in the test (see also *recipe*).

Likert scale A surveying response scale that measures affinity or agreement. Most commonly used with five response levels (strongly agree, agree, neither agree nor disagree, disagree, strongly disagree).

linear models A class of mathematical models that adds and subtracts the effects of all input variables and their combinations to estimate the corresponding value of the output variable.

list fatigue In e-mail marketing, when the response of a list to an offer or call-to-action declines after repeated mailings.

LTV See *lifetime value*.

M

main effects The effects of individually changing the values of single variables in a multivariate data sample. If a model only measures main effects, it assumes that there are no variable interactions (see also *variable interactions*).

managing by exception A management principle that focuses on problems or deviations from normal behavior as measured by a set of performance indicators.

marketese A copywriting style that embellishes the effects or benefits of a product or service in an attempt to make it appear more attractive to the target audience. Frequently uses superlatives and adjectives.

MBTI An abbreviation for "Myers-Briggs Type Indicator." A framework for describing behavioral styles based on cognitive predispositions.

mean The sum of all measured variable outcomes divided by the number of outcomes. Commonly called the average value.

microsite A special-purpose, small website that is designed to maximize conversion rates for an online marketing campaign or traffic source.

multivariate testing A type of landing page testing methodology where data is collected while simultaneously changing a number of different experimental variables (contrast with *A-B split testing*, see also *design of experiments*).

Myers-Briggs Type Indicator See *MBTI*.

N

negative interaction During multivariate testing data analysis, when the effect of two or more input variables combines to produce a noticeably worse outcome than would be predicted by the settings of the individual variables alone (see also *variable interaction*, *input variables*, contrast with *positive interaction*).

non-parametric A type of multivariate testing data analysis that tries to identify the best-performing recipe in the landing page search space without building a model involving the input variables (contrast with *parametric*).

normal distribution See *Gaussian distribution*.

null hypothesis In statistical testing, the assumption that there is no difference in outcomes based on changes to the tested input variables. If there is a significant observed effect, statistical tests will be able to *reject* the null hypothesis. Some advanced statistical techniques do not make use of a null hypothesis.

O

organic A type of search engine traffic that originates from nonpaid search results, often as a result of search engine optimization (see also *search engine optimization*).

output variables The measured quantities that are optimized in a landing page optimization experiment. The goal is to find out how modifying the input variables changes the output variables. Typical output variables include conversion rate, revenue per visitor, and profit per visitor. Also called "dependent variables."

parametric A type of multivariate testing data analysis that attempts to build a model based on the input variables and their combinations to predict the corresponding value of the output variables (see also *input variables, output variables,* contrast with *non-parametric*).

permission marketing Any marketing activity that is voluntarily accepted by a member of your target audience. Permission marketing must be anticipated, personal, and relevant (contrast with *interruption marketing*).

persona A detailed profile of a hypothetical person representing an important class of visitors to your site. The persona allows you to empathize with them and understand their needs. Often used as the basis for constructing a relevant and effective conversion experience.

positive interaction During multivariate testing data analysis, when the effect of two or more input variables combines to produce a noticeably better outcome than would be predicted by the settings of the individual variables alone (see also *variable interaction, input variables,* contrast with *negative interaction*).

probability distribution function In probability theory, the probability distribution function describes the set of possible outcomes for an event along with their likelihood. Also called a "probability density function" and abbreviated "PDF" (see also *event*).

probability theory A branch of mathematics that deals with the description and analysis of random events. Probability theory is the underlying machinery of statistics.

promo code Abbreviation for "promotional code," which allows the person presenting the code to get discounts or special deals not available to the general public.

quality assurance In landing page optimization, the function of testing alternative landing page designs to ensure that they have been properly been implemented. Abbreviated as "QA."

random variable In probability theory, an event drawn from a larger population of events that has a defined probability of occurrence and corresponding value. In landing page testing, the random variable is the item that you repeatedly sample (typically the conversion response value of a new visitor to your landing page design).

rate card Indicates current pricing for promotional advertising. Rate cards are commonly expressed in cost-per-impression (see *CPM*) or cost-per-click (see *CPC*).

recipe A unique combination of values for all of the variables in a multivariate test. Defines a unique version of the landing page being tested.

resolution The size of the improvements that can be reliably found in a landing page test with a certain number of total conversions sampled. The larger the data sample, the smaller the effects that can be resolved.

run of network Distribution of an online advertisement across the whole network of available websites for a particular advertising network.

S

sales force automation A type of software that allows you to track all important interactions with potential sales prospects and clients. Abbreviated as "SFA."

saturated main effect A type of parametric model that only considers main effects and thus assumes that variable interactions do not exist (see also *main effects, variable interaction*).

server-side Program code and scripts for constructing a Web page that execute on the Web server before the file is transferred to the Web browser for display (contrast with *client-side*).

SFA See *sales force automation.*

search engine optimization The process for trying to get your website to appear as high as possible in the search results for relevant keywords. Abbreviated as "SEO."

search engine results pages The pages that are displayed by a search engine in response to a keyword(s) typed in by the searcher. Abbreviated as "SERPs."

search engine spiders Automated computer programs that are the part of search engines that retrieve and index Web pages for later retrieval in response to queries.

search space size The total number of distinct recipes possible in a landing page test (see also *recipe*).

SEO See *search engine optimization.*

SERPs See *search engine results pages.*

service-level agreement Guarantees of a certain level of responsiveness and availability for an online service. Abbreviated as "SLA." SLAs are typically expressed in the maximum amount of time it can take to access the data, the percentage of time that the website should be operational, and a maximum response time for complaints or service requests.

signal-to-noise ratio The strength of a particular observed effect expressed as a ratio to the background noise associated with measurements of the effect. Abbreviated as "SNR."

staging environment A parallel implementation for a website or landing page that is used for testing new features or quality assurance before the content is moved to the live or operational environment. A staging environment should be as similar to the production environment as possible.

stochastic process In probability theory, a set of random events drawn from the related underlying distributions (see also *time series, event*).

T

Taguchi method A specific type of fractional factorial design of experiments (DOE) approach commonly used in manufacturing optimization, and sometimes applied to landing page optimization (see also *fractional factorial, design of experiments*).

third-party cookies Cookies left by websites other than the one that the Internet browser is visiting. These kinds of cookies are commonly used for tracking advertising campaigns and are often turned off by Web surfers (see also *cookies*, contrast with *first-party cookies*).

throttling The practice of restricting the percentage of available traffic that is allocated to certain recipes in a landing page optimization test, or restricting the percentage of traffic that is allocated to the test in general. Throttling can decrease the impact of testing poor design alternatives, but it makes the test take longer because data accumulates more slowly.

thumbnail image A small product image that is used on e-commerce website pages to show a large number of products. Larger images are subsequently displayed on the product detail pages.

time series A stochastic process with time based sampling (see *stochastic process*).

U

Universal Resource Locator A method for describing specific content (such as a Web page) that is available on the Internet. Abbreviated as "URL."

URL See *Universal Resource Locator*.

user-centered design A philosophy and practice that considers the needs and background of the intended user of an object or interface as central to the design process.

user experience A series of specific user interactions with a website that form a larger user experience. Abbreviated as "UX."

V

value The specific assignment for a variable in a landing page test (see also *variable*). Also called a "level" or "variation." The number of distinct values for a particular variable is called the "branching factor."

variable A specific landing page tuning element or page section that is part of a landing page test. Also sometimes called a "factor" in statistical testing (see also *value*).

variable interaction Variable interactions are said to occur when the effect of a variable value depends on the values of one or more other variables. In other words, the context in which something is seen will have an effect on its impact. Most fractional factorial approaches assume that there are no variable interactions. Many landing page tests have very strong variable interactions (see also *positive interaction*, *negative interaction*).

variance The square of the sampling noise during a statistical experiment. As the sample size increases, the variance decreases. The standard deviation is the square root of the variance.

W

Web analytics Software for analyzing and tracking the behavior of visitors to a website.

whitelist A set of e-mail addresses from which an e-mail program will always accept messages, regardless of whether the messages fail other spam-filtering criteria.

Z

Z-score A statistical measure of the difference between two quantities. The larger the Z-score, the less likely the two quantities are to have been drawn from the same population.

Index

Note to the Reader: Throughout this index **boldfaced** page numbers indicate primary discussions of a topic. *Italicized* page numbers indicate illustrations.

N

naming conventions in GWO, 331
"Narrow By" navigation bar, **80–81**, *80*
navigation for action, 100
need recognition, **77–78**, *77*
negative variable interaction, 192
neocortex, **126–127**
nested testing elements, **330**
new visitors, **116**
news feeds, 21
newsletters, **21**
newspaper writing, 133
Nielsen, Jakob, 132
"Noes" visitors, 22–23, *23*
non-parametric analysis, 217, *217*,
    234–235
    advantages, **235–236**
    characteristics, **221–222**
    disadvantages, **236**
    vs. parametric, 218
nonstationary time series, 177
normal distribution, **178–180**, *179*
normalized metrics, **205**
Norman, Don, *59–60*, 129
notification features in GWO, 331
null hypotheses, **187**

O

observational studies, 180
observed effects, 188
Observed Improvement in
    Combinations report, **325**
off-page search engine factors, 307
offers
    audience segmentation, **150**
    testing, **162**
offline acquisition activities, **12–13**
on-page search engine factors, 307
online acquisition activities, **8–11**
online and offline combined conversion
    activities, **19–20**
online video ads, **11**

onsite conversion factors, **16–19**
onsite search
    in problem identification, **120–122**
    Web analytics for, **120–121**
operational policies, I.T staff for, **252**
opportunity costs in insourcing vs.
    outsourcing, **259**
order independence
    fractional factorial parametric testing,
      230
    for navigation, 81
organization in accessibility, 131
outdoor advertising, 13
output variables, **198**
outsourcing
    vs. insourcing, **258–261**, **280**
    testing, **256–257**
overgeneralization in sampling, **173**
overlay information, 120
Overstock.com site, 94–95, *95*
overview section in test plans, 275–276,
    276

P

page layout, **137–138**
page quality score, 309–310
page sections
    GWO, 315, **318–319**, *318–320*
    reports, **326–327**
    scripts, 322–323
page size, 133–134
page structure testing, **152–153**
paid traffic, Web analytics for, **118–119**
paid units (PU) in subscriptions, **43**
paleo-mammalian system, 126
parallel pricing presentations, 167
parallel testing, 172
parametric analysis, **217–218**, *217*
    characteristics, **219–221**
    fractional factorial. *See* fractional
      factorial design
    full factorial, **232–234**
    GWO, 312, **327–328**

variable cost of affiliate leads (VCAL), **41**

variable cost of affiliate sales (VCAS), **40**

variable cost of nonaffiliate leads (VCNL), **41**

variable cost percentage (VCP)
  catalog sales, **40**
  conversion rate, **35**
  intermediate conversion actions, **45**
  subscriptions, **43**
  third-party lead generation, **41**

variable interactions, **192–195**, *193*
  A-B split testing, **216–217**
  fractional factorial parametric testing, **224–225**, 230–231, 233–234
  full factorial non-parametric testing, 235
  GWO, **327–329**
  parametric analysis, 219
  pitfalls, **294–296**
  in QA plans, **285**

variables
  contingent, 201
  price testing, **163–165**
  in test plans, **275–279**
  tuning methods, **198–204**, *199*
  values, **199–200**

variance, 178

variations
  GWO setup, **322–323**, *323*
  Page Sections reports, **326**

verifying improvement, **289–290**

video ads, **11**

visibility of landing pages, 254

visible browser window, **115–116**

visible choices, 96

visitor state in page flows, 157

visitors
  biased, **210–211**
  types, **22–23**, *23*
  wants, 78–79

comparisons, **84–85**
customization, 86
details, **85–86**
research, **79–84**, *80*, *82–83*
Web analytics for, **111–117**, *112–115*

visual design, **137**
  color, **139**
  graphics, **138–139**
  page layout, **137–138**

visual learning modality, **127–128**

visual mistakes, 113, *113*

Voltaire, 129

von Moltke, Helmuth, 291

W

walking price curves, **165**

warnings. *See* pitfalls

Web analytics
  audience demographics, **51–52**
  content, **119–120**, *121*
  problem identification. *See* problem identification methods
  traffic sources, **117–119**
  visitors, **111–117**, *112–115*

webmasters, **243–244**

Website Optimizer Authorized Consultant (WOAC) program, 313

"What" question for audience, 50

"When" question for audience, **49**

"Where" question for audience, **49**

whitelists, 20

whitepapers on visitor wants, 79

whitespace, 138

"Who" question for audience, **49**

"Why" question for audience, **49–50**

wizards for visitor wants, 79

Wooden, John, 192

written words, **132–133**
  format, **136–137**
  structure, **133–134**
  tone, **134–136**

Y

"Yesses" visitors, 22–23, *23*
yields in parametric testing, 224–225

Z

Z-scores, 184–186
Zappos.com site, 81–83, *82–83*